Challenges to Emerging and Established Powers

I0084250

This edited volume explores the analytical possibilities of contrasting Brazil and the United Kingdom as examples of emerging and established powers, respectively. It is organised around several themes focusing on the roles of Brazil and the United Kingdom in the management of global economic governance, international development, international security, the politics of regional integration, global climate change governance, and the political leveraging of sports mega-events. Each chapter explores Brazil's and/or the UK's particular foreign policies and their resulting impact on these key areas of global governance and politics. The conceptual focus is on these states' motivations as either status-seekers (Brazil) or status-maintainers (UK) in the context of a fast moving international landscape. The chapters in this book directly or indirectly indicate that these states wish to draw attention to their aspiring or established positions as key global players through either visible foreign policy action and/or symbolic rhetoric.

This book was originally published as a special issue of *Global Society*.

Marco Vieira is a Senior Lecturer in the Department of Political Science and International Studies at the University of Birmingham, UK. He has published in leading journals such as *Review of International Studies, Third World Quarterly, Environmental Politics, Foreign Policy Analysis, Global Society, Global Governance,* and *International Studies Review*. He is the co-author of *The South in World Politics* (2010).

Jonathan Grix is a Reader in Sport Policy and Politics in the School of Sport, Exercise and Rehabilitation Sciences, and Director of the Sport Policy Centre at the University of Birmingham, UK. His latest books include *Sport under Communism. Behind the East German "Miracle"* (co-authored with Mike Dennis, 2012), *Understanding UK Sport Policy in Context* (co-edited with Lesley Phillpots, 2014), and *Sport Politics: An Introduction* (2015).

Challenges to Emerging and Established Powers

Brazil, the United Kingdom and global order

Edited by
Marco Vieira and Jonathan Grix

Routledge
Taylor & Francis Group

LONDON AND NEW YORK

First published 2016 by Routledge

2 Park Square, Milton Park, Abingdon, Oxfordshire OX14 4RN
711 Third Avenue, New York, NY 10017

Routledge is an imprint of the Taylor & Francis Group, an informa business

First issued in paperback 2018

Copyright © 2016 University of Kent

All rights reserved. No part of this book may be reprinted or reproduced
or utilised in any form or by any electronic, mechanical, or other means,
now known or hereafter invented, including photocopying and recording,
or in any information storage or retrieval system, without permission in
writing from the publishers.

Notice:
Product or corporate names may be trademarks or registered trademarks,
and are used only for identification and explanation without intent to infringe.

British Library Cataloguing in Publication Data
A catalogue record for this book is available from the British Library

ISBN 13: 978-1-138-19594-3 (hbk)
ISBN 13: 978-1-138-39195-6 (pbk)

Typeset in Palatino
by RefineCatch Limited, Bungay, Suffolk

Publisher's Note
The publisher accepts responsibility for any inconsistencies that may have
arisen during the conversion of this book from journal articles to book chapters,
namely the possible inclusion of journal terminology.

Disclaimer
Every effort has been made to contact copyright holders for their permission to
reprint material in this book. The publishers would be grateful to hear from any
copyright holder who is not here acknowledged and will undertake to rectify
any errors or omissions in future editions of this book.

Contents

CONTENTS

Citation Information

The chapters in this book were originally published in *Global Society*, volume 29, issue 3 (July 2015). When citing this material, please use the original page numbering for each article, as follows:

Chapter 1
Introduction to the Special Issue: Challenges to Emerging and Established Powers: Brazil and the United Kingdom in the Contemporary Global Order
Marco Vieira and Jonathan Grix
Global Society, volume 29, issue 3 (July 2015), pp. 281–285

Chapter 2
Brazil's Role in Institutions of Global Economic Governance: The WTO and G20
Mahrukh Doctor
Global Society, volume 29, issue 3 (July 2015), pp. 286–300

Chapter 3
Global Economic Governance and the British Economy: From the Gold Standard to the G20
Chris Rogers
Global Society, volume 29, issue 3 (July 2015), pp. 301–320

Chapter 4
Organisation and Politics in South–South Cooperation: Brazil's Technical Cooperation in Africa
Adriana Erthal Abdenur
Global Society, volume 29, issue 3 (July 2015), pp. 321–338

Chapter 5
DFID, the Private Sector and the Re-centring of an Economic Growth Agenda in International Development
Emma Mawdsley
Global Society, volume 29, issue 3 (July 2015), pp. 339–358

Chapter 6
Emerging Brazil: The Challenges of Liberal Peace and Global Governance
Monica Hirst
Global Society, volume 29, issue 3 (July 2015), pp. 359–372

Chapter 7

Three Emerging Security Challenges for the UK
Page Wilson
Global Society, volume 29, issue 3 (July 2015), pp. 373–389

Chapter 8

Regionalism as an Instrument: Assessing Brazil's Relations with its Neighbourhood
Elena Lazarou and Bruno Theodoro Luciano
Global Society, volume 29, issue 3 (July 2015), pp. 390–408

Chapter 9

Europe's British Question: The UK–EU Relationship in a Changing Europe and Multipolar World
Tim Oliver
Global Society, volume 29, issue 3 (July 2015), pp. 409–426

Chapter 10

Brazilian Energy-Climate Policy and Politics towards Low Carbon Development
Eduardo Viola and Larissa Basso
Global Society, volume 29, issue 3 (July 2015), pp. 427–446

Chapter 11

The UK and Emerging Countries in the Climate Regime: Whither Leadership?
Sevasti-Eleni Vezirgiannidou
Global Society, volume 29, issue 3 (July 2015), pp. 447–462

Chapter 12

Interrogating States' Soft Power Strategies: A Case Study of Sports Mega-Events in Brazil and the UK
Jonathan Grix, Paul Michael Brannagan and Barrie Houlihan
Global Society, volume 29, issue 3 (July 2015), pp. 463–479

For any permission-related enquiries please visit:
http://www.tandfonline.com/page/help/permissions

Notes on Contributors

Adriana Erthal Abdenur (PhD Princeton, AB Harvard) is Professor of International Relations at the Pontifical Catholic University in Rio de Janeiro, and Senior Researcher at the BRICS Policy Centre. Her research focuses on the role of rising powers in international development (especially South–South cooperation) and security. Recent publications include articles in *Third World Quarterly, Journal of Peacebuilding and Development, Africa Review, Georgetown Journal of International Affairs*, and *Revista Brasileira de Política Internacional*. In 2015, she was named a "Research Productivity Scholar" by Brazil's National Council for Scientific and Technological Development (CnPQ). She is also a former Fulbright Research grantee and Fellow of the India China Institute, and from 2011 to 2013, she was General Coordinator of the BRICS Policy Centre.

Larissa Basso (Brazil) is a PhD candidate in International Relations at the University of Brasília and a member of the Brazilian Research Network International System in the Anthropocene. She holds Bachelor of Laws–LLB (2003) and Master in International Law–LLM (2008) degrees from the University of Sao Paulo, and an MPhil in Environmental Policy (2010) from the University of Cambridge. She is also an Attorney at Law since 2004. She has researched extensively on international trade and development; since 2009, her main research interests are sustainable development, environmental governance, climate change, and global energy governance in the transition to low carbon development.

Paul Michael Brannagan is a Doctoral Researcher of Sociology within Loughborough University's School of Sport, Exercise and Health Sciences, and a Teaching Fellow in Sport Policy and Politics at the University of Birmingham's School of Sport, Exercise and Rehabilitation Sciences. He is one of the few scholars concentrating on the contemporary influence of modern sport in the Middle East, with a particular focus on the state of Qatar and its acquisition of the 2022 FIFA World Cup finals. Through this, Paul has uncovered the crucial role sport is playing in Qatar's wider socio-political objectives.

Mahrukh Doctor is a Senior Lecturer in Political Economy at the University of Hull, and Adjunct Professor of Latin American Studies at the Johns Hopkins University (SAIS-Europe) in Bologna (Italy). Her research interests include political economy of Brazil (especially business–state relations) and regionalism in Latin America (especially Mercosur and EU–Mercosur relations).

Jonathan Grix is a Reader in Sport Policy and Politics in the School of Sport, Exercise and Rehabilitation Sciences, Director of the Sport Policy Centre, and

Head of the Sport Pedagogy and Sport Policy research and teaching group at the University of Birmingham. His latest books include *Sport under Communism: Behind the East German "Miracle"* (co-authored with Mike Dennis; Palgrave, 2012), *Understanding UK Sport Policy in Context* (co-edited with Lesley Phillpots; Routledge, 2014), and *Sport Politics: An Introduction* (Palgrave, 2015).

Monica Hirst is a Brazilian–US expert in International Affairs based in Buenos Aires. She is a professor in the Department of Economics and Administration at Quilmes National University and teaches in the master's programme in International Relations at Torcuato Di Tella University. She has consulted for the United Nations Development Programme (UNDP), the Ford Foundation, NOREF, the Andean Development Corporation, and the Foreign Ministries of Brazil, Argentina, and Colombia. She has published extensively on Brazilian foreign policy, Latin American–US relations, regional security and integration, emerging powers, and cooperation for development.

Barrie Houlihan is Professor of Sport Policy at Loughborough University, UK, and Visiting Professor at the Norwegian School of Sport Sciences. His research interests include the domestic and international policy processes for sport. He has authored or edited 20 books and over 50 journal articles. His most recent books are *Sport Policy in Britain* (with Iain Lindsey; Routledge, 2012) and *The Youth Olympic Games* (co-edited with D.V. Hanstad and M. Parent; Routledge, 2014).

Elena Lazarou is Assistant Professor of International Relations at the School of Social Sciences (CPDOC), Getulio Vargas Foundation (FGV), Rio de Janeiro, and Head of FGV's Centre for International Relations. She is also a Research Associate at ELIAMEP, Athens. She holds a PhD in International Studies and an MPhil in European Studies from the University of Cambridge.

Bruno Theodoro Luciano is Konrad Adenauer Fellow in European Studies at the Centre for International Relations, Getulio Vargas Foundation (FGV). He holds an MA in International Relations from the University of Brasília (UnB). His work focuses on regional integration, mainly on the European Union, South America and MERCOSUR, and on the role of direct elections in regional parliaments.

Emma Mawdsley is a Reader in Human Geography at the University of Cambridge. She works on the politics of international development and is the author of *From Recipients to Donors: Emerging Powers and the Changing Development Landscape* (2012). She has a particular interest in the UK and India as donors/development partners.

Tim Oliver is a Dahrendorf Fellow on Europe–North American relations at LSE IDEAS, and a non-resident fellow at the Centre for Transatlantic Relations at the Johns Hopkins University School of Advanced International Studies, Washington DC. For several years he was a senior lecturer in the Department of Defence and International Affairs at the Royal Military Academy Sandhurst. He has also taught at LSE and UCL, and has worked in the House of Lords, the European Parliament, RAND, and the German Institute for International and Security Affairs (SWP).

Chris Rogers joined the Department of Politics and International Studies at the University of Warwick as Assistant Professor of Public Policy and Political

Economy in September 2014. Prior to joining Warwick, Chris was first a Teaching Fellow and then a Leverhulme Early Career Fellow in the Department of Politics at the University of York. His research interests include British economic policy, critical state theory, and the co-operative movement. His recent book, *Capitalism and its Alternatives*, was published in 2014.

Sevasti-Eleni Vezirgiannidou is a Lecturer in International Organisations in the Department of Political Science and International Studies at the University of Birmingham. She has published in the field of International Relations and the environment, global environmental governance, US foreign policy, and US climate policy. She is the author of a book entitled *Environmental Governance: Regime Displacement in Space, Time and across Issue-Areas* (2010).

Marco Vieira is a Senior Lecturer in International Relations and Postgraduate Research Director in the Department of Political Science and International Studies (POLSIS) at the University of Birmingham. His research focuses on the role of emerging South powers in international politics/governance, South–South political cooperation, and international relations theory. He has published a number of peer-reviewed articles in leading journals such as *Review of International Studies*, *Third World Quarterly*, *Environmental Politics*, *Foreign Policy Analysis*, *Global Society*, *Global Governance*, and *International Studies Review*. He is the co-author of the book *The South in World Politics* (2010).

Eduardo Viola (Brazil) is a Full Professor of International Relations at the University of Brasília, a Senior Researcher of the Brazilian Council for Scientific Research (CNPQ), and the Coordinator of the Brazilian Research Network International System in the Anthropocene. He holds a PhD in Political Science (1982) from the University of Sao Paulo. He has published extensively on issues of globalisation and governance, democracy and democratisation in South America, Brazilian foreign policy, international environmental policy and politics, and the international political economy of climate change. Dr Viola has been Visiting Professor at Stanford, Colorado at Boulder, Notre Dame, Texas at Austin, Amsterdam, Campinas, San Martin, and Buenos Aires.

Page Wilson (BA [Hons] LLB Grad Dip Ed PhD) is an Assistant Professor at the University of Greenland, presently on leave from her post as Senior Lecturer in the Department of Defence and International Affairs at the Royal Military Academy Sandhurst. Her first book, *Aggression, Crime and International Security* (Routledge, 2009) mapped the evolution of the concept of aggression in the context of international security and law. The views expressed in her article are hers alone.

Introduction: Challenges to Emerging and Established Powers: Brazil and the United Kingdom in the Contemporary Global Order

MARCO VIEIRA and JONATHAN GRIX

The question of how new centres of power such as China, India and Brazil will affect the global order, and the international regimes and norms that sustain it, is fast becoming one of the most pressing of the 21st century. Most analyses, however, focus on individual emerging powers or groups such as the Brazil, Russia, India, China and South Africa partnership (BRICS). Rarely is this undertaken through an investigation of the actual differences and similarities in terms of particular emerging powers' perceptions and sources of influence vis-à-vis the established powers. Brazil and the United Kingdom are prime examples of new and old powers which are trying to adapt their foreign policies to the fast-changing context of global politics and governance. For issues as diverse as climate change, development assistance, humanitarian intervention and international security, both states are clearly and inescapably involved in reshaping and renegotiating the current rules of global governance.

This special issue compiles a series of articles that explore the analytical possibilities of contrasting Brazil and the United Kingdom as examples of emerging and established powers, respectively. It is organised around several themes focusing on the roles of Brazil and the United Kingdom in the management of global economic governance, international development, international security, the politics of regional integration, global climate change governance, and the political leveraging of sports mega-events. Each article explores Brazil's and/or the UK's particular foreign policies and their resulting impact on the key areas of global governance and politics touched on above. The conceptual focus is on these states' motivations as either *status-seekers* (Brazil) or *status-maintainers* (UK) in the context of a fast-moving international landscape. The articles in this issue directly or indirectly indicate that these states wish to draw attention to their aspiring or established position as key global players through either visible foreign policy action and/or symbolic rhetoric.

The first two articles, by Mahrukh Doctor and Chris Rogers, examine the contributions and central motivations of Brazil and the UK, respectively, in reforming global economic governance. In the opening article, Doctor argues that Brazil's foreign policy goals and positions have changed in the past decade from an almost exclusive focus on economic development to the current and increasingly important additional element of prestige and status recognition. Doctor empirically examines Brazil's positions at the World Trade Organisation (WTO) and the G20 to claim that "Brazil has shifted its foreign policy behaviour to the point where it sometimes seems to support positions that contradict its immediate material interests".

In his article, Rogers argues that the institutions of global economic governance, from the Gold Standard to the G20, have favoured and reinforced the ideological and material agendas of policy elites in the UK. Interestingly, Rogers claims that "by incorporating emerging economies in the framework of the G20, it has also served to legitimise liberalisation in nations on which countries reliant on financialisation, like Britain, depend for liquidity and the supply of commodities". Rogers' point is that the G20 served well the British goal of consolidating a common narrative and policy framework among developed and developing states around the idea of "globalisation as a fact that must be managed in a particular way". We can take away from Rogers' analysis that the UK has successfully managed to preserve, in the context of a much more diverse and unstable international environment, its influential position as a key ideological and political pillar of the post-WWII international economic order.

The next two articles, by Adriana Abdenur and Emma Mawdsley, deal with the Brazilian and UK approaches to international development cooperation. Abdenur's central argument is that in the past decade Brazil has more clearly and systematically used its particular model of South–South technical cooperation as a tool to promote broader foreign policy objectives. More specifically, she focuses on Brazil's involvement in Africa to demonstrate that "technical cooperation is increasingly used to bolster the government's global power aspirations and to resist Northern-led efforts to set international development norms".

Mawdsley's article turns to the British model of international development cooperation. She claims that in recent years the UK's Department of International Development (DIFD) has shifted its mandate to accommodate the government's private sector-led economic growth agenda. According to her critical assessment, "this strategy may well achieve growth outcomes in partner countries, but without sufficient conceptual rigour … or attention to the connective fabric between growth and development, the latter is more uncertain". The doubling of DIFD's budget for economic development (from 2012/13 to 2015/16) means this growth-led model of "international development" is likely to continue—a model which seeks to convince a domestic audience while maintaining international support.

The fifth and sixth articles in the issue, by Monica Hirst and Page Wilson, respectively, look at the role of Brazil and the UK in the global management of international and regional security. Hirst argues that Brazil has in recent years expanded the reach of its international security agenda to areas conventionally controlled by the Western powers. This has been achieved through a foreign policy based on a "double-track course of action, both of which may be considered fertile sources for the accumulation of soft-power assets". In her account, Brazil's soft power strategy relies on: 1) coalitions of emerging powers, namely the BRICS and the India, Brazil, South Africa Dialogue Forum (IBSA); and 2) "an enhanced involvement and responsibility in UN-led operations, accompanied by a robust portfolio of bilateral and multilateral accords with developing countries".

Wilson's article focuses more closely on identifying and discussing three particular areas which, according to the author, will most likely be central to the British national security agenda in the mid-21st century. These are: 1) cyber security threats; 2) changes in the balance of global power and its impact on a "rules-based" international system; and 3) growing economic inequality within the UK. With regards to the latter, Wilson claims that growing economic and social disparities can be "a motivation for actions that undermine the legitimacy of the UK's governing elites and state institutions".

The following two articles, by Elena Lazarou/Bruno Teodoro and Tim Oliver, discuss Brazil's and the UK's regional integration politics in South America and Europe, respectively. In their article, Lazarou and Teodoro seek to examine the particular features of Brazil's engagement in regional integration and cooperation. They identify five key foreign policy instruments, or models, which have been historically used by Brazilian foreign policy leaders in South American regionalism. These are "post-democratisation regionalism", "presidential regionalism", "reactive regionalism", "concentric/multilevel regionalism" and "instrumental regionalism". Following an analysis of these different models, they conclude that "regionalism serves more as an instrument to promote Brazil's global aspirations and preferences, rather than a norm-driven goal (end)".

Oliver's article focuses on the UK's (awkward) relationship with the EU. He argues that both the EU and the UK should consider and balance carefully the geopolitical and economic implications of the UK's potential withdrawal from the European Union, a possible outcome, if an in-out referendum is held by 2017. Oliver suggests that the UK's exit will have little or no impact on advancing the extremely entangled diplomatic, security and economic interests of the UK and the EU. On the other hand, London's withdrawal would represent a blow to the UK's already declining influence in global politics. In particular, a "Brexit" would negatively impact on the UK's bilateral relations with its main global ally, the United States of America.

The ninth and tenth articles, by Larissa Basso/Eduardo Viola and Sevasti-Eleni Vezirgiannidou, respectively, focus on the roles of Brazil and the UK on global climate change governance. Basso and Viola address Brazil's energy climate politics and policy from the early 1990s to 2014. The authors argue that Brazil has gone through three distinctive stages in terms of its positions on global climate negotiations. Brazilian negotiating positions ranged from an initial conservative and obstructionist stance in the early 1990s to a more accommodating reformist position from 2005 to 2010. In the current period, under Dilma Rousseff's administration, the authors claim that "Brazil has taken a step back, moving from moderate reformism to moderate conservatism, due to the discovery of deep oil reserves and the use of oil prices to maintain higher rates of economic growth".

In her article, Vezirgiannidou discusses the UK's engagement in global climate politics. In particular, she focuses on the UK's climate diplomacy towards emerging powers on two analytical levels: firstly, she looks at multilateral climate governance whereby the UK acts in cooperation with its EU partners; secondly, she analyses the UK's bilateral engagements with emerging states outside the multilateral governance framework provided by the United Nations Framework Convention on Climate Change (UNFCCC). She concludes that "despite continued divergence in international negotiations, domestic agendas are showing signs of convergence, and further bilateral cooperation can only build on and ameliorate these trends".

In the last article, Jonathan Grix, Paul Brannagan and Barrie Houlihan conceptually operate and critically engage with the concept of "soft power" to empirically demonstrate how and why the UK and Brazil have used sports mega-events to leverage their international political influence and seek to either maintain and consolidate their international status (the UK) or to boost it (Brazil). Two important points emanate from this final piece. First, the authors offer an analysis of the concept of "soft power" and the strategies used by a variety of advanced and "emerging" states to promote it. Second, the authors turn to sport by drawing on the hosting of sports mega-events (London Olympics, 2012; FIFA Soccer World Cup, Brazil, 2014; Rio Olympics, 2016) to shed light on how the UK and Brazil respectively manipulate(d) global sporting to achieve their soft power aims.

In aggregate, these articles offer interesting comparative insights (even if still analytically tentative at this stage of the research programme) into the roles and motivations of emerging and established powers in the context of a fast-moving international order. The interrelated issues of *status recognition* and *foreign policy adaptation*, to an uncertain international normative/institutional landscape, seem to be the common thread cutting across all the articles in the issue. Collectively these articles shed light on the variety of strategies in a range of areas used by Brazil in seeking a new-found status in the global order and the UK in attempting to maintain its position.

Acknowledgements

This special issue evolved out of a conference the editors organised at the Institute of Advanced Studies (IAS), University of Birmingham, 30–31 May 2014, in collaboration with the Centre for the Study of International Negotiations (CAENI) at the University of São Paulo. The original papers underwent significant revisions following comments by peer reviewers and the editors. This project was financially supported by the University of Birmingham-São Paulo Research Foundation (FAPESP) joint research fund. We are grateful to Rubens Duarte and Bruno Dalponte, PhD researchers in the Department of Political Science and International Studies (POLSIS) at the University of Birmingham, for their invaluable support in both capacities as research assistants and conference organisers. Finally, we thank Alexandre Christoyannopoulos, editorial assistant of *Global Society*, for his professionalism and dedication while assisting us in producing this volume.

Brazil's Role in Institutions of Global Economic Governance: The WTO and G20

MAHRUKH DOCTOR

The article evaluates the extent to which Brazil's foreign policy actions, negotiating positions and diplomatic strategies in global governance institutions contribute to supporting its national interest and foreign policy aims. It compares Brazil's preferences and behaviour in the World Trade Organization (WTO) and Group of 20 (G20). For decades, Brazil's primary national interest has been national economic development. The article argues that Brazil is moving from a material interests based definition of its prime national interest to a more complex one that includes both material and prestige/status based aspects. Research demonstrates that Brazil has become increasingly focused on gaining recognition as a leader of developing countries, sometimes even at the cost of realising its full material interests. It considers the value of constructivist international relations theory to understanding Brazilian foreign policy.

The past decade has seen a major shift in global economic dynamism and power distribution. Ideological as well as pragmatic factors colour established and emerging powers' attitudes towards the emerging world order. Moreover, the growing political, economic, and ideological diversity present in the international system has dissipated the like-mindedness that guided post-war collaboration on issues of global governance. The impacts of the global financial crisis, Eurozone troubles, and turbulence in emerging markets required both established and emerging powers to rethink their behaviour in arenas of global economic governance. Although there are a plethora of institutions, organisations and networks that deal with issues of global economic governance, this article focuses on the World Trade Organization (WTO) and Group of Twenty Leaders' Summit (G20). These organisations are particularly interesting, because even though they have different organisational logics, established and emerging powers formally sit as equals in both (i.e. with equal voting power). Moreover, Brazil plays an active and significant role in both of them.

The main aim of the article is to examine to what extent Brazil's foreign policy actions, negotiating positions and diplomatic strategies in global governance institutions contribute to supporting its national interest and foreign policy aims. It compares Brazil's preferences and behaviour in the WTO and G20 to explain how Brazil appears to be moving from a material based definition of its national interest to a more complex one that includes both material and prestige/status based aspects. It argues that by prioritising leadership of the Global South/developing countries, in addition to its own direct material interests, Brazil has shifted its foreign policy behaviour to the point where it sometimes seems to support positions that contradict its immediate material interests. The key sources for the analysis are public speeches and media interviews by top officials complemented by personal interviews with Brazilian diplomats. My aim is to provide evidence that provokes discussion rather than present definitive conclusions on the evolution of Brazilian foreign policy. The analysis is developed in four sections: (1) Brazil's traditional foreign policy aims and negotiating strategy; (2) Brazil's positions and actions in the WTO, with special reference to the "Bali package" signed in December 2013; (3) Brazil's positions and actions in the G20, with special reference to the St Petersburg Action Plan signed in September 2013; and (4) an evaluation of Brazilian diplomatic strategy and foreign policy achievements as well as some comments on whether established powers can hope to work with and accommodate Brazil's interests and preferences.

A secondary aim of the analysis is to consider whether traditional approaches to studying Brazilian foreign policy still provide a complete and convincing explanation for Brazil's evolving discourse and actions in the foreign policy arena. Traditionally, the academic literature emphasises liberal institutionalism when discussing Brazil's approach to issues of global economic governance, given its active engagement in international institutions and international regimes as well as its valuing of international law. However, recent diplomatic language and behaviour raise questions about the continuing validity of these interpretations, or at least their ability to provide an exhaustive explanation. The article briefly explores whether constructivism—with its emphasis on socially constructed relations and interpretations of international politics as well as attention to values, ideas and identities—might afford useful insights into understanding Brazil's positions in the WTO and G20.

Foreign Policy Aims and Strategy

The Brazilian Ministry of External Relations, known as the Itamaraty, has enjoyed considerable autonomy in handling Brazilian foreign policy. Regimes of all shapes and political inclinations typically adopted highly instrumental and pragmatic approaches to foreign policy. Although new elements have appeared (discussed later), they were accommodated within the traditional four features of Brazilian foreign policy. These features fundamentally shape Brazilian attitudes and actions in the WTO and G20.

The first feature and overarching goal of Brazilian foreign policy is to support the achievement of national development, more recently conceived of in terms of economic, social and environmentally sustainable development. Both Presidents Luiz Inácio Lula da Silva (2003–2010) and Dilma Rousseff (2011–2014; elected to a second term that began in 2015) have reiterated this often. Marco Aurelio Garcia, Foreign Policy Special Advisor to both presidents noted that Brazilian foreign policy "should not be understood as a way to project Brazil's presence in the world, but rather as a substantial part of Brazil's national project".[1] Moreover, as Brazil's economic and social progress gathered pace, Foreign Minister Antonio de Aguiar Patriota (2011–2013) pointed out: "times have changed, and we have changed with the times … Brazil broke new ground on social protection and the results are there for anyone to see".[2] Brazil claimed agenda-setting influence when its domestic Zero-Hunger programme was transformed into a global endeavour with the launch of the Zero-Hunger Challenge by UN Secretary-General Ban Ki-Moon at the Rio+20 Conference in 2012. Also, Rousseff gave increasing emphasis to science, technology and innovation in Brazil's dialogue and exchanges with the world.[3] Unsurprisingly, the strong developmentalist discourse within foreign policy thinking and the country's self-identity as a developing economy and emerging power make it an attractive leader for other developing countries to follow.

A second feature of Brazilian foreign policy relates to an emphatic defence of sovereignty and autonomy. Brazil's view is that autonomy refers not only to an obligation to respect national sovereignty/non-intervention in domestic affairs of other states, but also to maintaining policy flexibility in the domestic economic sphere. There is good reason to view Brazil as a "quintessential soft power"[4] privileging dialogue, mediation and bridge-building in its diplomacy. This emphasis on the possibility of cooperation without sole reliance on force and material capabilities is best explained by constructivism. It is not that constructivism dismisses the role of power and interests in driving state behaviour, but rather that it acknowledges that states do not always act in their direct immediate material interests.[5] These views resonate in recent Brazilian diplomacy.

A third feature is the priority given to multilateralism and universalism.[6] Foreign Minister Celso Amorim (1993–1994; 2003–2010) clearly stated that "we see multilateralism as the primary means of solving conflicts and making decisions internationally".[7] Brazil has a long history of participation in multilateral international institutions from the League of Nations to the United Nations (UN) as well as its many agencies and institutions. In a typical statement by a Brazilian Foreign Minister, Mauro Vieira (2015–) noted how Brazilian diplomacy was driven by the need to "defend the country's interests in a world marked by increasing opposition, challenges and risks … in harmony with the principles of multilateralism and

1. Cited by Jonathan Rathbone, "Foreign Policy: Big Ambitions", *Financial Times*, 14 November 2010, available: <www.ft.com/cms> (accessed 15 February 2015). Also see Celso Amorim, "Brazilian Foreign Policy under President Lula (2003-2010): An Overview", *Revista Brasileira de Politica Internacional*, Vol. 53, special edition (2010), pp. 214–240; Maria Regina Soares de Lima and Monica Hirst, "Brazil as an Intermediate State and Regional Power: Action, Choice and Responsibilities", *International Affairs*, Vol. 82, No. 1 (2006), pp. 21–40.

2. Antonio Patriota, Speech at the 39th Session of the Food Security Committee of the Food and Agriculture Organisation, Rome, 17 October 2012, available: <www.itamaraty.gov.br/discursos-artigos-entrevistas> (accessed 15 February 2015).

3. Antonio Patriota, "Diplomacia não é publicidade", Interview in *IstoÉ*, 23 July 2012, available: <www.itamaraty.gov.br/sala-de-imprensa> (accessed 15 February 2015).

4. Paulo Sotero and Leslie Elliot Armijo, "Brazil: To Be or Not to Be a BRIC", *Asian Perspectives*, Vol. 31, No. 4 (2007), pp. 43–70.

5. Ian Hurd, "Constructivism", in Christian Reus-Smit and Duncan Snidal (eds.), *The Oxford Handbook of International Relations* (Oxford: Oxford University Press, 2010), pp. 298–316.

6. A useful discussion of this is found in Tulio Vigevani and Haroldo Ramanzini Junior, "The Changing Nature of Multilateralism and Brazilian Foreign Policy", *The International Spectator*, Vol. 45, No. 4 (2010), pp. 63–71.

7. Amorim, "Brazilian Foreign Policy", *op. cit.*, p. 214.

international law … our interests are geographically and thematically universal".[8] Brazilian foreign policy also put much emphasis on universalism and multi-polarity, something that Patriota claimed "demonstrated an ability to place Brazil ahead of the curve, because it led to diversification of partners".[9] All the same, Brazil mainly was a "rule taker" in the international system throughout the twentieth century. Only recently has it sought to shape global governance structures as a "rule maker" and "agenda-setter", what Sean Burges correctly suggested was part of a psychological transformation and recovery of *auto-estima* in Brazil's foreign policy agenda.[10] So far, Brazil's demands for reform have mainly been mildly revisionist, unlikely to shake the influence of the established powers.[11] Brazil upholds its interests "with pragmatism, without renouncing our principles and values".[12] It is precisely this cooperative attitude towards multilateralism that makes Brazil the emerging power easiest to work alongside for the established powers. It displays "all the signs of a responsible leader on the rise".[13]

Two new elements have appeared alongside these traditional features of Brazilian foreign policy. First, there has been a gradual opening to societal interests and inputs, but with an emphasis on technocratic contributions that reinforce diplomatic relations and negotiating strategies. Second, foreign policy discourse has become more ideological, although the ideology-tinged language is often deployed at a rhetorical rather than practical level. Arguably, President Lula moved away from traditional pragmatism, when he turned to "South-South" diplomacy and promoting greater international equity and social justice. Indubitably, he introduced more political objectives into diplomacy, such as increasing Brazil's international prestige and gaining recognition as leader among developing countries.[14] Amorim argues that while established powers were likely to question this independent attitude, actually it was "fearless, not reckless—commensurate with Brazil's size and aspirations".[15] Thus, Lula did not set aside material power or instrumental calculations of Brazil's interest. However, his actions were shaped by his understanding of the world and Brazil's identity within it as well as the need to change them to boost Brazil's national interest. Understanding these types of behavioural imperatives is precisely the focus of the constructivist approach.

Although Rousseff toned down her predecessor's ideological and politicised approach, she did not abandon "South-South" leadership ambitions or development objectives in her foreign policy. As her Foreign Minister stated:

8. Mauro Vieira, Speech at Investiture ceremony in Ministry of External Relations, Brasilia on 2 January 2015, available: <www.itamaraty.gov.br/discursos> (accessed 15 February 2015).

9 Antonio Patriota in an interview with *Brazil Confidential*, January 2012, available: <www.itamaraty.gov.br/sala-de-imprensa> (accessed 15 February 2015).

10. Sean Burges, "*Auto-Estima* in Brazil: The Logic of Lula's South-South Foreign Policy", *International Journal*, Vol. 60, No. 4 (2005), pp. 1133–1151.

11. Andrew Hurrell, "Brazil: What Kind of Rising State in What Kind of Institutional Order", in Alan Alexandroff and Andrew Cooper (eds.), *Rising States, Rising Institutions: Challenges for Global Governance* (Washington, DC: Brookings, 2010).

12. Amorim, "Brazilian Foreign Policy", *op. cit.*, p. 214.

13. Amrita Narlikar, *New Powers: How to Become One and How to Manage Them* (London: Hurst, 2010), p. 134.

14. See for example, Sean W. Burges, *Brazilian Foreign Policy after the Cold War* (Gainsville: University of Florida Press, 2009).

15. Amorim, "Brazilian Foreign Policy", *op. cit.*, p. 217.

we have been on the outside looking in for most of our history, and we know how it feels to be outside looking in. And this is what I think creates a special sensitivity to keep in touch with what some people call the G-172, all UN members who are not members of the G20.[16]

Rousseff was the first to explicitly link the BRICS (Brazil, Russia, India, China and South Africa) countries to Brazil's diplomatic activity in South America, when she piggy backed the BRICS Fortaleza Summit in August 2014 on to a meeting of all 11 heads of state of the Union of South American Nations (UNASUR) in Brasilia. Although she was unable to maintain Lula's high profile on the international stage, both presidents benefited from the effective negotiating skills of Itamaraty diplomats.

So, how did the Itamaraty contribute to achieving Brazilian foreign policy aims? Hurrell and Narlikar discuss diplomatic negotiating strategies of emerging powers on a spectrum from strictly distributive ("value claiming") to integrative ("value creating").[17] Mostly (and traditionally), Brazil preferred a more integrative approach in negotiations. Since 2003, there have also been numerous instances where it adopted distributive strategies (often against the inclination of professional diplomats). Evidence shows that this usually occurred to show solidarity with fellow emerging powers or to maintain its identity and leadership position among developing countries (in other words when it wanted to please its "followers").[18] The next section discusses some examples of when Brazil acted as per the expectations and preferences of its followership rather than its immediate self-interest.

At his investiture ceremony, Vieira noted that "the valuable symbolism of our presence [*in various international institutions*] is no substitute for a results-driven diplomacy".[19] As such, Brazilian diplomats like using what may be called "insider activism" and "smart coalitions", i.e. groups organised on the basis of shared interests (rather than just identities), where the idea is to share information within the group so as to engage cooperatively across numerous issue areas. These types of actions reflected very technocratic approaches to negotiation and fit the Itamaraty style. Thus, Brazilian negotiators typically proposed research-backed alternatives framed within institutionalised legal frameworks rather than simply appealing to distributive justice or other values (in contrast to the diplomatic style of its presidents). They have also become more accepting of input from civil society organisations, especially if the latter's views are couched in technocratic language or provide information supportive of Itamaraty notions of the national interest (the crucial role of the highly competitive agribusiness sector is a case in point[20]).

---

16. Antonio Patriota, Transcript of Speech at the Woodrow Wilson Center, Washington, DC, 31 May 2011, available: <http://www.wilsoncenter.org/sites/default/files/1310524380.pdf> (accessed 15 February 2015).

17. Andrew Hurrell and Amrita Narlikar, "A New Politics of Confrontation? Brazil and India in Multi-lateral Trade Negotiations", *Global Society*, Vol. 20, No. 4 (2006), pp. 415–433.

18. For examples of this behaviour, see: Charalampos Efstathopolous, "Leadership in the WTO: Brazil, India and the Doha Development Agenda", *Cambridge Review of International Affairs*, Vol. 25, No. 2 (2012), pp. 269–293; and Kristen Hopewell, "Different Paths to Power: The Rise of Brazil, India and China at the World Trade Organization", *Review of International Political Economy* (2014), doi: 10.1080/09692290.2014.927387.

19. Mauro Vieira, *op. cit.* (italics are my words).

20. See Kristen Hopewell, "New Protagonists in Global Economic Governance: Brazilian Agribusiness at the WTO", *New Political Economy*, Vol. 18, No. 4 (2013), pp. 602–623.

Bearing the above in mind, the analysis now turns to examining Brazil's role in the WTO and G20.

Brazil in the WTO

As a global trader, Brazil played a key role in the General Agreement on Tariffs and Trade (GATT), and continued to do so in its successor, the WTO. Also, given the priority of development in Brazil's national interest, any evaluation of its engagement in the WTO can be expected to measure the material benefits emanating from its membership. From the beginning, it decided to actively lead in the current round of trade negotiations, the Doha Development Round (DDR), which was launched in November 2001. Two points need to be borne in mind. First, the WTO's core mandate is to set trade rules, which it does via a process of negotiating rounds. It then monitors the implementation of rules via mechanisms for trade review and dispute settlement. Second, the WTO is not a development agency. While Brazil accepts this in principle, it is less happy about the fact that "each of the previous eight rounds has resulted in asymmetrical deals favouring the largest most economically powerful states relative to (and sometimes at the expense of) their less powerful counterparts".[21] It is this sense of frustration with the "unfairness" or at least consistently asymmetrical outcomes of previous rounds that saw Brazil turn towards rejecting "done deals" by advanced economies, accepting a North–South division of interests, and embracing solidarity with developing countries in general terms.

Herein lay the heart of a process of strategy shifting that clearly emerged in the run up to the Cancun ministerial conference in 2003. In response to the joint European Union–United States agricultural proposal in mid-2003, the Brazilians turned to the recently created IBSA (India, Brazil, South Africa) Forum and proposed the creation of a coalition of developing countries to oppose it. This took shape as the G20-Trade at Cancun, a coalition which included India and others that often adopted stances at odds with Brazil's interests and positions in agricultural negotiations. Amorim clearly explained Brazil's shift in attitude when he wrote that Brazil was

> not interested in North-South confrontation … our platform is about levelling the playing field through the full integration of agriculture into the multilateral rules-based trading system. … developing countries will not be reduced to the role of supporting actors in discussions that affect their development prospects. Consensus cannot be imposed through pre-cooked deals that disregard previous commitments … Trade must be a tool not only to create wealth but also to distribute it in a more equitable way.[22]

Brazil's leadership of the G20-Trade was an excellent example of its new "Southern approach" and more politicised view of negotiations. Pedro da Motta Veiga shows

---

21. Rorden Wilkinson, "Of Butchery and Bicycles: The WTO and the 'Death' of the Doha Development Agenda", *The Political Quarterly*, Vol. 83, No. 2 (2012), pp. 395–401, at p. 396.

22. Celso Amorim, "The Real Cancun", *Wall Street Journal*, 25 September 2003, available: <http://online.wsj.com/news/articles/> (accessed 15 February 2015).

how Brazil watered down its own market access ambitions so as to accommodate its partners' concerns about food security and rural livelihoods.[23] Amorim spoke of it in terms of "two parallel battles", one at the negotiating table and the other to win hearts and minds of the public.[24] Thus, Brazil demanded that the WTO deliver on the Doha Development Agenda (DDA) and a fairer outcome for vulnerable rural populations in developing countries. Brazil was reasonably satisfied with the immediate outcome at Cancun, and Amorim happily noted at a talk in London that "it is not an exaggeration to say that the G20 for the first time in trade negotiations brought home the twin message on trade liberalisation and social justice".[25] After Cancun, Brazil and India were definitively brought into the inner circle of negotiations in the so-called G4/New Quad. Unlike India, Brazil had both offensive and defensive interests in the round and was therefore in a position to push for constructive solutions and bridge-building between North and South. Effectively, Cancun was a critical turning point and the two emerging powers were able to play agenda-setting roles in the DDR from 2003 onwards.

Before examining Brazil's positions on key issues in WTO negotiations, it is important to understand that traditionally the Itamaraty exercised a virtual monopoly on multilateral trade negotiations. Its diplomats and negotiators were largely insulated from domestic politics, and both government and civil society had little input on specific aspects of the negotiations. Business was consulted occasionally, but only when it suited the Itamaraty to do so. The Ministry of Development, Industry and Trade tried to muscle in on the negotiations, but was limited to providing technical details and sectoral statistical data.

While the above scenario broadly remains in place (with some adjustments for democracy), there have been some key alterations in practical terms during the DDR. Once it was clear Brazilian agricultural competitiveness allowed it to become a *demandeur* in trade negotiations, the Itamaraty became more open to agribusiness input into generating negotiators' technical positions. Negotiators worked closely with agribusiness sectoral organisations, such as the National Confederation of Agriculture (CNA) and Institute for International Trade Negotiations (ICONE).[26] However, it should not be forgotten that these exchanges were on the Itamaraty's terms. Interaction was based on technocratic criteria with a focus on knowledge and information-sharing. It would be a mistake to assume the Itamaraty had become open to broad societal interest representation. Thus, it could confidently partner India in the G20-Trade even though this implied adopting positions with negative commercial impacts on its own exporters (and even ordinary citizens). Thus, Itamaraty diplomats, alongside a group of technocrats (whether public or private sector), remain the key actors both defining and voicing Brazilian interests in the WTO. Crucially, their autonomy allows them

23. Pedro da Motta Veiga, "Case Study 7: Brazil and the G-20 Group of Developing Countries", in *Managing the Challenges of WTO Participation: 45 Case Studies* (Geneva: WTO Secretariat, 2005), available: <https://www.wto.org/english/res_e/booksp_e/casestudies_e/case7_e.htm> (accessed 15 February 2015).

24. Amorim, "Brazilian Foreign Policy", *op. cit.*, p. 219.

25. Celso Amorim, "The Foreign Policy of the Lula Government", Lecture at the London School of Economics, London, 17 March 2004, available: <http://www.lse.ac.uk/newsAndMedia/news/archives/2004/Brazilian_ForeignMinister_Transcript.aspx> (accessed 15 February 2015).

26. See Hopewell, "New Protagonists in Global Economic Governance", *op. cit.*, for a detailed examination of Brazilian agribusiness influence on trade negotiations.

to be flexible, but also consistent and coherent over time and across issues in negotiating Brazil's interests.

One can gain a better understanding of Brazilian interests in the DDR by examining its positions in three main issue areas. The first issue relates to Brazil's insistence that WTO negotiations be dealt with as a "single undertaking" or in other words, nothing is agreed until all is agreed. This principle ensures that negotiators cannot pick and choose what suits them, opting out of agreements where they might be "losers". However, after years of stagnation in the Doha Round and increasing frustration with the comatose condition of negotiations, Brazil actually went along with the idea of an "early harvest" at the Bali ministerial conference in December 2013. It believed that a limited but symbolic move forward might serve as an inducement for further agreement. All the same, at the Bali Opening Plenary, Foreign Minister Luis Alberto Figueiredo (2013–2014) was quick to point out that

> the early harvest model has already run its course and should not be repeated. We should now revert to a more ambitious goal … done with a clear sense of priorities. And our first priority remains the removal of the most distorting trade measures, particularly in agriculture, that hamper full integration of developing countries into world trade.[27]

Thus, Brazil compromised on specific aspects of the negotiations to support its broader principles and longer-term ambitions.

The second issue relates to Brazil's status as a developing country. It faces a real diplomatic dilemma in view of the conflicting requirements for recognition as an emerging power alongside continuing status as a developing country. In recent years, there has been considerable pressure on Brazil to "graduate" out of receiving WTO mandated special and differential treatment (SDT) as a developing country. Although a middle income economy, it insists that the large number of poor and the high levels of regional poverty and inequality keep it economically vulnerable and deserving of developing country status. However, on closer examination and in my interviews with diplomats, it soon becomes clear that it is not the loss of the material provisions, but the loss of identity as a developing country that is at stake. Brazil resists "graduating" because it fears that it would mean losing legitimacy as the representative and leader of developing countries. These concerns partly explain Brazil's actions in Bali, as discussed below.

The third set of issues relates to Brazil's resistance to adding new issues to WTO negotiations before older ones are resolved. It is specifically adamant that advanced economies make progress towards ending export subsidies and liberalising trade in agricultural goods. Basically, it resists creating new WTO disciplines around what are essentially behind border issues (such as government procurement, investment, labour and environmental standards, etc.), where monitoring compliance is difficult (this logic allowed room for trade facilitation to be an exception among new issues). Moreover, even if Brazil were inclined to more flexibility on some counts, it was unlikely to cross sides and risk losing support from many developing countries (not to mention other emerging powers).

---

27. Luiz Alberto Figueiredo, Statement of Minister of External Relations of Brazil, WTO Bali Ministerial Conference, Bali, 4 December 2013, available: <http://www.wto.org/english/thewto_e/minist_e/mc9_e/stat_e/bra.pdf> (accessed 15 February 2015).

While the headlines were hogged by the Indians and Americans during the Bali meeting, it was a Brazilian (albeit in the position of WTO Director General) that played a significant role in getting all the delegations to agree to the 10 texts covering three areas in the negotiations: trade facilitation; agriculture; SDT for least developed countries (LDCs). It was generally acknowledged that Roberto Azevêdo, who only became Director General in September 2013, deserved huge credit for his effort before and during the ministerial conference to get an agreement. He emphasised the importance of transparency and inclusivity in preparation of the conference texts. He is said to have met with 45 delegations during the Bali meeting and even extended it by a day to ensure all were on board to sign the first legally binding agreement in the history of the almost 19-year-old organisation (at the time).

Brazil was quietly satisfied with Azevêdo, the Itamaraty-trained diplomat, who had been their chief negotiator at the WTO in Geneva. However, given the above concerns and positions, was Brazil satisfied with the content of the "Bali package"? The Trade Facilitation Agreement (TFA) was the main legally binding part of the texts agreed at Bali. Generally, Brazil had decided to adopt a positive line on Section I of the trade facilitation text, which dealt with technicalities of cross-border trade. Brazil saw this as an opportunity to improve its trade related bureaucracy: upgrading customs procedures, increasing coordination between various government agencies, and benefiting exporters in terms of diminished red tape and faster processing of traded goods. Shortly after signing the agreement, Brazil clarified that nine of the 12 articles in TFA-Section I were already implemented, while the other three would soon follow.[28] Moreover, in the spirit of TFA-Section II (assistance for relevant capacity building in developing countries), Brazil almost immediately offered technical and financial assistance to some of its African and Latin American trade partners (thus bolstering its development cooperation credentials).

Although Brazil realised that TFA was a major priority of the advanced economies, it conditioned its agreement on some sweeteners being added for developing countries, such as a peace clause on food security (public stockholding and subsidised food aid for the poor and support for vulnerable farmers), an agreement on cotton, a trade in services waiver and preferential rules of origin for LDCs as well as a best endeavour promise for duty free quota free (DFQF) market access for LDCs. More interestingly, Brazil seemed willing to forgo its own interests on some of these issues. Most prominently, it set aside demands for ending subsidies for agriculture in specific cases and agreed to allow DFQF for LDCs (the latter item created apprehension in the domestic textile and apparel sector).

In many ways, the "Bali package" reflected WTO business as usual, where gains were asymmetrical (the North got a legally binding agreement on its priority; the South received best endeavour promises).[29] All the same, it provided Brazilian negotiators and trade experts much food for thought. Specifically: should Brazil rethink its position on single undertaking and SDT? Are small harvest and

---

28. The three incomplete aspects relate to article 3 (consultation solutions), article 7 (express dispatch) and article 11 (free transit). See Sandra P. Rios and Fabrizio Sardelli Panzini, "O Pacote de Bali: Implicações para a política commercial brasileira", CINDES *Breves*, No. 82 (2014), available: <www.cindesbrasil. org> (accessed 15 February 2015).

29. Rorden Wilkinson, Erin Hannah and James Scott, "The WTO in Bali: What mc9 Means for the Doha Development Agenda and Why It Matters", *Third World Quarterly*, Vol. 35, No. 6 (2014), pp. 1032–1050.

plurilateral agreements better than no agreement at all? What would "graduating" mean for Brazil's leadership of the South? How should it respond to its exclusion from negotiations for mega-regional accords (such as the Trans Pacific Partnership and the Trans-Atlantic Trade and Investment Partnership), which threaten to transform the global governance of trade? Some of these themes are taken up in the conclusion.

Brazil in the G20

In the aftermath of the Asian Financial Crisis in the late 1990s, Brazil was invited to participate in the G20-Finance. In the following years, this group of finance ministers and central bank governors of 20 systemically important economies met on a regular basis. Brazil happened to be hosting a G20-Finance meeting when the global financial crisis hit in September 2008. Brazil's Finance Minister Guido Mantega (2006–2014) immediately suggested that the same group of economies meet at a leaders' summit to address the challenges of responding to the crisis.[30] Thus, Brazil was particularly pleased when US President George Bush (2001–2008) agreed to upgrade the G20 into a leaders' summit, the first of which was held in Washington, DC in November 2008. The upgrade effectively meant that Brazil could also shake off the unequal status it had been given as one of the "Outreach Five" in the G7/8 led "Heiligendamm process".[31]

Brazil's influence in the G20, as also in the BRICS group, relies on presidential diplomacy and networking, in direct contrast to the technocratic approach utilised in the WTO. This implies much depends on the personality and style of the president (and not just on institutionalised roles played by trained diplomats). In keeping with the nature of these informal club-like groups, Brazil often uses G20 and BRICS summits (often held close together) as a sounding board for Brazilian foreign policy preferences and pragmatically avoids making any sticky alignments or binding commitments within these groups. This approach works exceptionally well in the BRICS group, since it keeps options open by "playing up what the BRICS have in common and playing down issues on which they disagree".[32]

Brazil was comfortable with the gradual shift in the G20's focus from that of "crisis breaker" to "steering committee" for global economic and financial governance. In the G20, it consistently demanded reform of the international financial institutions, especially International Monetary Fund (IMF) quota and voting shares, greater control over international capital flows and regulation of the banking sector, action on global imbalances and exchange rate volatility, orderly exit from quantitative easing (QE), and a better balance between monetary and fiscal policy approaches to addressing post-crisis recovery.[33] Brazil's positions in

---

30. This was not the first time that a leaders' summit was proposed. Already in 2004, the Canadian Prime Minister Paul Martin had suggested the value of holding such a meeting.

31. Denise Gregory and Paulo Roberto Almeida, "Brazil and the G8 Heiligendamm Process", in Agata Antkiewicz and Andrew Cooper (eds.), *Emerging Powers in Global Governance: Lessons from the Heiligendamm Process* (Waterloo, ON: Centre for International Governance Innovation, 2008), pp. 137–162.

32. Andrew Cooper and Asif Farooq, "BRICS and the Privileging of Informality in Global Governance", *Global Policy*, Vol. 4, No. 4 (2013), pp. 428–433, at p. 432.

33. A clear expression of these concerns appears in Dilma Rousseff's speech at the 67th Opening of the UN General Assembly, New York, 23 September 2012, available: <www.itamaraty.gov.br/discursos> (accessed 15 February 2015).

the G20 responded to its specific macro-economic concerns and global economic conditions at the time of each summit, but there also was a consistent underlying thread to its arguments. Moreover, it repeatedly made clear that it not only enjoyed participating as an equal at the top table of global economic governance, but also accepted the responsibilities that came with this status. It understood the crucial importance of the G7 trusting it would act as a responsible stakeholder rather than exhibit ideologically motivated radical revisionist stances. In fact, Brazil made every effort to justify its place in the G20 on the basis of efficiency and effectiveness rather than equity alone.

At the G20 Seoul Summit (November 2010), Brazil raised the alarm about exchange rate misalignments and "currency war".[34] It highlighted the need for fiscal consolidation, but without cutting off incipient fragile recoveries around the world. At the G20 Cannes Summit (November 2011), Rousseff agreed to consider contributing to European rescue funds, but only within the context of the IMF (she rejected any call for direct contribution into the European Stability Fund). By February 2012, Mantega made it clear that Brazilian contributions would be on two conditions: strengthening the EU's "firewall" and implementing IMF voting share reform. Brazil rejected the German position that the two issues should be treated separately. At the G20 Los Cabos Summit (June 2012), Brazil, alongside all its BRICS partners, agreed to increase contributions to the IMF. Brazil pledged US$10.2 billion. Few could have predicted even a decade ago that Brazil would not only become a creditor nation, but also be contributing funds to bailing out international banks and European governments. Obviously, its deteriorating macro-economic performance in 2014–2015 has dampened confidence in Brazil.

Alongside its fellow emerging powers, Brazil met with some success on its fundamental demand for a greater voice for emerging powers in the IMF. In 2006, Brazil's IMF quota share was raised from 1.42% to 1.78%; in 2010 it was further increased to 2.32%.[35] Once this was implemented, Brazil would rank tenth in the IMF distribution of quota shares, an important acknowledgement of its rising status in the global economy. Disappointingly, although actively engaged in various high profile debates related to global financial and currency related issues, it seldom achieved a favourable response from the established powers. More intriguingly, it often failed to get consistent (or even any) support from its fellow BRICS countries on a range of issues: from "currency wars" to what it believes is an impending "monetary tsunami". Thus, both government and diplomats remain frustrated with the paucity of tangible achievements in reforming various aspects of the global financial architecture.

Notwithstanding these frustrations, so far, Brazil has put considerable effort into complying with obligations agreed in the action plans and communiqués signed at G20 summits. The University of Toronto's G20 Information Centre provides regular reports on compliance of each G20 participant on a selected range of collective

---

34. Guido Mantega is credited with first using this term. NB Brazil also took this issue to the WTO, thus making an explicit link between exchange rate policy and trade competitiveness.

35. Note that China's quota share jumped from 2.98% to 6.39% and India's from 2.44% to 2.75% in the 14th General Review of Quotas at Seoul. Once these are implemented all the BRIC economies will be among the top 10 quota shareholders of the IMF. As of 27 January 2015, 163 members having 79.64% of total quota had consented, although the US had not yet ratified the agreement; see <www.imf.org/external/np/sec/misc/consents.htm> (accessed 15 February 2015).

commitments in the 12 months after the signing of the action plan at the end of each summit. As per its evaluations, Brazil generally scores quite highly, usually in the top half of the 20 states monitored for the compliance report.[36] The latest full compliance report refers to the St Petersburg Action Plan (September 2013). It focused on a range of issues including global growth and job creation, QE exit, cooperation against tax evasion and "financing for investment" (especially securitisation of infrastructure loans and public–private partnerships). Compliance was monitored for 16 priority commitments, and the final compliance report noted that the G20 achieved an average compliance score of +0.44 or 72% (better than final compliance scores for the London, Pittsburgh and Toronto summits). The UK and Germany scored highest with 88% compliance, while Brazil only achieved 66% compliance, unusually putting it in the lower half of the group.[37]

Although Brazil's interests overlap with those of advanced economies in some areas, it believes it has a revisionist vocation and a representative function (as the voice of developing countries) at the G20. This sometimes limits its choices and actions. All evidence suggests that it is highly unlikely to push for radical changes in global governance structures, but it strongly advocates revising them to create a more inclusive international system.

Brazil was sceptical that the informal network structure of the G20 was the obvious arena to manage the process. In 2008, Amorim expressed this view clearly: "The G20 was a positive step in [*dealing with the financial crisis, but it*] will not meet the expectations and interests of all. The UN can and should contribute to this debate."[38] Brazilian diplomats have always preferred to engage in more formal multilateral institutions, where their material resources, negotiating skills, and technocratic approach are most likely to prosper. So although Brazil is likely to be proactive and willing to engage with the concerns of established powers on broader issues of global governance that deal with the provision of global public goods (including issues such as climate change, food security and health), it would rather not turn to the G20 as *the* forum for elaborating international regimes around these issues. Significantly, Brazil might accept discussing these matters at the G20, but it still insists on sticking to the formal multilateral organisations for decision-making in these spheres.

Evaluating Brazil's Success

The above analysis showed Brazil played an active role in both the WTO and the G20, institutions with very different characteristics and memberships. Its achievements in both organisations suggest the range and flexibility of its policy-makers and diplomats. In both cases, its positions and actions displayed revisionist preferences, but via constructive engagement and consistent adherence to international law. Although it favoured formal institutions that allowed for technocratic

36. G20 Information Centre Compliance Reports; see <www.g20.utoronto.ca/compliance> (accessed 15 February 2015). Also, note information on the methodology for calculating these scores.

37. G20 Research Group, "2013 St Petersburg G20 Summit Final Compliance Report" (Toronto: G20 Information Centre, University of Toronto, 15 November 2014), available: <www.g20.utoronto.ca/compliance/2013stpetersburg> (accessed 15 February 2015).

38. Celso Amorim, Speech at the Follow-up International Conference on Financing for Development to Review the Implementation of the Monterrey Consensus, Doha, 30 November 2008available: <www.un.org/webcast/ffd/2008/statements/081130_brasil_en.pdf> (accessed 15 February 2015); emphasis added.

arguments, it did equally well in club-like settings where personal relationships and informal discussions provided opportunities to influence key players. Moreover, in both settings, it became more evident over time that Brazil's shifting strategy often tied in to its desire to be recognised as representative and leader of the Global South. Thus, although focused on bridge-building and constructive dialogue with established powers, when push came to shove it increasingly sided with its "followers" rather than staying focused on its own immediate national interest (as best illustrated on issues of food security and DFQF).

On the one hand, one could argue Brazil was becoming a prisoner of its followers' expectations. It even seemed willing to sacrifice immediate development interests in exchange for gaining recognition as leader of developing countries and benefiting development elsewhere (not that these interests are mutually exclusive). On the other hand, the Itamaraty argues that solidarity with developing countries "is not contradictory with defence of our own interests ... It will bring benefits to Brazil ... This dialectic relation between national interests and the exercise of solidarity has been a fundamental aspect of President Lula's foreign policy".[39] Crucially, South-South cooperation expands Brazil's participation and stature in international politics, and provides a platform for more assertive behaviour demanding global governance reform.

The starting point for any evaluation of its achievements should surely be whether it performs well in terms of its self-defined foreign policy goals. The first section of the article set out three main aims of its foreign policy: domestic development, international rule-making influence, and finding recognition as a major emerging power with rising prestige in the international community. These aspects form the basis of the following brief evaluation.

Although this article cannot develop a full analysis of development outcomes, it would be fair to say that the full arsenal of trade and industrial policies, not to mention social policies (e.g. the well-known conditional cash transfer programme, *Bolsa Família*), did not produce the expected and hoped-for results. Both the academic literature and media reports identify a range of obstacles hampering development and also citizen dissatisfaction (e.g. the street protests in 2013 demanding better public services, improved infrastructure, enhanced job opportunities, etc.). However, it is difficult to lay the blame for development outcomes on foreign policy.

In terms of international rule-making influence, Brazil certainly played a vital role in international institutions from WTO to G20 and beyond in the past 15 years. Its influence as a rule-maker stemmed from its many identities: largest economy in Latin America, major developing country, leader of the Global South, and member of the BRICS. Both established powers and developing countries often consulted it formally and informally on a wide range of issues affecting multiple international regimes and global governance structures. More importantly, Brazil had not only the technical capacity but also the willingness to contribute with constructive interventions to shape global governance institutions. Its diplomatic traditions, emphasising dialogue and bridge-building while respecting autonomy, were essential to its image as a pragmatic and sensible negotiating partner.

---

39. Amorim, "Brazilian Foreign Policy", *op. cit.*, p. 225.

However, recent years have seen Brazil's positions being fashioned by an overt desire to be identified as a key emerging power and acknowledged leader among developing countries. In practical terms, this ambition has manifested itself in the shift to more distributive bargaining strategies, demonstrating its influence as a blocking rather than a constructive force. The dangers of such a strategy are many, most importantly: does it make sense to allow concerns with identity and status to subvert more pragmatic material interests? Moreover, such negative approaches to gaining influence might solidify one's reputation as a veto player, but only reveal weak capabilities as a rule-maker or positive agenda-setter. From the point of view of established powers, it might make sense to engage Brazil sooner rather than later, so as to avoid it entrenching more confrontational patterns of behaviour. This would strengthen systemic legitimacy (because of Brazil's developing country and regional leadership credentials), and also "send an important signal to other aspiring powers on the merits of choosing less disruptive pathways to power".[40]

Finally, have these domestic and international achievements (or failures) led to an overall increase in Brazil's international prestige? Yes, the past decade has seen Brazil emerge as an essential interlocutor and it is likely to be included in most discussions related to global economic governance. Brazilian citizens have assumed the leadership/directorship of key multilateral institutions such as the WTO and the UN Food and Agriculture Organization (FAO). It is part of the prestigious club of emerging powers, the BRICS. As such, it is an equal contributor to the new BRICS development bank and the contingency currency reserve pool announced at the BRICS Summit in Fortaleza in July 2014. Brazil is also a strategic partner of the European Union and separately with a number of European states.

However, Brazil's growing influence cannot be taken for granted. On the one hand, the current negotiations for mega-regional trade agreements deliberately exclude Brazil (as well as the other BRICS members). Although not yet finalised, and depending on what is signed, these agreements could shape global trade and investment flows (without any Brazilian input) even as they bypass the multilateral regime (Brazil's priority arena for such discussions). On the other hand, it bears noting that Atlantic facing European established powers (including the UK) are in some sense competing with the growing influence of the Pacific Rim countries. Brazil shares European geopolitical and geo-economic frustrations on this point and much can be said for boosting the strategic relevance of the Atlantic to include South Atlantic states (especially Brazil and South Africa).[41] Brazil also needs to be aware that Western established powers may prefer to accommodate emerging powers in informal groups such as the G20, rather than to extensively reform formal international organisations that have "substantive missions or voting mechanisms".[42] As already mentioned, Brazil does not favour acting in these informal institutional spaces.

Finally, does constructivism provide a better explanation than more traditional international relations theories? The analysis demonstrated how strategic

---

40. Narlikar, *op. cit.*, p. 136.

41. See Robert Dover and Erik Jones, "The Role of the EU in Promoting a Broader Trans-Atlantic Partnership", Report prepared for European Parliament Directorate General for External Policies (Brussels: European Parliament Policy Department, 2013).

42. G. John Ikenberry and Thomas Wright, "Rising Powers and Global Institutions", Century Foundation Report (New York: The Century Foundation, 2008), p. 30.

behaviour and national interest are socially constructed, based on how state actors perceive the world, the identities they hold about themselves and others, and their shared understandings about the institutions in which they participate. A direct focus on material interests does not provide a thorough explanation of Brazilian foreign policy and negotiating positions. Instead, as constructivists argue, these are better analysed as a response to social relationships (a sense of community), historical experience (collective memory), and a drive for social recognition and prestige.[43] It is these features that come across in the rhetoric and practice of South-South diplomacy and the push for recognition as a major power. Constructivism presents the best alternative to materialism, while not abandoning rationalism.[44] It also seeks to explain how norms, ideas and the rhetoric of statecraft can see an alternative to anarchy and focus on developing "communal cooperation in the future".[45] This is best exemplified in the acceptance among developing countries and the WTO of Lula's message linking market access to social justice and the ability of Brazilian diplomats to embed this in their coalition management strategies.

To conclude, the above analysis has shown that Brazil's leadership style is based on particular development-friendly values and solidarity with its followership. However, this is unlikely to be enough to gain major power status. Brazil needs to do more. It must rethink the norms and concepts that drive its foreign policy positions. It needs to move beyond simply incrementally adapting to a changing context. It must actively engage in deeper processes of learning that meaningfully change its attitudes and actions. It should reconsider its leadership strategy and seek to overcome the tension inherent in its developing country identity and its emerging power status. Graduation fears might result in Brazil's marginalisation fears becoming a reality. For all of Brazil's talk of engaging with a changing world, it sometimes seems that Brazil itself is afraid to change.

Acknowledgements

Many thanks to my reviewers for their very useful comments, and to Marco Vieira for organising a thought-provoking conference at the University of Birmingham in May 2014.

---

43. Alexander Wendt, *Social Theory of International Politics* (Cambridge: Cambridge University Press, 1999).

44. Hurd, *op. cit.*, pp. 311–312.

45. Jennifer Sterling-Folker, "Competing Paradigms or Birds of a Feather? Constructivism and Neoliberal Institutionalism Compared", *International Studies Quarterly,* Vol. 44, No. 1 (2000), pp. 97–119.

Global Economic Governance and the British Economy: From the Gold Standard to the G20

CHRIS ROGERS

The paper considers the extent to which the G20 process has assisted British state managers with key problems of economic management. It conceptualises the state as the political form of capital and argues that the institutions of global economic governance have helped British state managers reconcile the objectives of accumulation and legitimation from the Gold Standard to the G20. In particular, it argues that the technocratic approach adopted by the G20 from the finance ministers' meetings to the leaders' summits has provided British policymakers with a discourse of international expert consensus that reinforces domestic economic strategy based on financialisation, and in the process contributes to the depoliticisation of welfare state retrenchment and labour market discipline in the context of liberalisation and globalisation.

Introduction

Throughout the twentieth and twenty-first centuries, the development of the global economy has been punctuated by crises that have been explained in terms of the deficiencies of global economic governance, and responded to with revisions to that framework. In the shadows of the Asian financial crisis, meetings of the G20 group of finance ministers emerged from the G7 and G8 as it was agreed that "key emerging economies were insufficiently included in global economic management efforts" and subsequently, it was argued these meetings proved the G20's "worth as a way of opening up and rationalizing the international dialogue"[1] on global governance. In the wake of the global financial crisis that emerged in 2007, George W. Bush's invitation to leaders of the G20 saw the finance ministers' meeting of 2008 serve "as a prepatory session for the subsequent meeting at the leaders' level".[2]

As Eric Helleiner noted, "many analysts speculated that it might generate a new 'Bretton Woods moment'", while both the French President, Nicholas Sarkozy and the British Prime Minister, Gordon Brown, "held up the hope of a 'new Bretton Woods' in the lead up to the first G20 leaders' summit in November 2008".[3] Nonetheless, in spite of some reforms in global economic governance, including the

---

1. Gordon S. Smith, "G7 to G8 to G20: Evolution in Global Governance", *CIGI 20 Papers No. 6* (Ontario: CIGI, 2011), p. 5.
2. *Ibid.*, p. 6.
3. Eric Helleiner, "A Bretton Woods Moment? The 2007–2008 Crisis and the Future of Global Finance", *International Affairs*, Vol. 83, No. 3 (2010), pp. 619–636.

expansion of resources for the International Monetary Fund (IMF) and regulatory reform reflecting a shift from microprudential to macroprudential ideational paradigms,[4] the G20 has not produced a Bretton Woods moment of this kind and the prospect of it doing so in the future seems remote. Indeed, Eichengreen has argued that the modest approach of the G20 "will not be hailed as a New World Financial Order", even if it might go some way to making the global economy more secure.[5] In contrast to approaches such as these, which have examined the evolution of the G20 process in terms of its institutional development, this paper asks how the G20 process has helped British policymakers confront economic challenges, and the extent to which it has posed new ones.

The paper understands the state as the political form of capital accumulation.[6] This leaves state managers facing a contradiction between accumulation and legitimation that is exacerbated by the tension between the global character of capital and the national character of political authority.[7] This is because accumulation in the context of international competition relies on market discipline, and the consequences of market discipline include things like low wages, precariousness of employment and unemployment, which have the potential to pose problems for political authority. The central argument of the paper is that institutions of global economic governance from the Gold Standard to the G20 have consistently assisted British state managers in their attempts to mediate these tensions in the context of its relative economic decline. It argues that the G20's technocratic approach to global economic governance does not question the normative basis of liberalisation or globalisation, and therefore implies both that these processes *must* be accepted and that there is a "correct" set of policies to govern them—which includes the acceptance of market discipline and balanced budgets. The paper suggests that this discourse serves to reinforce domestic discourses of globalisation that depoliticise the social consequences of economic restructuring in Britain by allowing policymakers to defer to a language of international expert consensus.

In other words, the paper accepts a broadly shared view of global economic governance as consisting of the institutions and processes through which states negotiate solutions to common problems, but emphasises the role these institutions can also play in domestic political strategies. While the institutions of global economic governance include organisations such as the IMF, the World Bank, the Organisation for Economic Co-operation and Development and the G20 (among others), and a full discussion of the role these institutions play in the promotion of domestic political strategies would be desirable, the constraints of a journal article mean that such an analysis is not possible here. The G20 provides the primary focus for this paper.

The first section briefly historicises the way in which various institutions of global economic governance have assisted Britain with managing its relative

---

4. See Andrew Baker, "The New Political Economy of the Macroprudential Ideational Shift", *New Political Economy* (2012), doi: 10.1080/13563467.2012.662952.

5. Barry Eichengreen, "New World Pragmatism", *The Guardian*, 24 October 2008, available: <http://www.theguardian.com/commentisfree/2008/oct/24/marketturmoil-creditcrunch>.

6. The theoretical position reflects the Open Marxist tradition of state theory, captured in works such as Werner Bonefeld, "Social Constitution and the Form of the Capitalist State", in Werner Bonefeld *et al.* (eds.), *Open Marxism: Volume I* (London: Pluto, 1992), pp. 92–122 and Peter Burnham, "Capital, Crisis, and the International State System", in Werner Bonefeld and John Holloway (eds.), *Global Capital, National State, and the Politics of Money* (Basingstoke: Palgrave Macmillan, 1995), pp. 92–115.

7. See John Holloway, *Crack Capitalism: The Meaning of Revolution Today* (London: Pluto, 2005), p. 14.

economic decline by depoliticising the consequences of attempts to restructure its economy since the Gold Standard era. The second section presents data to demonstrate the extent to which the tension between accumulation and legitimation stemming from Britain's relative economic decline has remained a key challenge for the British state since the 1990s, which was mediated through financialisation. The third section shows how British domestic policy has adopted a technocratic approach to globalisation, that the G20 agenda reflects this, and has contributed to depoliticising the consequences of Britain's attempts to restructure its economy by endorsing the domestically promoted view that liberalisation and globalisation are processes that place an effective constraint on the kind of policies the state can pursue. The fourth section discusses the contribution the G20 agenda has made to Britain's attempts to restructure its economy by encouraging the development of complementary strategies in emerging economies.

The British Economy from the Gold Standard to the G20

If, as Bonefeld has phrased it, we understand that "the purpose of capital is to make profit, and the state is the political form of that purpose",[8] the focus of our analysis of challenges faced by emerging and established powers in global economic governance must shift from the form of the institutions, to the political and economic problems states are confronted with as they attempt to create conditions for accumulation. This approach is distinct from realist traditions in the political economy of international relations[9] and domestic interest/societal approaches to the development of the forms of global economic governance[10] because it does not focus on the pursuit of power or the way in which the state responds to powerful domestic pressure groups. Rather, it is concerned with the tensions between accumulation and legitimation that stem from the fact that the former depends on a disciplined labour force (with low wages, precariousness of employment, etc.) and the latter on consumer demand based on high and stable earnings. This section briefly shows how institutions of global economic governance can be understood to have helped mediate that tension since the era of the Gold Standard.

The classic account of the operation of the Gold Standard and its contradictions is found in Polanyi's *The Great Transformation*. Polanyi conceived of the Gold Standard as a means of facilitating the expansion of trade through the use of commodity money, which contradicted the management of domestic currencies. This is because whenever changes in the terms of trade threatened the exchange rate, domestic price deflation was required in order to bring the system back into balance.[11] This process was facilitated by central banks, whose function was to cushion "the immediate effects of gold withdrawals on the circulation of notes as well as of the diminished circulation of notes on business".[12] However, since domestic deflation

---

8. Werner Bonefeld, "Global Capital, National State, and the International", *Critique*, Vol. 36, No. 1 (2008), p. 64.

9. For example, Robert Gilpin, *The Political Economy of International Relations* (Princeton, NJ: Princeton University Press, 1987).

10. For example, Stefan A. Schirm, "Global Politics are Domestic Politics: A Society Approach to Divergence in the G20", *Review of International Studies*, Vol. 39 (2013), pp. 685–706.

11. Karl Polanyi, *The Great Transformation: The Political and Economic Origins of Our Time* (Boston: Beacon Press, [1944] 2001), pp. 202–203.

12. *Ibid.*, p. 203.

carried with it domestic social and political consequences, in a context where adherence to the Gold Standard was "axiomatic" and where "the supreme directive of the bank was always and under all conditions to stay on gold",[13] attempts to stabilise exchanges in the context of downward movements in prices had devastating social consequences and exposed the myth of the self-regulating market.

Polanyi's analysis therefore gives primacy to the notion that the operation of the Gold Standard prompted defensive countermoves that undermined its existence. Given the onset of the Great Depression, Polanyi's account fits with a conventional narrative that understands Britain's return to gold in the inter-war period as a policy failure rooted in a mistaken ideological belief in the myth of the self-regulating market. However, given the economy was suffering from "increasing problems associated with the onset of relative economic decline, a growing dependency on industries of diminishing international importance, and a progressive rise in labour dissatisfaction", which were compounded by the politicisation of economic policy during the First World War,[14] it is possible to construct an alternative narrative. For instance, Kettell has argued that Britain's return to gold at the pre-war parity of $4.86

> was seen by Britain's state managers as the key element of a governing strategy designed to deal with these problems by imposing a firm anti-inflationary discipline on capital and labour, and by displacing any adverse social and political consequences of this process away from the state through a "depoliticisation" of economic conditions and policy-making.[15]

In other words, commitments to the institutions of global economic governance generally deemed to have been an abject failure, can be interpreted as a way in which British policymakers were able to discipline labour to extract competitive advantage while offsetting responsibility for the social consequences of these policies to the technical imperatives of exchange rate management.

The relationship between the Bretton Woods institutions and the British economy can also be understood in a similar way. It is often argued that the introduction of the par-value system of fixed-but-adjustable exchange rates and capital controls served as a means of insulating policymakers from the discipline of international financial markets so they might pursue domestic policy objectives, including full employment. This position is typified by Ruggie's description of the settlement as a reflection of "the shared legitimacy of a set of social objectives to which the industrial world had moved, unevenly but 'as a single entity'".[16] However, this particular institutionalised form of governing the global economy also allowed British state managers to take important steps toward restructuring its economy without precipitating a crisis of legitimation.

The keystone in this endeavour was capital controls, which were particularly significant for Britain given the size of overseas sterling balances accumulated during

---

13. *Ibid.*, p. 206.

14. Steven Kettell, *The Political Economy of Exchange Rate Policy Making: From the Gold Standard to the Euro* (Basingstoke: Palgrave Macmillan, 2004), p. 5.

15. *Ibid.*, p. 5.

16. John G. Ruggie, "International Regimes, Transactions, and Change: Embedded Liberalism in the Postwar Economic Order", *International Organization*, Vol. 36, No. 2 (1982), p. 398.

the Second World War. In the period between 1945 and 1962, these were consistently above £3 billion and frequently above £3.5 billion,[17] and would have exposed the exchange rate to downward pressure in the context of Britain's relative economic decline if they could be freely converted. This became immediately apparent in 1947 as a run on the pound resulted from America's insistence that Britain introduce current account convertibility as a condition of receiving a $3.75 billion loan.[18] The capital controls permitted by Bretton Woods meant Britain was therefore insulated from destabilising capital flows to which it was especially exposed. This allowed it to manage the depreciation of sterling, while the fact that the IMF had to approve currency devaluations meant that any declines in the pound's purchasing power could be attributed to structural factors. This could help to depoliticise both the consequences of economic restructuring and the increasing labour discipline that this implied, as well as increasing costs of living, by deferring to the Fund's view that restructuring and devaluation were economically necessary.

Following the collapse of the fixed exchange rate regime in the early 1970s and the failure of the British state to successfully restructure its economy in the long run during the stagflation, which ultimately resulted in domestic political unrest during the 1978–79 Winter of Discontent, the Thatcher governments relied more obviously on the strength of the state in order to achieve its goals. For instance, confrontation with the trade unions represented an explicit politicisation of industrial relations as a means of disciplining labour. Nonetheless, in the context of the liberalisation of finance and floating exchange rates, the British state continued to use the institutional forms of global economic governance to pursue domestic accumulation strategies without provoking political dissatisfaction from the early 1990s. The most notable example of this was through membership of the Exchange Rate Mechanism (ERM) under John Major in the period 1990–92, which established counter-inflationary credibility while offsetting responsibility for its deflationary consequences onto the international commitments implied by ERM membership.[19]

Challenges for the British Economy

The previous section showed how the institutions of global economic governance have supported British state managers' strategies aimed at addressing contradictions between accumulation and legitimation through the politics of depoliticisation in the context of its relative economic decline. In order to assess the extent to which the same can be said of Britain's participation in the G20, it is first necessary to outline the challenges faced by the British economy since the 1990s. This section uses a range of official statistics in order to show how reconciling the tension between accumulation and legitimation in the context of relative economic decline has remained a significant challenge for the British economy.

The most obvious indicator of a state's competitiveness is reflected in its national accounts in the form of the current account balance, and as Figure 1 shows, Britain

17. The figures are reported in Chris Rogers, *The IMF and European Economies: Crisis and Conditionality* (Basingstoke: Palgrave Macmillan, 2012), p. 72, and original data can be found in The National Archives T 267/29, *Treasury Historical Memorandum* No. 16, January 1972.

18. Peter Burnham, "Re-evaluating the Washington Loan Agreement: A Revisionist View of the Limits of Postwar American Power", *Review of International Studies*, Vol. 18, No. 2 (1992), p. 245.

19. See Werner Bonefeld and Peter Burnham, "The Politics of Counter Inflationary Credibility in Britain, 1990–94", *Review of Radical Political Economics*, Vol. 30, No. 1 (1998), pp. 32–52.

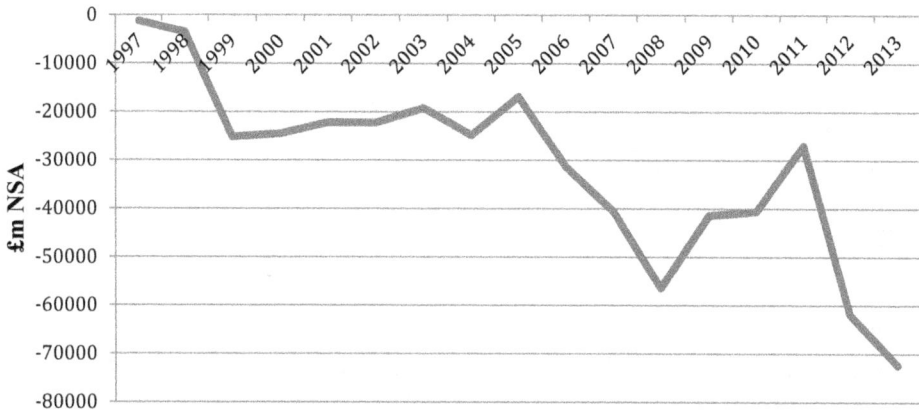

Figure 1. UK Current Account Balance 1997–2013.
Source: Office for National Statistics, "Pink Book—Current Account (Series HBOG) Last Updated 20 January 2015" (2015), available: <http://www.ons.gov.uk/ons/rel/bop/united-kingdom-balance-of-payments/2014/tsd-pink-book-2014-time-series.html> (last accessed 3 March 2015).

has not recorded a surplus since before 1997. However, Britain's consistent propensity to import more goods and services than it exports is a reflection of more fundamental issues within the economy. As Figure 2 shows, production in Britain has also become steadily more expensive as unit labour costs, a function of wages and productivity, has gradually increased across the whole economy, and while unit wage costs in the manufacturing sector showed some decline in the mid-2000s, they too began to increase from late 2007.

From the point of view of international comparison, British productivity has also lagged significantly behind other major economies. As Figure 3 demonstrates, the British economy has been consistently outperformed by Germany, Italy and the USA in terms of productivity measured by gross domestic product (GDP) per hour worked, and remains significantly behind the G7 average (excluding the UK). Reflecting the relatively high costs of production in Britain, and the fact that it continues to lag behind other economies in terms of its productivity, rates of profitability in Britain have stagnated since the late 1990s in the manufacturing private non-financial corporations sector, and in the services private non-financial corporations sector, shown in Figure 4. In combination, these conditions have meant that the British economy has been allowed to operate under capacity as measured by its output gap—the difference between realised and potential GDP—in 14 of 23 years since 1990.[20]

---

20. See OECD, "Output Gaps: Deviation of Actual GDP from Potential GDP as a Percentage of Potential GDP", *Economic Outlook*, No. 95 (2014), available: <http://stats.oecd.org/Index.aspx?QueryId=51655#>. It is worth noting that the use of the output gap as an official statistic is also interesting in itself, both because of the difficulties involved in measuring potential GDP and because of its role in determining figures for newly fashionable "structural deficit" statistics, where it has been suggested that overly pessimistic assumptions about the permanent loss of capacity during the crisis have been used to inflate the structural deficit and therefore bolster the case for austerity measures. See Hugo Radice, "Enforcing Austerity in Europe: The Structural Deficit as a Policy Target", *Journal of Contemporary European Studies*, Vol. 22, No. 3 (2014), pp. 318–328.

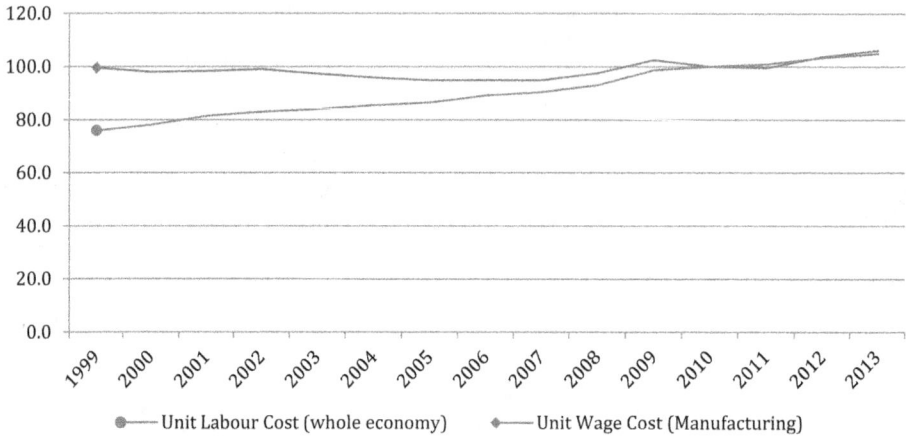

Figure 2. Unit Labour Cost Indices, Seasonally Adjusted, 2010 = 100.
Source: Office for National Statistics, "LPRODHIST: Historical Series of Labour Productivity" (2014), available: <http://www.ons.gov.uk/ons/datasets-and-tables/index.html?
pageSize=50&sortBy=none&sortDirection=none&newquery=LPRODHIST&content-type=
Reference+table&content-type=Dataset> (last accessed 3 March 2015).

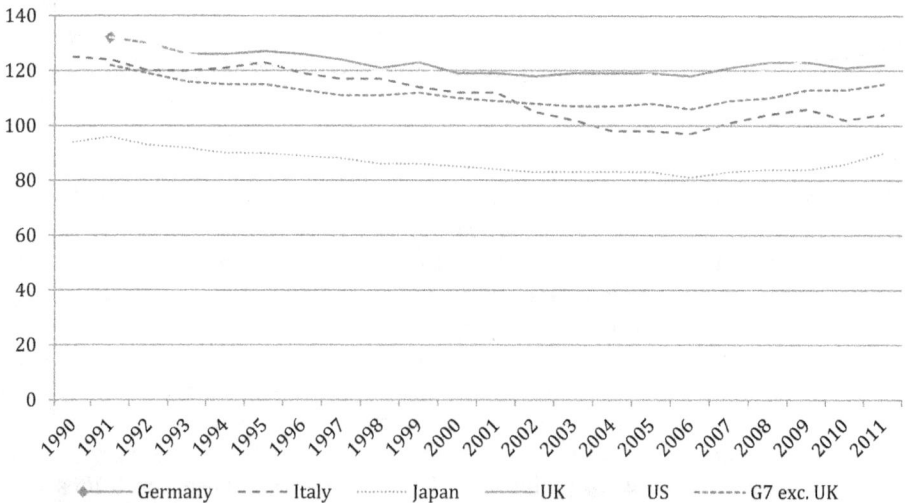

Figure 3. GDP per Hour Worked (Current Price), UK = 100.
Source: Office for National Statistics, "International Comparisons of Productivity—Final
Estimates for 2011" (2013), available: <http://www.ons.gov.uk/ons/datasets-and-tables/
index.html?pageSize=50&sortBy=none&sortDirection=none&newquery=international
+comparisons+of+productivity+final+estimates+2011> (last accessed 3 March 2015).

In combination, this data suggests that one of the overarching problems that the
British economy faces can be characterised in terms of labour discipline, which has
been insufficient to keep costs of production down and rates of profit high enough
to realise sufficient rewards for investors. As such, one of the principle challenges
for British state managers has been to exert greater discipline over labour to restore

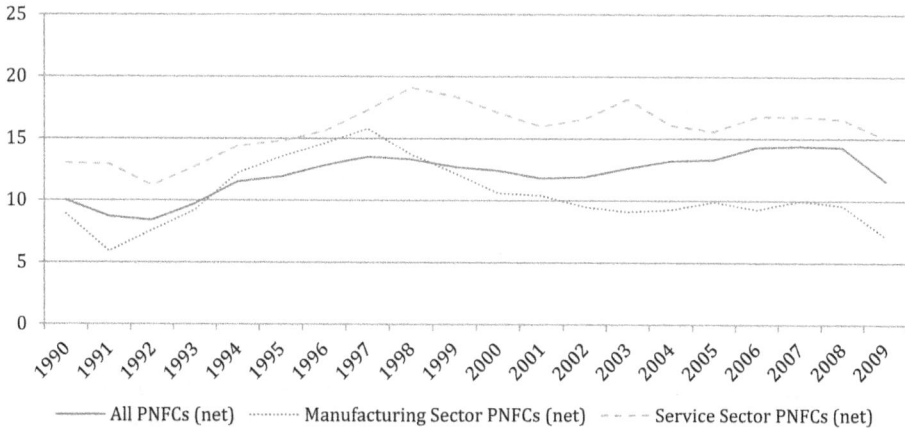

Figure 4. Annual Rate of Return of Private Non-financial Corporations (PNFCs) (%).
Source: Office for National Statistics, *Profitability of UK Companies 1st Quarter 2010* (Newport: ONS, 2010), Table 1, p. 6.

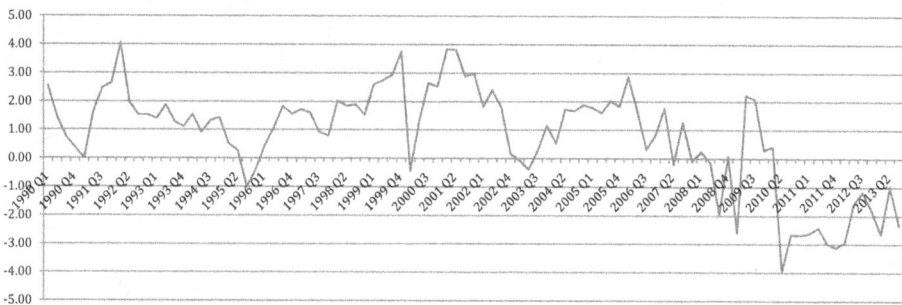

Figure 5. Average Weekly Wage Growth (Deflated by Retail Price Index (RPI), Percentage Increase on Previous Year).
Source: Data from Office for National Statistics, "An Examination of Falling Real Wages 2010–2013" (2014), Figure 2, p. 3, used under terms of the Open Government Licence.

some measure of competitiveness in the real economy. This has been reflected in only modest gains in real average weekly earnings, which have been punctuated by periods of negligible growth or declines (Figure 5), and levels of unemployment that have only fallen below 5% in two years since 1990 (Figure 6).

These indicators provide a prime illustration of the central contradiction in capitalist economies: that in order to create conditions for profitable accumulation state managers must extract sacrifices from the labour force on whose support their legitimacy depends. Strategies are therefore required in order to limit the extent to which discontent at these sacrifices come to be directed at the state's political legitimacy. Throughout the late 1990s and the early 2000s, this was principally managed through the politics of financialisation, which Crouch has described as a system of "privatised Keynesianism"[21] and Finlayson has called a system of

---

21. See Colin Crouch, "Privatized Keynesianism: An Unacknowledged Policy Regime", *British Journal of Politics and International Relations*, Vol. 11, No. 3 (2009), pp. 382–399.

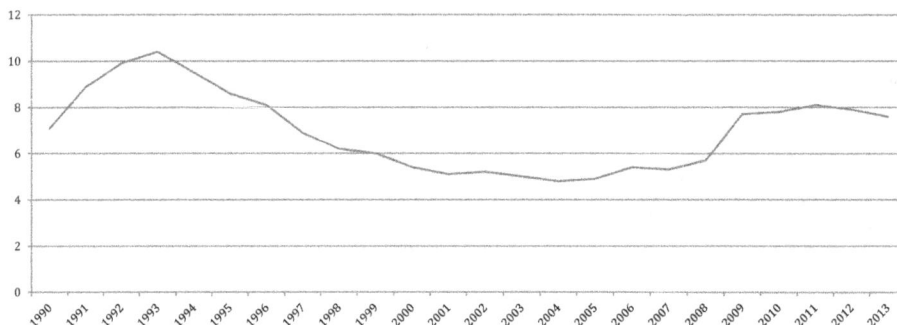

Figure 6. Unemployment 16+ (%).
Source: Office for National Statistics, "Series MGSX" (2015), available: <http://www.ons.gov.uk/ons/site-information/using-the-website/time-series/index.html> (last accessed 3 March 2015).

"asset-based welfare".[22] These systems, it has been argued, were fundamentally dependent on the systematic substitution of state-provided welfare services with market-based means of maintaining consumption, principally the use of revolving short-term unsecured debt and increasing paper wealth in the form of equity in property inflated by rising house prices. Figures 7 and 8 illustrate the extent to which the British economy was increasingly reliant on financialisation and the ways in which it was facilitated, by showing the increasing levels of household debt as a percentage of net disposable income and the declining rate of interest, first, on 2-year fixed rate 75% loan to value mortgages and second, on credit card debts.

This set of circumstances played a key role in sustaining the increase in house prices that saw the Land Registry's House Price Index nearly triple in the period between December 1995 and July 2007 (Figure 9). However, while this strategy was able to insulate British governments from political pressure that was otherwise likely to stem from their willingness to use levels of unemployment consistently upwards of 5% in order to impose discipline in labour markets in the context of increasing welfare conditionality, it was clearly not a sustainable strategy. This is illustrated by the dissonance between the rate of increase of house prices on which privatised Keynesianism and the system of asset-based welfare were based and the much lower rate of increase in wages, which was ultimately reflected in the increasing indebtedness of households. Ultimately, this state of affairs was unsustainable, as increases in wages failed to keep pace with indebtedness and undermined debt serviceability, with concomitant implications for the housing market on which the boom had been based, as well as the highly leveraged positions of British financial institutions with exposure to mortgage-backed securities.

Data on Britain's recent economic performance therefore shows a number of things. On the one hand, it paints a picture of an economy in decline, with attendant consequences for standards of living and potentially, for political legitimation. On the other, it paints a picture of an economy that has managed to mute the potential for political dissatisfaction to be directed at the state by using financialisation to sustain consumption as other policies have allowed the economy to frequently run below

---

22. See Alan Finlayson, "Financialisation, Financial Literacy, and Asset-Based Welfare", *British Journal of Politics and International Relations*, Vol. 11, No. 3 (2009), pp. 400–421.

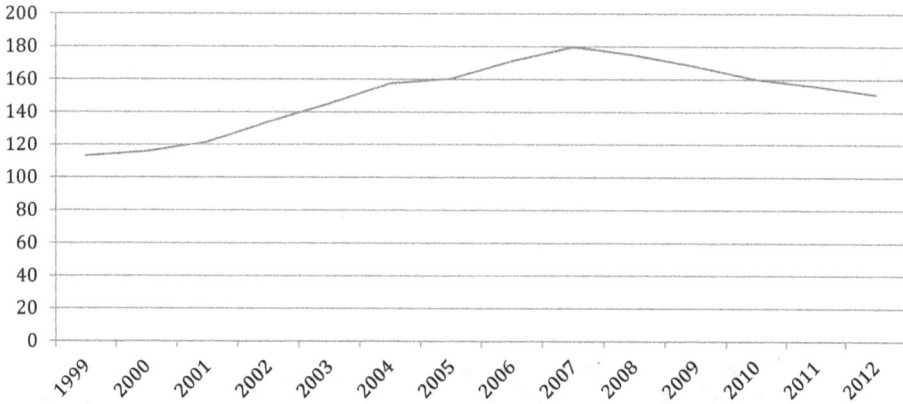

Figure 7. Household Debt as Percentage of Net Disposable Income.
Source: OECD data, available: <http://data.oecd.org/hha/household-debt.htm> (last accessed 3 March 2015).

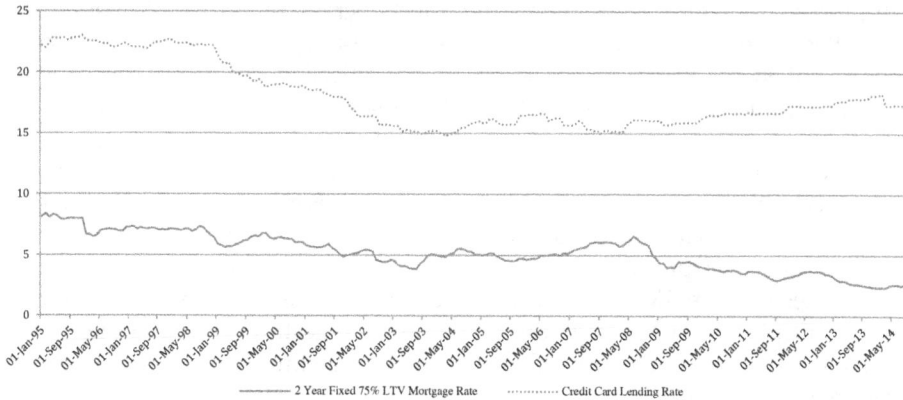

2 Year Fixed 75% LTV Mortgage Rate   Credit Card Lending Rate

Figure 8. UK Interest Rates.
Source: Bank of England Statistics Database, available: <http://www.bankofengland.co.uk/boeapps/iadb/Index.asp?first=yes&SectionRequired=I&HideNums=-1&ExtraInfo=true&Travel=Nix> (data generated 15 September 2014).

capacity, unemployment to remain above 5% and the trend in real wages to be punctuated with periodic declines. The next section considers the extent to which the evolution of the G20 process can be understood to have played a role in endorsing and legitimising the domestic policies that allowed this situation to develop.

From Finance Ministers' Meetings to Leaders' Summits

The central argument of the paper is that institutions of global economic governance may help domestic political authorities with the legitimation of policies designed to address tensions between accumulation and legitimation. In the first section, it showed ways in which British state managers have benefitted from such strategies historically, and the second section showed how this tension remains an ongoing problem in Britain. This section argues that, since 1999, the

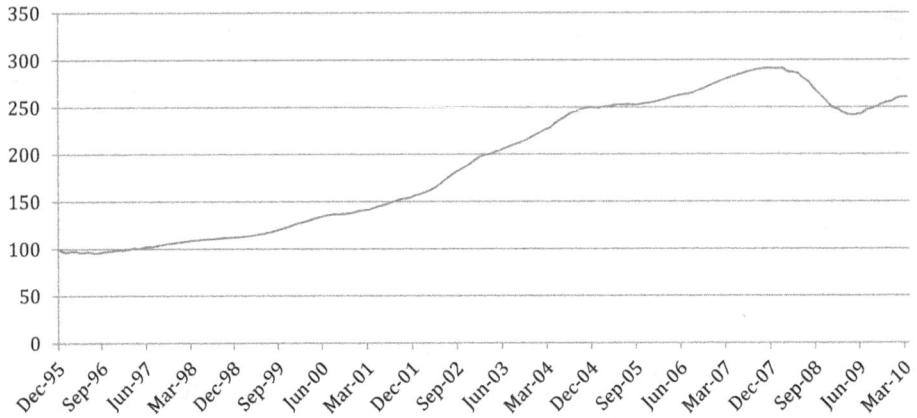

Figure 9. House Price Index for England and Wales.
Source: Land Registry data, available: <http://landregistry.data.gov.uk/app/hpi> (last accessed 3 March 2015).

G20 process has contributed to creating a technocratic discourse of liberalisation that reflects, endorses and reinforces the domestic growth model adopted in Britain, and in the process contributes to depoliticising the social consequences that stem from the politics of austerity it implies. This analysis comes with the important caveat that the G20 is not the only significant institution in global economic governance, and that the technocratic approach that has endorsed the British strategy is neither uniform nor wholly uncontested. For instance, the IMF and the European Central Bank have been instrumental in managing the Eurozone sovereign debt crisis by providing finance and injecting liquidity into the European banking sector. The IMF has also introduced debate over the desirability of capital controls to manage large capital inflows, suggesting a degree of normative contest and incremental ideational change[23] in the institutions of global economic governance more broadly defined.

The argument is not, therefore, that "global economic governance", broadly defined, has supported the domestic economic strategy in Britain by providing policymakers with an international expert view that endorses their strategies as "correct" in technical terms and serves to depoliticise the consequences of those strategies as a result. Rather, the argument here is that particular institutions of global economic governance *may* play this role, that there are numerous historical instances where there is evidence to support this claim and that the G20 is another instance in which it is possible to conceive of institutions of global economic governance supporting domestic political strategy by providing an external endorsement of policies being introduced that is couched in the language of technical "correctness".

Finance Ministers' Meetings

It is commonly acknowledged that the emergence of the G20 finance ministers' meetings reflected a need for the institutions of global economic governance to

23. See Manuella Moschella, "The Institutional Roots of Incremental Ideational Change: The IMF and Capital Controls over the Global Financial Crisis", *British Journal of Politics and International Relations* (2014), doi: 10.1111/1467-856X.12049.

recognise the significance of emerging economies, and to incorporate them into dialogue on global economic management to realise benefits for all.[24] Following the establishment of the ad hoc G22 and G33 processes, the G7 nations were aware "of the merit in engaging systemically important emerging-market economies in a regular informal dialogue" on the basis of their "growing importance in the global economy" and because "their vulnerabilities had been exposed by earlier crises".[25] The G20 itself was therefore established with the mandate to promote "cooperation to achieve sustainable world economic growth for all", which was ratified at the Berlin meeting in 1999.[26] Alongside it, although without formal connection,[27] the Financial Stability Forum was established in order to assist in the construction and coordination of international standards,[28] and in combination provided a new and more inclusive[29] international framework for governing the global economy.

The way in which this task was undertaken, however, was fundamentally dependent on the way that the emergence of crises in emerging markets in 1997 was understood. This was clearly demonstrated in the initial meetings, which resulted in a consensus "that in order to reduce a country's vulnerability to financial crises, sound macroeconomic policies, including appropriate exchange rate and debt management policies, were essential", and should be supplemented with "improved financial sector regulation and supervision, including the observance of internationally accepted standards and codes".[30] From the perspective of the G20, it was not capital account liberalisation itself that was at the root of the problem. Rather, it was argued that outflows of capital reflected poor market sentiment which emerged from the fact that "the development of supervisory and regulatory systems in many emerging economies had not kept pace with the challenges posed by the opening of capital accounts", while prevailing exchange rate regimes "proved brittle in the face of persistent capital outflows".[31]

As Eric Helleiner notes, this interpretation of the Asian financial crisis was not necessarily shared by emerging market economies, which felt it was necessary "to reduce their countries' vulnerability to global financial markets" and reignited interest in capital controls and reserve accumulation.[32] However, emphasis

---

24. See *inter alia* John Kirton, "What is the G20?", University of Toronto G8 Information Centre (1999), available: <http://www.g8.utoronto.ca/g20/g20whatisit.html>; John Kirton, "From G7 to G20: Capacity, Leadership and Normative Diffusion in Global Financial Governance", paper prepared for International Studies Association Annual Convention, Hawaii, March 2005, p. 4, available: <www.g8.utoronto.ca/scholar/kirton2005/kirton_isa2005.pdf>; Mark Beeson and Stephen Bell, "The G20 and the Politics of International Financial Sector Reform: Robust Regimes or Hegemonic Instability?", *CSGR Working Paper No. 174/05* (2005), p. 4, available: <http://wrap.warwick.ac.uk/1943/>; Smith, *op. cit.*, p. 5.

25. Group of Twenty, "The Group of Twenty: A History" (2008), p. 16, available: <http://www.g20.utoronto.ca>.

26. *Ibid.*, p. 19.

27. *Ibid.*, p. 45.

28. Helleiner, *op. cit.*, p. 630.

29. The inclusivity of the G20 has been contested, on the grounds that "it contains no representation either from the poorest and smallest developing countries or from the European like-minded countries (the Nordics and Dutch)", because it lacks accountability and transparency systems, and because its origins lie in the G7. See Gerald K. Helleiner, "Markets, Politics, and Globalization: Can the Global Economy be Civilized?", *Global Governance*, Vol. 7, No. 3 (2001), p. 253.

30. Group of Twenty, *op. cit.*, p. 29.

31. *Ibid.*, p. 11.

32. Helleiner, "A Bretton Woods Moment?", *op. cit.*, p. 628.

nonetheless came to rest on the sequencing of capital account liberalisation,[33] which is to say an emphasis on the implementation of adequate regulatory standards before the capital account was liberalised, rather than on an examination of the benefits of the process itself. As the implications of the Asian financial crisis receded, the focus of the G20 gradually shifted towards social priorities because it appeared that discussions on crisis prevention and resolution had "run their course, at least for the time being".[34] After 2004, this new emphasis revolved around the G20 Accord for Sustained Growth, which included agreement among members on "the importance of price stability and fiscal discipline, strong domestic financial institutions, prudent debt management, competition, global trade liberalisation, flexible labour markets, education, and social safety nets".[35]

The approach adopted to global economic governance in the aftermath of the Asian financial crisis can be described as technocratic because it placed emphasis on the way in which liberalisation was facilitated rather than the desirability of liberalisation itself. Liberalisation and globalisation were therefore accepted as facts, which required the implementation of particular kinds of policies if benefits were to be realised. This approach provided an international institutional endorsement of policies that British state managers had been adopting in order to try and increase its economy's competitiveness while sustaining levels of consumption by encouraging financialisation and developing a system of asset-based welfare. For instance, the G20's technocratic approach to managing globalisation clearly resonated with the notion of "The Third Way", and its suggestion that the primary task of government was to help citizens negotiate the challenges presented by the "revolutions of our time",[36] including globalisation. It was even more firmly manifested in the policy discourse by Ed Balls' assertion that "The rapid globalization of the world economy has made securing credibility more rather than less important",[37] and that credibility was effectively dependent on "low and stable inflation and sound public finances".[38]

Through its treatment of the process of globalisation as a technical matter that needed to be managed in order to maximise its advantages, rather than as a site of normative contest, the G20's approach effectively mirrored New Labour's treatment of globalisation as a non-negotiable external constraint. This is part of what Gerald K. Helleiner has described as a "great deal of nonsense [that] has been written and said about globalization in recent years",[39] since it erroneously treats liberalisation as an unavoidable fact rather than as the product of political, economic and social decision-making.[40] Rather, the vulnerability of governments to capital flight has been used to justify the imposition of counter-inflationary discipline on the domestic economy, as well as to normalise the logic of market discipline that has been used to justify labour market flexibility and increasingly conditional approaches to public expenditure on the grounds of prudence.

---

33. Group of Twenty, *op. cit.*, p. 29; Beeson and Bell, *op. cit.*, p. 13.
34. Group of Twenty, *op. cit.*, p. 40.
35. *Ibid.*, p. 40.
36. See Anthony Giddens, *The Third Way* (Cambridge: Polity, 1998), p. 68.
37. Ed Balls, "Open Macroeconomics in an Open Economy", *Scottish Journal of Political Economy*, Vol. 45, No. 2 (1998), p. 122.
38. *Ibid.*, p. 116.
39. Helleiner, "Markets, Politics, and Globalization", *op. cit.*, p. 243.
40. *Ibid.*, p. 244.

Domestically, the principal forms this took were central bank independence, which served to depoliticise the consequences of deflationary policies adopted to secure a low and stable rate of inflation on confidence grounds,[41] and the invocation of globalisation as an irrevocable constraint to "render the contingent necessary".[42] Internationally, the probity of this approach was endorsed by the position of the G20, while its technical treatment of liberalisation and approaches to crisis prevention and resolution also served to legitimate a growth model based on financialisation because it implied it could be stabilised with the adoption of appropriate regulatory policies. In this way, British policymakers were able to draw attention to an international consensus among experts that justified its claims that there were no alternatives to increased labour market discipline and the substitution of state-based welfare systems with financialisation. As such, the development of the G20 in the period between 1999 and 2007 was able to assist British state managers in their attempts to balance the imperatives of capital accumulation and political legitimation through its endorsement and reinforcement of an economic common sense in which the immutable reality of market discipline and the precariousness of work and welfare provision was firmly entrenched.

Leaders' Summits

Between 1997 and 2007, the finance ministers' meetings established a technocratic view of global economic governance, but following the crisis of 2007, the involvement of international leaders in G20 hinted at the possibility of a thorough repoliticisation of policymaking. However, this did not occur, and initial injections of liquidity that briefly offered the prospect of a return to Keynesianism ultimately proved to be little more than temporary measures geared to preventing the system's outright collapse, rather than an indication of serious normative contestation about economic management. This is reflected in the relatively quick change in the G20's role from "recession buster" to "steering committee",[43] and indicates that leaders' involvement in the G20 does not appear, in the case of the UK, to be so much an attempt to shape the debate as to consolidate the *status quo ante*, and to effectively transmit responses framed in technocratic terms to domestic constituencies.[44]

The G20's transition from "recession buster" to "steering committee" reflected a return to "business as usual" rather than a fundamental challenge to the way in which the system operated, as attention turned quickly from diagnoses and treatment of the crisis to a much broader range of issues related to maximising the benefits of the open economy for the broadest possible range of people. The

---

41. See Peter Burnham, "New Labour and the Politics of Depoliticisation", *The British Journal of Politics and International Relations*, Vol. 3, No. 2 (2001), pp. 127–149.

42. Matthew Watson and Colin Hay, "Rendering the Contingent Necessary: The Discourse of Globalisation and the Logic of No Alternative in the Political Economy of New Labour", *Policy & Politics*, Vol. 31, No. 3 (2003), pp. 289–305.

43. Andrew F. Cooper, "The G20 as an Improvised Crisis Committee and/or a Contested 'Steering Committee' for the World", *International Affairs*, Vol. 86, No. 3 (2010), pp. 641–642; see also Andrew F. Cooper and Colin I. Bradford Jr., "The G20 and the Post-Crisis Economic Order", *CIGI G20 Papers No. 3* (June 2010).

44. I am grateful to an anonymous reviewer for suggesting development of this point.

G20's role as "recession buster" was clearly central in the summit declarations from Washington and London in 2008 and 2009, respectively. In the first instance, the G20 committed to increasing global liquidity, to strengthen the capital base of significant financial institutions and to support the international financial institutions' (IFIs) role in helping the global economy. It particularly involved the coordination of fiscal stimulus and monetary policy to offset deflationary pressures and sustain global demand, and commitments to ensure reform of the IFIs so that they had the necessary resources and legitimacy to succeed.[45] By the conclusion of the London summit, the G20 had delivered on its commitments to coordinate fiscal stimulus and interest rate cuts to stimulate growth, but perhaps most significantly trebled the resources of the IMF to $750 billion, and pledged "to support a new [Special Drawing Rights] allocation of $250 billion, to support at least $100 billion of additional lending by the [Multinational Development Banks], to ensure $250 billion of support for trade finance", constituting in total "an additional $1.1 trillion programme of support to restore credit, growth, and jobs in the whole economy".[46] The coordination of domestic fiscal and monetary policies and the injection of liquidity into the global economy that stemmed from the expansion of the IFIs' resources allowed the leaders to declare in Pittsburgh later that year simply that "it worked".[47]

In addition to preventing the exacerbation of the crisis in so far as possible, the second task taken on by the G20 related to the diagnosis of the crisis, and measures to attempt a recurrence in the future. The diagnostic element of this work was made clear from the outset of the 2008 Washington Declaration, which stated that the crisis stemmed from the fact that:

> market participants sought higher yields without an adequate appreci-
> ation of the risks and failed to exercise proper due diligence. At the
> same time, weak underwriting standards, unsound risk management prac-
> tices, increasingly complex and opaque financial products, and consequent
> excessive leverage combined to create vulnerabilities in the system. Policy-
> makers, regulators and supervisors, in some advanced countries, did not
> adequately appreciate and address the risks building up in financial
> markets, keep pace with financial innovation, or take into account the sys-
> temic ramifications of domestic regulatory actions.[48]

In essence, this diagnosis reduced the origins of the crisis to matters of conduct and matters of regulation. On the surface, this may appear to set a broad agenda. However, it excludes reflection on or reconsideration of the fundamental purpose of market activity. The aim is simply to "correct" prevailing forms of social and economic relations that have historically shown themselves to be prone towards crisis, rather than attempt to think about different forms of organisation. It is an explicit treatment of the logic of no alternative as fact, which set the stage for a technocratic response to the crisis, involving strengthening of banks' capital adequacy requirements, proposals to reform the trade of over the counter products like credit

---

45. G20, "Declaration Summit on Financial Markets and the World Economy", 15 November 2008, pp. 1–3.
46. G20, "London Summit—Leaders' Statement", 2 April 2009, p. 1.
47. G20, "Leaders' Statement: The Pittsburgh Summit", 24–25 September 2009, p. 1.
48. G20, "Declaration Summit on Financial Markets and the World Economy", *op. cit.*, p. 1.

default swaps (CDS), the regulation of shadow-banking activities including hedge funds, and revisions and streamlining of standards for credit rating agencies (CRAs) and accountancy firms.[49]

The technocratic approach broadly reflected the proposals of mainstream economists.[50] As a result, it has been noted that "the policy agenda did not in fact go much beyond pre-existing international initiatives"[51] and it certainly did not "propose an alternative growth model".[52] It is correct to question whether institutions like the G20 have the remit to engage in such activities. However, it is telling that very little consideration about the social usefulness of particular kinds of market activity has been undertaken by domestic political elites who do have the democratic mandate to do so, leaving technocratic discourses of institutions like the G20 relatively unchallenged. In this respect, the technocratic focus of the G20's response to the financial crisis reflected the fact that "Anglo-American elites face serious disincentives in retreating from financialization, securitization and the access to credit and housing finance [...] because these processes have become integral elements of the social and welfare settlements in these societies".[53] In the process, this served to endorse the financialised growth model on which British state managers had been relying in order to reconcile their attempts to increase competitiveness and secure domestic political legitimacy, just as the technocratic approach of the finance ministers' meetings had done before 2008. However, the G20 leaders' declarations also did more than this.

In particular, the leaders' declarations' increasing emphasis on fiscal responsibility and the threat that tax havens and tax evasion posed to domestic tax bases served to consolidate long-standing views about the significance of prudent fiscal policy, which has been used to justify welfare state retrenchment and impose market discipline on domestic constituencies. This strongly suggests that initial injections of liquidity were indicative of crisis measures rather than borne of serious normative contest. On fiscal policy, the Toronto declaration of 2010 noted that the G20 was "communicating 'growth friendly' fiscal consolidation plans in advanced countries that will be implemented going forward",[54] and is representative of the euphemistic way in which G20 leaders have referred to the politics of austerity. On the tax front, Christians has noted "there is no evidence that even the complete elimination of tax havens [...] would fill the revenue gap created during (and before) the crisis",[55] casting doubt on whether references to

---

49. See Eric Helleiner and Stefano Pagliari, "Towards a New Bretton Woods? The First G20 Leaders Summit and the Regulation of Global Finance", *New Political Economy*, Vol. 14, No. 2 (2009), pp. 275–287 and Eric Helleiner and Stefano Pagliari, "The G20 Leaders' Summit and the Regulation of Global Finance: What was Accomplished?", *CIGI Policy Brief No. 11* (December 2008).

50. For instance, see Mathias Dewatripont, Xavier Freizas and Richard Portes (eds.), *Macroeconomic Stability and Financial Regulation: Key Issues for the G20* (London: Centre for Economic Policy Research, 2009) on, among other topics, global liquidity, fiscal stimulus, zero interest rate policy, central counter-party clearing for CDS, regulation of CRAs and accountancy firms.

51. See Helleiner and Pagliari, "The G20 Leaders' Summit", *op. cit.*, p. 1, also Helleiner and Pagliari, "Towards a New Bretton Woods?", *op. cit.*, p. 277.

52. Andrew Baker, "Restraining Regulatory Capture? Anglo-America, Crisis Politics and Trajectories of Change in Global Financial Governance", *International Affairs*, Vol. 86, No. 3 (2010), p. 655.

53. *Ibid.*, p. 655.

54. G20, "The G-20 Toronto Summit Declaration", 26–27 June 2010, p. 2.

55. Allison Christians, "Taxation in a Time of Crisis: Policy Leadership from the OECD to the G20", *Northwestern Journal of Law & Social Policy*, Vol. 5, No. 1 (2010), p. 24.

protection of the tax base by the G20 amount to anything more than a platitude to social constituencies bearing the brunt of austerity.

What we see in the G20's approach to fiscal policy is therefore part of what Baker has described as "politically driven nonsense"[56] and Blyth has thoroughly debunked as a contradictory form of class politics, in the form of austerity, which constitutes a "dangerous idea".[57] Nonetheless, it has formed a centrepiece of David Cameron and Nick Clegg's coalition government since its formation in 2010, when its founding principles published in *The Coalition: Our Programme for Government*, described deficit reduction as "the most urgent issue facing Britain".[58] Moreover, Cameron has explicitly used the G20's endorsement of deficit reduction as a necessary precondition for restoring economic growth in his remarks to Parliament. For instance, in 2012 he noted that at the G20, "As at the G8, there was absolute agreement that deficit reduction and growth are not alternatives. You need the first to get the second."[59] After Seoul, he argued that "Countries with larger deficits need to act on them and do so now", and that this "was exactly the view of the G20".[60] Again in 2013 he noted that the St Petersburg Action Plan "contains all of the features of the plan we have been following in Britain since the coalition government came into office", and in particular "the importance of dealing with our debts".[61]

The fact that the British government runs a budgetary deficit and is in debt is beyond doubt—in July 2014 the Office for National Statistics reported Public Sector Net Borrowing for the financial year to date of £32.4 billion and net debt of £1,299 billion, or 76.5% of GDP[62]—however, what those figures mean about the necessity of austerity is open to contest because of the contested nature of "sustainability". As Burnham has noted, before austerity measures were introduced:

> Public sector net debt, excluding the financial interventions, was approximately 58% of GDP—within the Maastricht Treaty's Excessive Deficit guideline of 60%. The figure of 58% of GDP was not excessive when compared with Britain's postwar debt which topped 237% of GDP in 1946 and remained above 60% until 1970. Only with the financial interventions included did the debt figure rise to approximately 150% of GDP and this took no account of the newly acquired government assets.[63]

---

56. Andrew Baker, "Why Austerity is not Common Sense but Politically Driven Nonsense" (2010), available: <https://www.qub.ac.uk/schools/SchoolofPoliticsInternationalStudiesandPhilosophy/FileStore/Stafffiles/AndrewBaker/Filetoupload,224825,en.pdf> (last accessed 3 March 2015).

57. Mark Blyth, *Austerity: The History of a Dangerous Idea* (Oxford: Oxford University Press, 2013).

58. David Cameron and Nick Clegg, *The Coalition: Our Programme for Government* (London: Cabinet Office, 2010), p. 15.

59. David Cameron, "Prime Minister's Statement on G20", 25 June 2012, available: <https://www.gov.uk/government/news/prime-ministers-statement-on-g20>.

60. David Cameron, "Statement on G20 Summit in Seoul", 15 November 2010, available: <https://www.gov.uk/government/speeches/statement-on-g20-summit-in-seoul>.

61. David Cameron, "G20 Summit: Prime Minister Statement to the House of Commons", 9 September 2013, available: <https://www.gov.uk/government/speeches/g20-summit-prime-minister-statement-to-the-house-of-commons-2>.

62. See Office for National Statistics, "Statistical Bulletin: Public Sector Finances July 2014" (2014), Table 1, available: <http://www.ons.gov.uk/ons/dcp171778_374935.pdf>.

63. Peter Burnham, "Towards a Political Theory of Crisis: Policy and Resistance across Europe", *New Political Science*, Vol. 33, No. 4 (2011), pp. 502–503.

Not only was Britain's debt position not particularly high by historical standards when financial interventions were excluded, the frequent invocation of comparisons between household debt and government debt in Britain are entirely inappropriate since governments with their own central banks can "determine the supply of a currency they preside over" and makes it "next to impossible for a government with its own central bank to go bankrupt".[64]

In other words, British politicians have not used the G20 to repoliticise policymaking—they have used it as a platform from which to reiterate the position that there is no alternative to prudence. In combination, the G20's technocratic approach to the diagnosis and treatment of the crisis and the gradual shift in emphasis to fiscal sustainability provided international endorsement of a domestic growth strategy that was based on the twin pillars of financialisation and fiscal austerity. In the process, it serves to endorse the view that greater exposure of labour to market forces, which includes the reality of stagnating wages, unemployment, precariousness of employment and a diminishing social safety net, is a reality that has to be accepted but can be managed by implementing the correct policies. In the process, it presents inherently political decisions about the way that the economy is managed as apolitical technical decisions, and in doing so not only serves to address problems of competitiveness related to Britain's relative economic decline, but also insulates the government itself from the negative consequences that stem from it. As a result, it can be argued that the G20's response to the crisis served to legitimise the British growth strategy through the construction and consolidation of a discourse that depoliticised the politics of austerity on the grounds that "there is no alternative". In this sense, the evolution of the G20 process has served as an external anchor to which British state managers have deferred in order to help justify their strategies to address one of the core contradictions it faces.

Global Capital, National State and the G20

The paper has so far argued that as the political form of accumulation, the state is confronted with a challenge to create and maintain conditions for accumulation and legitimation, which are co-dependent but contradictory, since competitiveness is dependent on labour market discipline. It has argued that the institutions of global economic governance have assisted British state managers with reconciling this tension from the Gold Standard to the G20 by helping to depoliticise the politics of economic policymaking, in particular by constructing and reinforcing views of globalisation as an unavoidable reality that can be managed by implementing appropriate policies designed by technical experts. However, while the paper has suggested British state managers have benefitted from the institutional arrangements of global economic governance in this way, the paper has suggested that this cannot be accounted for by realist traditions in the political economy of international relations. As such, an important question remains. Given that "Historically, international financial regulation has been dominated by British and US officials because of the pre-eminent position of London and New York as international financial centres",[65] why would G7 members "incorporate political

---

64. Baker, "Why Austerity is not Common Sense", *op. cit.*, p. 4.
65. Helleiner and Pagliari, "The G20 Leaders' Summit", *op. cit.*, pp. 10–11.

authorities from outside the G-7 into the governance of the regime?"[66] As Porter has phrased it, this "appears to be an irrational weakening by powerful states of their own political dominance".[67]

The answer to this question lies in the practical implications of the tension that exists between the global character of accumulation and the national character of political authority. As nodes in the global flow of capital, individual states pursuing strategies to reconcile tensions between accumulation and legitimation are dependent on the adoption of complementary strategies being implemented elsewhere. In practice, it is not possible for one or more states to adopt a growth strategy based on financialisation unless they have access to liquidity to finance consumption, and commodities are available for purchase. Similarly, manufacturing-based economies cannot provide jobs for their people unless there is effective demand for the goods produced. In other words, the reconciliation of accumulation and legitimation in the domestic sphere is fundamentally dependent on the prevalence of complementary strategies in the international sphere.

This kind of dynamic is most commonly referred to in terms of the imbalances between China and the USA, which has seen the Chinese surplus effectively recycled through the USA in order to create effective demand in the former and sustain levels of consumption in the latter. In the process, this temporarily allowed for the reconciliation of accumulation and legitimation in both the USA and China, although without regard to the ability of American debtors to repay or the limits of China's international market, such that it has been described as a contradictory form of de facto cooperation between the two states.[68] Beeson and Bell have astutely noted that "both sides are locked into a symbiotic relationship upon which they all depend", even if this looked, and has ultimately been proven "unsustainable in the long term".[69] However, the problem of imbalances "is not just a US–China story. The UK, Spain, and Australia have had large current account deficits; Germany, Japan, and several Asian emerging market countries as well as some commodity exporters have had large surpluses",[70] and this fact helps explain why the G20 has been mobilised as the premier forum of global economic governance with a much broader base of participants.

This is because the G20's technocratic approach to global governance does not only assist countries like Britain through its consolidation of the notion that there is no alternative to greater market discipline at the domestic level. It also helps to foster legitimacy for liberalisation within the emerging economies on which deficit countries like Britain depend not only for liquidity, but also for the supply of commodities, by bringing them into the process. In this way, just as the G20 process has helped states like Britain negotiate the tensions between accumulation and legitimation at a domestic level, it has also served to help it negotiate the tensions between the global character of accumulation and the national character of political authority by legitimising the idea of the open and liberal economy on which it depends overseas.

---

66. Tony Porter, "The G-7, the Financial Stability Forum, the G-20, and the Politics of International Financial Regulation", paper prepared for the International Studies Association Annual Meeting, Los Angeles, 15 March 2000, p. 12.

67. *Ibid.*, p. 12.

68. See Gyu Cheol Lee, "The Political Economy of the Sino-American Imbalance", unpublished PhD dissertation, University of York, UK, 2014.

69. Beeson and Bell, *op. cit.*, p. 19.

70. Dewatripont, Freixas and Portes (eds.), *op. cit.*, p. 5.

Conclusions: Second Time as Farce?

The paper has used an understanding of the state as the political form of capital in the context of a tension between the global character of accumulation and the national character of political authority as its underlying framework. It has argued that the institutions of global economic governance from the Gold Standard to the G20 have assisted British state managers in their attempts to reconcile the tension between accumulation and legitimation as it has sought to regain competitiveness by imposing labour market discipline and the politics of austerity. In particular, it argued that the technocratic approach to global economic governance in general and liberalisation in particular has served to depoliticise the consequences of increasing market discipline and the politics of austerity at the domestic level by consolidating views of globalisation as a fact that must be managed in a particular way. By incorporating emerging economies into the framework of the G20, it has also served to legitimise liberalisation in nations on which countries reliant on financialisation, like Britain, depend for liquidity and the supply of commodities. In one sense then, the G20 process appears to have addressed many of the political challenges faced by the British state in the face of its relative economic decline, and continues to do so. However, given the proven fragility of the growth model it has contributed to consolidating, the possibility remains that its real contribution will be to history repeating itself, in Marx's famous phrase, "first as tragedy, then as farce".[71] In order to prevent this, decisive action on global imbalances is required, and while this is on the G20 agenda, it remains to be seen whether national states—Britain among them—are ready to accept the domestic political consequences of adjustment in the absence of a clearly articulated alternative growth model.

Acknowledgements

I am grateful to helpful comments from the anonymous reviewers of *Global Society*, which have helped to improve the paper.

Disclosure Statement

No potential conflict of interest was reported by the author.

---

71. See Karl Marx, *The Eighteenth Brumaire of Louis Bonaparte*, Marx/Engels Internet Archive (1852), p. 5, available: <https://www.marxists.org/archive/marx/works/download/pdf/18th-Brumaire.pdf>.

Organisation and Politics in South–South Cooperation: Brazil's Technical Cooperation in Africa

ADRIANA ERTHAL ABDENUR

How is Brazilian South–South technical cooperation organised, and how does this structure relate to the politics of cooperation? Focusing on the recent surge in Brazilian technical cooperation in Africa, I argue that the organisational structures involved in Brazilian technical cooperation are tightly intertwined with the political motivations behind the provision of such cooperation. Although individual ministries and other government divisions have provided technical cooperation since the 1960s, in the past decade the federal government has worked to harness this dispersed cooperation so as to advance broader foreign policy goals. In addition to helping legitimise the social policies implemented domestically by specific ministries, technical cooperation is increasingly used to bolster the government's global power aspirations and to resist Northern-led efforts to set international development norms. However, this harnessing effort has run into internal and external constraints that cast doubt on the Brazilian government's ability to instrumentalise cooperation as a foreign policy tool.

Introduction

The organisational structures involved in Northern bilateral aid are highly variable, but the typical point of departure for comparative analyses of aid bureaucracies is the centralised agency that coordinates aid efforts abroad.[1] The burgeoning scholarship on South–South development cooperation has noted a wide gamut of bureaucratic arrangements among providers, from China's inter-agency foreign cooperation coordination mechanism (which includes some 30 ministries and institutions) to India's establishment, within the Ministry of External Affairs, of an official agency for international development cooperation.[2]

Untangling such structures and their associated dynamics is important not only because of the recent surge in South–South development cooperation, which has provoked major shifts within international development debates, but also

The author wishes to thank the Jovem Cientista programme of the Fundação Carlos Chagas Filho de Amparo à Pesquisa do Estado do Rio de Janeiro (FAPERJ) and the Bolsa de Produtividade programme of Brazil's Conselho Nacional de Desenvolvimento Científico e Tecnológico (CNPq) for supporting this research.

1. See, for example, William Easterly and Tobias Pfutze, "Where Does the Money Go? Best and Worst Practices in Foreign Aid", *Journal of Economic Perspectives*, Vol. 22, No. 2 (2008), pp. 29–52.

2. Deborah Brautigam, *The Dragon's Gift* (Oxford: Oxford University Press, 2009); and Sachin Chaturvedi, "India's Development Partnership: Key Policy Shifts and Institutional Evolution", *Cambridge Review of International Affairs*, Vol. 25, No. 4 (2012), pp. 557–577.

because official discourses about South–South cooperation claim that it is fundamentally different from (and more effective than) Northern aid. If there are indeed major divergences between cooperation and aid, they might stem at least in part from the way in which these initiatives are coordinated.

Analysis of how Brazilian technical cooperation in Africa is organised suggests that the interplay between the agencies tasked with implementing this cooperation and the federal government has changed over the past decade. Namely, although individual ministries and other state divisions have provided technical cooperation abroad since the 1970s, the Workers' Party-led government of Luiz Inácio Lula da Silva (2003–10) worked to harness this disperse cooperation so as to better align them with foreign policy priorities. However, this harnessing effort has run into internal as well as external constraints, meaning that Brazil's technical cooperation remains essentially *capillary*—driven primarily by the implementing institutions and the broader networks in which they exist rather than the coordinating agency. Although this capillarity confers Brazilian technical cooperation a degree of agility, in the long term the lack of adequate coordination casts doubt on the effectiveness and durability of Brazil's technical cooperation efforts.

The attempt to instrumentalise technical cooperation is closely intertwined with the government's global power aspirations: its attempts to expand Brazil's influence regionally and globally by deepening ties to other developing countries while distancing itself from the advanced economies.[3] One important consequence of this effort to harness technical cooperation is that it raises the government's stakes in presenting Brazilian cooperation as fundamentally different from Northern aid. Most notably, Brazil has steadfastly resisted efforts by the Development Assistance Committee (DAC) of the Organization for Economic Co-operation and Development (OECD) to codify global development norms through the aid effectiveness agenda. At the same time, Brazil's provision of South–South development cooperation is also driven by a variety of subnational and sectoral interests.[4] Untangling these motivations and locating them within particular organisational structures may clarify both continuities and inconsistencies in Brazil's role as a development cooperation provider.

The next section of this paper offers an overview of how the development literature has treated the interplay between organisational structures and political drivers of aid, and it provides some background on Brazilian technical cooperation. Then, Brazil's technical cooperation in Africa is analysed in light of the Workers' Party's rising power strategy. The conclusion explores some of the key implications of these changing structures and dynamics for Brazil's role in global debates about development norms.

Bureaucracy and Politics in Aid and Cooperation

Organisational Dynamics in International Development

Bilateral donor agencies vary widely in organisational form, and these different configurations are often suggestive of how other state interests, including foreign

---

3. See, for instance, Sean Burges, "Brazil's International Development Co-operation: Old and New Motivations", *Development Policy Review*, Vol. 32, No. 3 (2014), pp. 355–374.

4. Cristina Yumie Anoki Inoue and Alcidez Costa Vaz, "Brazil as 'Southern Donor': Beyond Hierarchy and National Interests in Development Cooperation?", *Cambridge Review of International Affairs*, Vol. 25, No. 4 (2012), pp. 508–534.

policy and international trade priorities, shape the provision of aid. Many such institutions consist of a nodal agency that is either fully or partially tasked with managing that country's official development assistance (ODA). However, the status of that agency within the broader state bureaucracy is highly variable. The UK's Department for International Development (DFID), for instance, has full ministerial status, whereas the Danish International Development Agency (DANIDA) is now located within Denmark's Ministry of Foreign Affairs, as is the case with most such agencies. In the cases of New Zealand and South Korea, the same ministries responsible for coordinating aid are tasked with trade relations. Elsewhere, as in the USA and Japan, the aid architecture is highly fragmented among different parts of the state bureaucracy.[5]

Far from static, these arrangements are also susceptible to change across time, and there have been cases of rather dramatic relocations and restructurings. Such shifts can take place in response to changing domestic politics as well as external circumstances. The global economic crisis that began in 2008 provoked a temporary decline in ODA, and certain donors (among them Ireland) responded by aligning their aid programmes more closely with their economic interests abroad. In 2013, Canada's government announced the "amalgamation" of the Canadian International Development Agency (CIDA) into the Department of Foreign Affairs and International Trade. Others, including the UK and the Netherlands, have either restructured their aid towards a narrower assortment of developing countries, or reduced their overall flows altogether.

Anecdotal evidence suggests that organisational structures also vary widely among providers of South–South cooperation—a reflection of how varied this modality of development cooperation has become.[6] Some states, such as South Africa, Indonesia and India, have recently launched new coordination agencies for their international development cooperation. In other cases, as in Brazil and Turkey, existing agencies have been expanded and/or granted broader responsibilities. However, these institutions do not necessarily play the same role of protagonism (or quasi-protagonism) within their countries' provision of international cooperation as most established donor agencies within their respective countries' aid efforts. The relatively loose arrangement in place in many South–South cooperation providers may be largely due to the fact that, until recently, these countries were net recipients of aid. In contrast, donor agencies have been subject to institutional isomorphism forces through participation in multilateral organisations, like the OECD DAC, that generate pressures for bureaucratic structures and practices to conform to agreed-upon standards.[7] In contrast, South–South cooperation agencies have operated predominantly along bilateral channels. In addition, the boom in South–South cooperation is relatively recent; as a result, these institutions frequently lack the robust regulatory framework, dedicated career staff and systematised knowledge-building procedures that are common among established donor agencies.

5. Emma Mawdsley, *From Recipients to Donors: Emerging Powers and the Changing Development Landscape* (London: Zed Books, 2012).

6. Paolo de Renzio and Jurek Seifert, "South–South Cooperation and the Future of Development Assistance: Mapping Actors and Options", *Third World Quarterly*, Vol. 35, No. 10 (2014), pp. 1860–1875.

7. Thomas B. Lawrence and Roy Suddaby, "Institutions and Institutional Work", in Stewart R. Clegg, Cynthia Hardy, Thomas B. Lawrence and Walter R. Nord (eds.), *The SAGE Handbook of Organization Studies* (London: Sage, 2006).

However, South–South coordinating agencies have not emerged in total isolation. First, they have typically played a role in the country's received assistance, through which they interact with donor agencies and multilateral institutions, albeit as recipient country agencies. For most of its existence, for instance, Brazil's Agência Brasileira de Cooperação (ABC) was more involved in coordinating received assistance than in the provision of South–South cooperation. Second, recent years have brought about growing dialogue and collaboration among South–South cooperation agencies, both through bilateral channels and multilateral platforms such as the BRICS (Brazil, Russia, India, China and South Africa) coalition.

Typically, a coordinating agency is overlaid onto a more fragmented structure, and centralising coordination involves wrestling some control away from government divisions that seek to maintain their current functions in providing South–South cooperation. There are exceptions; for instance, China's South–South development cooperation is spread across a number of state and semi-state ministries and agencies that are tasked with different aspects of development cooperation.[8] Elsewhere, however, it might also be more appropriate to begin an analysis of how South–South cooperation is organised not by honing in on a "central" coordinating agency—which might not yet be so central after all—but rather with the wider bureaucratic ecology in which that agency operates and changes over time.

Although South–South development cooperation encompasses activities as diverse as trade, investment and currency agreements, in this paper the focus is on official technical cooperation, here defined as international cooperation initiatives undertaken by state actors that aim to build human and institutional capacity for purposes of socio-economic development. Technical cooperation entails a wide variety of initiatives, from project financing to personnel training, technological transfer and joint research. The term technical cooperation was endorsed by the United Nations (UN) in 1959, replacing the older term "technical assistance", which had come to be regarded as excessively asymmetrical.

Decentralised Cooperation: Early Brazilian Technical Cooperation with Africa

This paper focuses on Brazil, whose South–South technical cooperation has changed considerably over time, both in scope and in organisational dynamics. These changes—analysed in greater detail in the next section—have taken place within a context of intensifying relations between Brazil and other developing countries, including in Africa. Despite the surge in Brazil–Africa cooperation since the turn of the millennium, these ties are far from a novelty; ties between Brazil and Africa boast a long history that merits summarising so as to contextualise current Brazilian technical cooperation on the continent.

Brazil's links to Africa date back to the transatlantic slave trade, with African populations contributing to Brazil demographically and culturally; some 4 million Africans reached Brazilian ports to work as forced labour on the colonial plantations, mines and households. There was also some movement in the opposite direction, with Brazilians either participating directly in the slave trade, hiring themselves out as mercenaries in Africa or moving to Western Africa after the

---

8. Brautigam, *op. cit.*

official end of slavery in Brazil.[9] Despite these links, after the colonial period in Brazil, contact remained scarce. During much of the Cold War, in fact, Brazil sided with Portugal against the independence bids of former fellow colonies in Africa. At the UN, for instance, Brazil repeatedly voted against self-determination in Angola, Mozambique, Guinea-Bissau and other colonies.[10] In addition, Brazil never became a full-fledged member of the Non-Aligned Movement, although it has participated in meetings as an observer state. During that period, Brazil's relations with other developing countries, including those emerging in Africa, were carried out either bilaterally or through *tiermondiste* movements like the Group of 77 (G-77), and related efforts to launch the United Nations Conference on Trade and Development (UNCTAD).

During the early 1960s, during a short-lived left-wing government, Brazilian ruling elites sought to counterbalance Brazil's relations with (and heavy dependence upon) the USA by deepening ties to other developing countries, including those in Africa. This orientation was overturned by the military regime that installed itself in Brazil after a *coup d'état* in 1964 and remained in power for 27 years. In the mid-1970s, however, in part due to new economic pressures created by the 1973 oil shock, Brazil once again looked to Africa for new partnerships, especially in the procurement of oil. Despite still being under military rule, Brazil stopped backing Portugal's opposition to African demands for independence and began recognising newly independent states in Africa—including Portugal's former colonies. Brazil worked to strengthen its relations even with countries, such as Angola and Mozambique, where leftist governments came to power.[11]

At the vanguard of these deepening ties were a handful of Brazilian state and private companies that began making substantial investments in Africa. At that time, Brazil was still a net oil importer, and as part of the country's energy source diversification strategy, the state-owned oil company, Petrobras, started investing in Angola in 1979. Five years later, Brazilian construction firm Odebrecht began building a hydroelectric dam in Angola. Although they were at the leading edge of Brazil–Africa, these firms benefitted from the Brazilian government's new interest in Africa. Formal agreements, high-level visits and other diplomatic gestures helped to smooth the path for business deals. Concurrently, divisions of Brazilian government began offering some technical assistance to African partner institutions, especially by bringing African students, government officials and development experts to study and train in Brazilian universities and institutions. These activities were designed not only to increase contact and mutual understanding, but also to assist African states (especially lusophone countries) to build up capacity in specific sectors.

Rather than being centralised or coordinated through a single agency, these cooperation efforts were driven by specific ministries and agencies, each running its own programme without much cross-pollination. Initiatives were designed and implemented as secondary activities by staff whose primary work entailed the formulation and execution of domestic policies. Thus, early Brazilian technical

---

9. Luiz Felipe Alencastro, "Brazil in the South Atlantic: 1550–1850", trans. Emilio Sauri, *Mediations*, Vol. 23, No. 1 (2007), pp. 157–174.

10. José Flávio Sombra Saraiva, "The New Africa and Brazil in the Lula Era: The Rebirth of Brazilian Atlantic Policy", *Revista Brasileira de Política Internacional*, Vol. 53 (2010), pp. 169–182.

11. Pio Penna Filho and Antônio Carlos Moraes Lessa, "O Itamaraty e a África: as origens da política africana do Brasil", *Revista Estudos Históricos*, Vol. 39 (2007), pp. 57–81.

cooperation was highly decentralised and conducted by government divisions pursuing their own interests (for instance, legitimation of domestic policies) rather than following the guidelines of broad foreign policy objectives. This technical cooperation had only loose ties to foreign policy, although the Ministry of External Relations (MRE) encouraged initiatives in those countries with which Brazil was trying to deepen diplomatic relations. However, the MRE lacked a specific division dedicated to international cooperation, and whatever functions in international development it carried out at that point involved the receiving of assistance rather than the provision of South–South cooperation.

In addition, Brazil's considerable domestic challenges, including high levels of poverty and sharpening inequalities, constrained the resources it could allocate to this early South–South development cooperation. Brazil's first initiative towards implementing an "International Technical Cooperation System"—the 1950 launch of the National Commission for Technical Assistance (CNAT), an inter-ministerial group—was tasked with clarifying and prioritising the demands for external technical assistance requested by Brazilian institutions, rather than coordinating them as such. This incipient architecture was broadly reformed in 1969, when a decree was issued centralising the basic tasks of international technical cooperation (negotiations, planning, coordination, promotion and monitoring) within the Secretariat of Planning of the Presidential Office (SEPLAN) and within the MRE.[12] Nonetheless, this mechanism was still geared at received assistance rather than South–South cooperation, and at any rate its de facto coordinating capacity remained extremely limited. In 1984, additional reforms were implemented, without clear centralisation; the MRE's Technical Cooperation Division was tasked with the political coordination of cooperation, while the Sub-secretariat for International Economic and Technical Cooperation (SUBIN) was responsible for project prospection, analysis, approval and monitoring.[13]

As far as debates about South–South cooperation were concerned, in the 1960s and 1970s Brazil was an active participant in UN discussions about the role of technical cooperation between developing countries (TCDC). Brazil advocated for the creation of the Special Unit for TCDC within the United Nations Development Programme (UNDP) and contributed towards the 1978 Conference on Technical Cooperation between Developing Countries and its outcome document, the Buenos Aires Plan of Action.[14] However, the UN development system remained somewhat marginal to Brazil's own development model, which focused on fostering endogenous growth through investment in large-scale infrastructure. By 1983, out of the 4,353 projects that UNDP financed around the world, Brazil received only 0.7% of the total resources.[15] Technical cooperation, in other words, was not among the foreign policy priorities of that era.

Brazil's official provision of South–South technical cooperation began in 1973, as foreign policy began placing greater importance on ties to other developing countries. Despite the growing belief among diplomats that the provision of

---

12. MRE, "Agência Brasileira de Cooperação: Histórico" (n.d.), available: <http://www.abc.gov.br/SobreAbc/Historico> (accessed 10 July 2014).

13. *Ibid.*

14. MRE, "Histórico da Cooperação Técnica Brasileira" (n.d.), available: <http://www.abc.gov.br/CooperacaoTecnica/Historico> (accessed 25 July 2014).

15. Amado Cervo, "Socializando o desenvolvimento: uma história da cooperação técnica internacional do Brasil", *Revista Brasileira de Política Internacional*, Vol. 37, No. 1 (1994), pp. 37–63.

technical cooperation could become an important foreign policy tool, SUBIN's location outside of the Ministry of Foreign Affairs meant that, in practice, that alignment remained tenuous. Moreover, Brazil's role in international development was gradually changing: even as its access to assistance, especially of the financial kind, was slowly reduced, more demands began emerging from other developing countries for Brazilian technical cooperation.[16] Some of the planning and documentation mechanisms developed at SUBIN to deal with received assistance began to be adapted for the provision of technical cooperation. Yet, as a Brazilian diplomat put it, "it gradually became evident that the structure put in place for SUBIN was no longer adequate for taking on the new tasks that were being attributed to it". There was no legal framework in place to regulate the provision of technical cooperation, resources remained inadequate and the absence of specialised staff contributed to institutional weaknesses. A diplomat remarked that, because technical cooperation initiatives remained separate from foreign policy priorities like commercial promotion, "this gave the impression at SUBIN and at MRE that the country was not benefitting from the benefits of cooperation provision, especially in the commercial realm".[17]

Adding to the continued capillarity of Brazilian technical cooperation was the fact that demands for cooperation were made directly to those specific ministries and agencies, without mediation by the MRE. Individual ministries and agencies within the Brazilian government bureaucracy were motivated to engage in international cooperation by the belief that doing so would allow them to legitimise their domestic initiatives. Participation in international cooperation, especially as providers of knowledge and exchange, was viewed as a mark of prestige; it also entailed international travel and connections at a time when the Brazilian economy was extremely closed.

For instance, the Ministry of Finance started bringing Africans from lusophone countries, especially Angola and Mozambique, to study at its public administration school, the Escola de Administração Fazendária (ESAF) in Brasília. ESAF was itself created through external help, having been founded in 1975 with technical assistance from Germany's Technical Cooperation agency (GTZ) and later, from Canada.[18] ESAF's early engagement with technical cooperation thus took place concomitantly to its receiving of Northern aid, not only from Germany but also Canada. Another example of this early decentralised cooperation was the gradual insertion of Brazil's National Public Health School (ENSP), a part of the Oswaldo Cruz Foundation (known as Fiocruz), into international networks of technical cooperation, starting with efforts led by the World Health Organization to promote knowledge exchange in public health. During the 1980s, ENSP created a National and International Technical Cooperation sector meant to boost the institution's receipt and provision of technical cooperation. The move took place at the initiative of institutional leaders at Fiocruz; although the institution is linked to the Ministry of Health, the decision was made independently of the ministries

---

16. Carlos A.I. Puente, *A cooperação técnica horizontal brasileira como instrument da política externa: a evolução da cooperação técnica com países em desenvolvimento—CTPD—no period 1995–2005* (Brasília: FUNAG, 2010).

17. *Ibid.*, p. 104.

18. Renata C. Valente, *A GTZ no Brasil: uma etnografia da cooperação alemã para o desenvolvimento* (Rio Janeiro: Editora E-papers, 2010).

involved in coordinating technical cooperation (Ministry of Planning and the MRE).[19]

In the late 1980s, multilateral organisations that provided aid sought to transform the way in which development projects were implemented globally. As part of the drive to instil greater ownership and local accountability in development assistance, those organisations moved from "direct execution", in which they had maintained responsibility for the financial and administrative management of projects as well as the technical aspect of the cooperation; instead, they began placing a greater portion of their programmes under the control of developing country governments. This new strategy boosted the transference of know-how, practices and informal norms related to the management of international development cooperation.

Against this backdrop of changing administrative practices and aid structures, in 1987, the Brazilian federal government dissolved the previous structures involved in coordinating technical cooperation and created the Brazilian Cooperation Agency (Agência Brasileira de Cooperação—ABC). The new agency, launched as a subdivision of the Alexandre de Gusmão Foundation (FUNAG) under the umbrella of the MRE, was intended to coordinate both assistance received and South–South technical cooperation and was tasked with better aligning technical cooperation to foreign policy priorities. Yet ABC did not start out as a particularly robust agency. Partly because of Brazil's lack of formal regulation for international cooperation in Brazil, many of the functions of this coordination ended up with the UNDP Brasília office, which had assisted the MRE with the creation of the ABC in the first place. At any rate, the focus at the time was on received assistance, since Brazil was still a net recipient of aid.

The vulnerability of these ties became apparent during the "lost decade" of development, during which Brazil's foreign debt and commitments to the Bretton Woods Institutions' structural adjustment policies reoriented policymaking towards domestic affairs and towards fulfilling the country's commitments towards the International Monetary Fund (IMF) and the World Bank. In the 1980s, a gradual transition back to democracy put an end to Brazil's 21 years of military rule, but economic stagnation, high inflation and sharpening social inequalities continued to present considerable policy challenges even as the Cold War came to an end. In light of these pressing concerns and austerity guidelines, the provision of technical cooperation (and, more broadly, Brazilian interests in Africa) lost considerable steam.

In the 1990s, South–South cooperation was not among Brazil's foreign policy priorities, which tended to privilege ties with the North (with the notable exceptions of Mercosur and certain regional powers, such as China, India and South Africa). Brazil–Africa relations generally retracted as trade and investment stagnated, a number of Brazilian diplomatic representations were closed or downsized and many technical cooperation programmes were either scaled back or terminated. However, the 1994 *Plano Real*—a suite of measures that finally stabilised the Brazilian economy—set the foundation for economic growth, which resumed more vigorously after the turn of the millennium in part due to the growth of exports, fuelled by rising demand from China. By the 2000s, Brazil transitioned from a

19. ENSP, "Cooperação Internacional" (n.d.), available: <http://www.ensp.fiocruz.br/portal-ensp/cooperacao-internacional/assessoria/> (accessed 15 September 2014).

net recipient of aid to net provider of cooperation[20]—a change in status recognised by the UN, which began referring to Brazil (along with other major providers of South–South cooperation, like China and India) as one of the new "pivotal states" in the field of development—countries able to "serve as catalysts for implementing TCDC".[21]

The Surge in Brazil–Africa Technical Cooperation

Brazil's Global Player Aspirations

By the time that Brazil's first Workers' Party-led government came to power, in 2003, the field of international development had experienced another significant shift. In the aftermath of the Cold War, a considerable proportion of ODA had been redirected towards Eastern European countries. After the start of the US-led War on Terror, in 2001, humanitarian aid and growing concerns with conflict zones restructured global aid flows, in effect channelling resources away from development and towards security efforts.[22]

In Brazil, the Workers' Party's domestic policies turned out to be quite conservative (relative to its campaign promises). In its foreign policy, however, Lula's government openly pursued the goal of transforming Brazil into a global power.[23] Part of the strategy involved lessening dependence on the USA and other advanced economies by strengthening cooperation with other developing countries. South–South cooperation, broadly writ, became a cornerstone of Brazilian foreign policy under the Workers' Party. Brazilian leaders believed that the Washington Consensus era had constrained the country's policy autonomy, and that—far from resolving the problems of the Lost Decade—the market-driven prescriptions of that period had fuelled socio-economic inequality and discontent. Deepening ties to other developing countries was seen as a way to diminish dependency and unleash new forms and levels of development.

Unlike during the Cold War, when developing countries rallied around the idea of South–South cooperation yet lacked the resources to turn the concept into concrete initiatives at a large scale, in the new millennium South–South development cooperation drew on considerably greater economic and political leverage. In Brazil's case, the domestic economy went through a period of relatively high growth, enabling it to pay off its IMF debt and become, in fact, a net contributor (even as it began accumulating new debt). Domestically, the government implemented policies designed to redress some of the sharp social inequities, for instance, by expanding redistributive policies such as the Bolsa Família conditional cash transfer programme, which had first been launched during the government of Fernando Henrique Cardoso (1996–2001). Economic growth helped to lift millions of Brazilians out of extreme poverty and propelled them into the country's booming middle classes.

Although Brazilian foreign policy had long sought to expand the country's influence and opportunities abroad, the Workers' Party-led government openly endorsed

---

20. Puente, *op. cit.*

21. UNDP, "New Directions for Technical Cooperation among Developing Countries", New York, 7 April 1995, p. 2.

22. Mark Duffield, *Development, Security and Unending War* (London: Polity, 2007).

23. Guilherme Stolle Paixão e Casarões, "A Mídia e a Política Externa no Brasil de Lula", *Austral: Revista Brasileira de Estratégia e Relações Internacionais*, Vol. 1, No. 2 (2012), pp. 211–236.

the identity of rising power and expanded efforts on a number of fronts. It also made Brazil's long-standing ambition of securing a permanent seat at the United Nations Security Council (UNSC) into a cornerstone of Lula's foreign policy.[24] Against this backdrop, South–South development cooperation was viewed as (among other things) a way to mobilise support for Brazil's bid, although the link was never made explicit by official government discourse.[25] Yet there were other reasons why the government decided to boost relations with other developing countries. Since the 1990s, Brazilian leaders had developed certain scepticism towards the "good governance" paradigm, arguing that this was a thinly veiled way to justify the imposition of political conditionalities that served the interests of donor countries rather than recipient states. Under the Workers' Party-led government, this critical perspective helped fuel a discourse of respect for national sovereignty and an increasingly oppositional stance towards Northern aid, particularly when accompanied by efforts to set global norms for international development, as in the case of the OECD aid effectiveness agenda.[26] Finally, the 2008 onset of the global economic crisis, whose initial shocks affected advanced economies more than emerging ones, emboldened Brazil's promotion of a state-centric approach to development and reinforced rising power calls for reform of global governance institutions.

Africa has long become a space of certain protagonism in debates and initiatives in international development—including South–South cooperation, which expanded dramatically across the continent after China revamped its African cooperation policy in the mid-1990s. In the 2000s, Africa assumed an important role within Brazil's rising power strategy. In part, this happened because of the barriers to regional leadership that the Workers' Party-led government encountered within South America; expectations of ideological alignment with other leftist governments were often frustrated by contestation of Brazil's bid for regional leadership. For instance, Argentina, which in the 1990s had become a key partner of Brazil, made it clear that it would not support the Brazilian bid for a permanent seat at the UNSC. Due in part to this contestation, in many respects Brazil has been more successful in gaining visibility within certain global debates than at the regional level, for instance, helping to found the G-20 grouping and participating in ambitious new trans-regional coalitions, such as the BRICS and the India Brazil South Africa Dialogue Forum (IBSA).[27]

Brazil's frustrated leadership bid within South America pushed it to expand its international influence elsewhere. It thus turned across the South Atlantic

---

24. Brazil withdrew from the League when this bid was frustrated in 1926. President Roosevelt promised Brazilian leaders that Brazil would gain a permanent seat at the UNSC, but the proposal was shot down by the UK and the Soviet Union. Eugênio V. Garcia, *Sexto membro permanente: O Brasil e a criação da ONU* (Rio de Janeiro: Contraponto, 2012).

25. Four decades earlier, China had pursued a similar strategy in Africa, offering development cooperation as a way to cement ties and muster support for its bid to replace Taiwan as the legitimate representative of China at the UN, including the Security Council.

26. This goal of autonomy is not equivalent to complete rejection of Northern aid; in addition to continuing receiving assistance, especially from multilateral organisations, Brazil has expanded its participation in triangular cooperation arrangements, including those that involve donor agencies. This participation is also coordinated by ABC.

27. Andrés Malamud, "A Leader Without Followers? The Growing Divergence between the Regional and Global Performance of Brazilian Foreign Policy", *Latin American Politics and Society*, Vol. 53, No. 1 (2011), p. 24.

towards Africa. Not only did Brazil have decades-long relations with several African countries, there was also a certain demonstration effect: namely, China had already shown that Africa, far from a "hopeless continent", was fertile ground for South–South cooperation initiatives, and that high growth rates in parts of the continent represented robust economic opportunities.

Brazilian entrepreneurs began referring to Africa as the "new frontier" for investment. For some companies, however, Africa was anything but novel terrain: Odebrecht and Petrobras, for instance, had infrastructure projects in Angola since the 1970s. Nevertheless, in the 2000s investments and trade between Brazil and Africa also increased; commercial flows surged from US$4 billion in 2000 to US $20 billion in 2010.[28] Minerals dominated Brazilian imports from Africa and agricultural commodities made up the majority of exports, with semi and manufactured products, including arms and military equipment, also experiencing a boost. It was against this backdrop that the Brazilian government increasingly mobilised technical cooperation in pursuit of broader foreign policy goals in Africa.

Harnessing South–South Technical Cooperation

As part of its effort to deepen ties to other developing countries, the Brazilian government resorted to both organisational and discursive strategies. With respect to the organisation aspect, a series of changes were implemented to the MRE, whose budget nearly doubled, so as to broaden the reach of Brazilian diplomacy. The diplomatic corps was rapidly expanded from around 1,000 to 1,400 individuals, and dozens of embassies and other diplomatic representations were inaugurated or reopened, most of them in Africa. In addition, Lula undertook an active presidential diplomacy abroad, privileging South America and Africa. During his tenure as President, Lula made 13 trips to Africa, visiting 28 countries (some of them more than once), and his foreign minister made 67 visits to 34 African states.[29] By the end of his second mandate, the number of Brazilian embassies on the continent reached 37 —more than the UK had in Africa.[30] This engagement was met with enthusiasm by many African states; since 2003, 17 new African embassies were opened in Brasilia, bringing the total to 33 diplomatic representations.[31]

With regard to cooperation, the government also increased the resources allocated to South–South technical cooperation. Although the way that Brazil defines the categories of its international development cooperation does not correspond exactly to those used by donors and other aid providers, government figures show a substantial increase in Brazil's provision of South–South cooperation during the 2000s. According to a government think tank report that surveyed most government divisions involved in South–South development cooperation, from 2005 to 2010, Brazil spent around 6.6 billion reais on international development cooperation. More than half of this amount consisted of contributions to

28. Susana Carrillo, *Bridging the Atlantic—Brazil and Sub-Saharan Africa: South–South Partnering for Growth* (Washington, DC: World Bank/IPEA, 2011).

29. MRE, "Balanço da Política Externa 2003–2010—Resumo Executivo" (2011); and MRE, "Balanço de Política Externa 2003–2010—África—Defesa" (Brasília, 2011).

30. Under Rousseff, an embassy was also opened in Malawi.

31. Carrillo, *op. cit.*

international organisations, such as UN agencies,[32] and another 20% went towards peacekeeping operations. The rest was allocated to humanitarian assistance, technical cooperation and scholarships for foreign students.[33] In 2010 alone—when Brazil's annual gross domestic product (GDP) growth rate reached a decade peak of 7.5%—some 1.6 billion reais were channelled to South–South cooperation—an increase of 91% compared to the previous year.

The geographic distribution of this cooperation funding reflects the regional priorities of Brazilian foreign policy during this period. Partnerships with Africa accounted for 22.6% of the total spent (far behind the 68.1% allocated to Latin America and the Caribbean).[34] Within Africa, the largest allocations were made to lusophone countries: Mozambique (11%), São Tomé and Príncipe (6.7%), Guinea-Bissau (5.7%) and Cape Verde (3.6%). This distribution reflects not only the historic bilateral ties Brazil has with these countries, but also the growing importance within Brazilian foreign policy of the Community of Portuguese Language Countries (CPLP), which during the 2000s came to be viewed by Brazilian diplomats as a springboard for expanding Brazil's influence in lusophone Africa.[35]

The official figures also show some diversification in the range of Brazilian implementing agencies carrying out technical cooperation in Africa. Among the 44 government agencies whose South–South expenditures appear in the Instituto de Pesquisa Econômica Aplicada (IPEA) cooperation report, the MRE itself spent by far the most among any government body—over 80 million reais—followed by the Federal Police and a number of ministries (including those devoted to Health, Agriculture and Development); key implementing institutions also included the Brazilian Corporation of Agricultural Research (Embrapa) and Fiocruz.[36]

Some of these institutions, such as Embrapa and Fiocruz, are hybrid organisations, combining characteristics and objectives from the public and private sector. As semi-autonomous institutions under the umbrella of specific ministries (Agriculture and Health, respectively), these organisations are tasked with a variety of activities related to domestic policy, including training and pure and applied research. Among Embrapa's goals is to develop new techniques and varieties to help boost Brazilian agricultural exports. Fiocruz provides support not only to the Brazilian public health system (the Sistema Único de Saúde, SUS), but also to the national pharmaceutical industry. Both Embrapa and Fiocruz have long histories of participating in international cooperation, not only as recipients but also as partners within broad international networks and as providers of technical cooperation. They each also collaborate with private sector partners, both

---

32. A large part of these contributions are self-supporting contributions, whereby the Brazilian government pays UN agencies to deliver services within its own borders. See Flavia Galvani and Stephen Morse, "Institutional Sustainability: At What Price? UNDP and the New Cost-Sharing Model in Brazil", *Development in Practice*, Vol. 14, No. 3 (2004), pp. 311–327.

33. Amanda Rossi, "Em 5 anos, Brasil gasta R$6,6 bilhões em cooperação", *Estado de São Paulo*, August 2013, available: <http://www.estadao.com.br/noticias/impresso,em-5-anos-brasil-gasta-r-6-6-bilhoes-em-cooperacao,1060682,0.htm> (accessed 10 December 2014).

34. IPEA, "País investiu R$ 1,6 bi na cooperação internacional", 1 August 2013, available: <http://www.ipea.gov.br/portal/index.php?option=com_content&view=article&id=19209> (accessed 10 July 2014).

35. Interview with Brazilian diplomat, Brasília, October 2014.

36. IPEA relatorio COBRADI, p. 33.

in Brazil and abroad.[37] This means that some of Brazil's most important implementing agencies are keenly attuned to private sector dynamics as well as to policy debates and are embedded within networks of research centres with decades of experience in international cooperation, both North–South and South–South.

Although these institutions have a fair degree of autonomy in the design and implementation of international cooperation activities, they also figure prominently within the MRE's efforts to promote Brazil as "an important source of technical knowledge and imaginative solutions that can be applied in countries with a 'know-how' deficit" and in its insistence that the cooperation they implement "is not assistentialist, has no profit motives nor commercial goals".[38] This official discourse also presents Brazilian cooperation as demand-driven, with projects designed and implemented in response to specific needs identified by partner states. In practice, however, the government also engages in broad promotion of Brazilian technical cooperation, which helps to generate demand for these initiatives. For instance, Brazil's diplomatic representations abroad disseminate information about Brazil's "innovative policies", and Lula, in particular, used his state visits to present Brazil as a transformative agent in African development. There were also efforts to promote Brazilian technical cooperation at home. The MRE's Rio Branco Institute, tasked with selecting and training career diplomats, has expanded its exchange programmes for African students and designed new short courses for early career diplomats, all of which incorporated guest lectures and discussions of Brazilian technical cooperation.[39]

Greater stress was also placed on the concept of horizontal cooperation, often through claims that these initiatives lack the deep asymmetries that characterise Northern aid. In addition, the Brazilian government has emphasised two elements: solidarity with African partners, especially by highlighting Brazil's past status as a former colony and its shared historical and cultural bonds with Africa; and compatibility, by claiming that its own development experiences are more similar to those of African countries. Finally, Brazil's official discourse has increasingly differentiated Brazilian cooperation from Northern aid by insisting that its non-imposition of political conditionalities is more respectful of the national sovereignty of partner states.[40] These claims resonate with the positions adopted by Brazilian foreign policy as far back as the Cold War, but they also seem compatible with the South–South cooperation discourses of other rising powers, including China, and of coalitions such as the BRICS.

The stance on national sovereignty also allowed the Brazilian government to deepen cooperation with a broad assortment of political regimes, from fellow democracies to autocratic governments. Although Brazilian firms had long invested in countries viewed by the international community, including the UN mechanisms, as chronic violators of human rights, Lula in particular made

---

37. Carlos R. De Carli, "Embrapa: Precursora da Parceria Público-Privada no Brasil", Master's thesis, Universidade de Brasília, Centro de Desenvolvimento Sustentável, Brasília, 2005. See also: *A Tarde*, "Farmanguinhos faz acordo para produzir antibiótico", 23 November 2012.

38. ABC, "CGPD" (n.d.), available: <http://www.abc.gov.br/SobreAbc/Direcao/CGPD> (accessed 10 July 2014).

39. FUNAG, *I Curso para diplomatas africanos* (Brasília: Ministério das Relações Exteriores, 2011).

40. Carolina Milhorance, "A política de cooperação do Brasil com a África Subsaariana no setor rural: transferência e inovação na difusão de políticas públicas", *Revista Brasileira de Política Internacional*, Vol. 56, No. 2 (2013), pp. 5–22.

highly visible efforts to burnish ties to states viewed by the West as "pariah" or "non-compliant" regimes. Brazilian diplomats argued that the name-and-shame or isolation policies pursued by many Northern states and international non-governmental organisations (NGOs) are counterproductive, and that engaging these states via dialogue and South–South development cooperation is more constructive.[41] In Africa, Brazil deepened ties with Zimbabwe, Equatorial Guinea and Libya, combining diplomatic dialogue with expanded development cooperation.[42]

More broadly, South–South cooperation became a way for the government to brand Brazil as an important source of social policy innovations—what officials frequently refer to as "social technologies"—offering alternatives to Western aid. This discourse was important not only to the individual government divisions that had long driven much of Brazil's technical cooperation abroad, but also to the federal government, as the Lula government worked to promote Brazil's identity as a rising power both at home and abroad.

At the organisational level, the attempt to harness capillary cooperation entailed forging closer partnerships between the federal government and implementing agencies such as Fiocruz and Embrapa, which possess the technical know-how to carry out concrete projects.[43] One example that illustrates the interplay between Brazilian foreign policy and the interests of the implementing agency is the antiretroviral (ARV) factory that Brazil has helped to build in Mozambique. The factory, designed to foment local production of generics for AIDS/HIV as well as other illnesses, was part of a cooperation agreement signed in 2008; despite multiple delays and being only partially completed, the plant was formally inaugurated in 2013, with partial financing from the Brazilian mining company Vale. The project is aligned not only with Brazil's domestic approach to HIV/AIDS, which relies on a combination of prevention and treatment with generics, but also boosts the position defended abroad by Brazilian diplomacy that developing countries have a right to produce generic medications in cases of epidemics. This reasoning has pitted the Brazilian government against the interests of the big pharmaceutical industry and the positions of Northern governments, but Brazil's position is endorsed by a number of developing countries with similar stances. By disseminating its own model in Africa, Brazil not only works to legitimise its approach to HIV/AIDS, particularly in light of the ongoing international controversies, but also to garner support among other developing countries for its stance on intellectual property issues as they relate to public health epidemics.[44]

In addition to increasing expenditures and expanding the array of cooperation projects in Africa, the Brazilian government also expanded the ABC, granting it larger staff and resources. To better align the country's official technical cooperation with its foreign policy priorities, starting in 2004 the ABC was tasked with

---

41. Interview with Brazilian senior diplomat, Brasília, May 2014.

42. Adriana Erthal Abdenur and Danilo Marcondes de Souza-Neto, "Brazil's Development Cooperation with Africa: What Role for Democracy and Human Rights?", *Sur: International Journal of Human Rights*, Vol. 10, No. 19 (2013), pp. 17–35.

43. One side effect of these partnerships is the incipient but growing institutionalisation and professionalisation of South–South cooperation within implementing agencies: both Fiocruz and Embrapa have created divisions dedicated to international cooperation, with public selection of staff specifically dedicated to international cooperation.

44. André de Mello e Souza, "Saúde pública, patentes e atores não estatais: a política externa do Brasil ante a epidemia de AIDS", in Leticia Pinheiro and Carlos Milani (eds.), *Política externa brasileira. As prática da política e a política das práticas* (Rio de Janeiro: FGV, 2012).

prioritising certain types of projects and programmes, namely: technical cooperation with developing countries that are strategic to Brazilian foreign policy; projects that are linked to the national programmes and priorities of recipient countries; projects of greater impact and influence; projects that have local counterpart resources and/or effective participation of partner institutions; and partnerships with institutions that are genuinely national in scope.[45]

The MRE also worked to channel more technical cooperation through the agency by signing formal agreements and memoranda of understanding with partner states. Nevertheless, efforts to strengthen ABC's coordination capacity continue to run into certain barriers. First, the lack of a legal framework regulating the country's official technical cooperation abroad constrains the resources that can be spent on projects, as well as the amount of time that professionals may spend on this type of work. Partly as a result, the ABC still "outsources" many functions to the UNDP in Brasília. Second, lead staff turnover at ABC is high, partly by design: career diplomats work there only temporarily and are then allocated to other divisions. Third, the agency's coordinating reach remains limited, as evidenced by the high number of international cooperation projects carried out by government divisions that take place without ABC playing a role. These limitations mean that, despite the harnessing attempts by the federal government, Brazilian technical cooperation remains strongly capillary in nature, driven primarily by implementing institutions such as Fiocruz and Embrapa rather than ABC or the broader MRE.

This capillarity may be reinforced, in some contexts, by the enlistment of civil society entities such as NGOs, labour unions, professional associations and research centres as implementing institutions. For instance, the Serviço Nacional de Aprendizagem Industrial (SENAI), a vocational and professional training organisation, has been tasked with the creation of professional capacity-building centres in several African countries (so far, in Angola, Cape Verde and Guinea-Bissau; there are also plans underway for new centres in São Tomé and Príncipe and Mozambique).[46] ABC has also partnered with the Pastoral da Criança, an NGO affiliated with the Catholic Church but funded primarily by the Health Ministry, to provide community leadership training and other services in several African countries, including Guinea-Bissau.[47] These partnerships help to make up for the resource constraints as well as the lack of regulation of Brazil's South–South development cooperation.

More than just a branding exercise, technical cooperation has been viewed as a kind of currency for obtaining support for positions and initiatives within multilateral settings. In a typically implicit quid pro quo, Brazil promises development cooperation projects and African heads of state either announce or reiterate their support for Brazil's bid for a UNSC permanent seat or for Brazilian candidates to leadership positions at international organisations. While African support contributed towards the elections of Brazilian agronomist José Graziano da Silva as Director-General of the World Food Programme and Brazilian diplomat Roberto

45. ABC, "CGPD—Coordenação Geral de Cooperação Técnica entre Países em Desenvolvimento—Histórico" (n.d.), available: <http://www.abc.gov.br/SobreABC/Direcao/CGPD> (accessed 10 December 2014).

46. ABC, "SENAI—Serviço Nacional de Aprendizagem Industrial" (n.d.), available: <http://www.abc.gov.br/Projetos/CooperacaoSulSul/Senai> (accessed 10 July 2014).

47. ABC South–South Cooperation Project Database: BRA/04/044-A100—Missão para Desenvolvimento e Detalhamento de Projetos de Cooperação em Guiné Bissau—Pastoral da Criança.

Azevêdo to the post of Director-General of the World Trade Organization, in other instances the effectiveness South–South cooperation provision as a political strategy is less certain. On the UNSC issue, for instance, despite frequently voicing support for Brazil's bid for a permanent seat, most African states have not aligned with the proposals that Brazil has advanced through its informal alliance with India, Germany and Japan (the group known as the G-4), favouring instead other reform models.[48]

In seeking to advance Brazil's global player ambitions, the Workers' Party-led government mobilised technical cooperation in order to help legitimise its ambitious (and often, controversial) foreign policy. This federal-level political driver, superimposed onto the objectives of specific implementing institutions, became even more important as political opposition groups and civil society entities began contesting the Workers' Party foreign policy, including elements of its South–South development cooperation. For instance, Brazilian NGOs have partnered with Mozambican counterparts to sharply criticise the ProSavana project, a triangular cooperation initiative carried out in partnership with the Japanese Cooperation Agency (JICA) and the Mozambican government. The project, which aims to implement a vast agricultural corridor in the province of Nacala dedicated to the export of agricultural commodities, drew inspiration from Brazil's own experience in large-scale agricultural reengineering, namely, the transformation of large swaths of South-western Brazil (the arid *cerrado*) into export-oriented monoculture. Civil society entities have questioned not only the heavy influence of major corporate interests in the design of ProSavana, but also what they perceive to be insufficient attention to local stakeholder, including small farmers.[49] Such contestation introduces additional non-state interests into Brazilian technical cooperation in Africa that also complicate efforts to appropriate Brazil's technical cooperation as a tool of foreign policy.

Implications for Development Governance

The Brazilian government has stressed that its cooperation practices are fundamentally different from those of Northern aid providers, and that it is thus not merely a "new donor". As a result, since Lula's first mandate, Brazil has distanced itself from what it perceives as Northern-dominated efforts to codify the principles and norms of international development. Most notably, although Brazil signed the 2005 Paris Declaration,[50] more recently the government has declined to join efforts led by the OECD's DAC to set norms for the field through the "aid effectiveness" agenda. Although Brazilian diplomats emphasise that the government is not opposed to all of the principles promoted by the DAC, they insist that certain elements— such as the imposition of political conditionalities in the name of good governance—are incompatible with the guiding concepts of Brazilian foreign policy,

48. Richard Gowan and Nora Gordon, "Pathways to Security Council Reform", Center on International Cooperation, New York, May 2014.

49. Fátima Mello, "O que o Brasil quer com o Pró-Savana?", FASE, 12 March 2013, available: <http://www.fase.org.br/v2/pagina.php?id=3837> (accessed 10 July 2014).

50. Although Brazil signed the Paris Declaration, it claims to have signed it only in the condition of aid recipient, and not as provider of South–South cooperation. German Development Institute, "Brazil as an Emerging Actor in International Development Cooperation: A Good Partner for European Donors?", Briefing Paper, Bonn, May 2010.

such as non-intervention. Not only has Brazil bristled at being pigeonholed into the category of donors, it has also refused to bandwagon with the initiative, which it views as lacking legitimacy because it takes place outside of the UN. At the 2014 Global Partnership in Mexico, the head of ABC stated unequivocally that Brazil was only there as an observer, and not as a full participant.[51]

The impact of Brazil's reticence is magnified by the fact that, since the late 2000s, it has aligned more closely with other rising powers that also regard the current governance architecture in the field of international development with a degree of suspicion. Of all of the BRICS, only Russia had established connections with the DAC, and these links have stagnated since the start of the Crimean crisis in 2014. Neither China (which has already become the largest South–South cooperation provider) nor India sent representatives to the meeting in Mexico.[52] Even if other major developing economies have actively joined the process— among them Mexico, Indonesia and Nigeria—the BRICS states are increasingly moving away from the DAC paradigm. The July 2014 announcement that the BRICS would launch a New Development Bank only underscored the growing distance between these states and the current Western-led discussions about international development norms.

This position has become particularly salient at the federal level, especially in foreign policy, but the discourse is now frequently echoed by implementing institutions, for instance, in their resistance to adopt monitoring and evaluation models championed by the DAC.[53] However, this does not mean that the instrumentalisation of technical cooperation for foreign policy purposes always goes smoothly; since the implementing institutions often have their own goals, there is the occasional tug of war between the MRE diplomats and the sector specialists who design and implement initiatives abroad, either within the implementing institution or at the corresponding ministry. Such tensions have emerged anew with wide-reaching budget cuts implemented under the Dilma Rousseff administration, which have affected not only the execution of technical cooperation projects, but also the broader operations of the ministry itself.[54]

Conclusion

This paper has analysed Brazil's technical cooperation with Africa by tracing key changes in its organisational structure and dynamics. While early Brazilian technical cooperation was driven primarily by individual ministries and other government divisions—therefore, more capillary than centralised—under the Workers'

51. Thomas Fues and Stephan Klingebiel, "Unrequited Love: What is the Legacy of the First Global Partnership Summit?", German Development Institute, Bonn, 17 April 2014.

52. *Ibid.*

53. The MRE has not been entirely opposed to implementing monitoring and evaluation (M&E) practices in its South–South technical cooperation; rather, it has begun to foster homegrown models. In 2014, for instance, it launched a tender for the development of a M&E framework for the Cotton 4 project, which provides agricultural support to Benin, Burkina Faso, Chad and Mali. See ENAP, "Termo de cooperação para a construção do marco analítico de avaliação do projeto Cotton 4", available: <http://repositorio.enap.gov.br/handle/1/854> (accessed 10 December 2014).

54. *Folha de São Paulo*, "Diplomats Criticize 'Anomaly' at Brazilian Foreign Affairs Ministry", 29 September 2014, available: <http://www1.folha.uol.com.br/internacional/en/brazil/2014/09/1524298-diplomats-criticize-anomaly-at-brazilian-foreign-affairs-ministry.shtml> (accessed 10 December 2014).

Party the federal government has sought to better align Brazilian technical cooperation with its foreign policy. The ABC's project portfolio has vastly expanded over the past 10 years, channelling initiatives that are implemented abroad by state as well as non-state actors. This expanding cooperation has been conducted under a discourse of South–South cooperation that seeks to present Brazil as a hotbed of development innovation, particularly with respect to social policies—which are at the heart of the Workers' Party's domestic agenda. Technical cooperation has thus served not only to legitimise the social policies implemented at home, but also—increasingly—to bolster the positions taken by Brazil's foreign policy, including Brazil's global power aspirations.

Against the backdrop of Brazilian technical cooperation's changing configuration and politics, Africa has come to play a crucial role. In many ways, countries in Africa—especially but not exclusively lusophone partners—have become testing grounds for the Brazilian government's ability to promote its ideas and garner influence abroad. Offering technical cooperation to African partners has been viewed both as a way to broaden support for Brazilian positions within multilateral institutions, as a way to garner goodwill bilaterally, and as a way to contest Northern-led development norms. By framing Brazilian technical cooperation as more horizontal, more compatible and possibly more effective than aid, the Brazilian government discourse about South–South cooperation seeks to set Brazil apart from DAC donors.

However, efforts to boost federal-level coordination and thus instrumentalise technical cooperation as a tool of foreign policy have run into institutional and legal limitations, as well as some political contestation. In other words, it is both the case that the government uses South–South technical cooperation to legitimise its foreign policy, and that this technical cooperation is informed (although no means determined) by foreign policy priorities.

Disclosure Statement

No potential conflict of interest was reported by the author.

DFID, the Private Sector and the Re-centring of an Economic Growth Agenda in International Development

EMMA MAWDSLEY

This article examines the way in which the UK's Department for International Development (DFID) is returning an economic growth agenda to the centre of its mandate. The private sector is pitched as the primary engine of this strategy, with a growing place for corporations, consultancies and the financial sector in particular. The shift can be understood as a strategic response to an increasingly challenging domestic context, and to a turbulent external arena for the "traditional" donors. This strategy may well achieve growth outcomes in partner countries, but without sufficient conceptual rigour, regulatory oversight or attention to the "connective fabric" between growth and "development", the latter is more uncertain. DFID's direction reflects wider trends in international development norms, finances and actors. While in some regards we could say that the "traditional" donors are "returning" to older development models, they are doing so with new tools and in new contexts. An optimistic assessment is that this will result in a more effective "beyond aid" development agenda, but there is a significant risk of capture by state-corporate interests that will not aim for or achieve progressive, just development outcomes.

Introduction

In a keynote speech delivered with evident symbolic flourish at the London Stock Exchange in January 2014, the secretary of state for the UK's Department for International Development (DFID), Justine Greening, stated:

> Economic development is not a completely new direction for DFID but in the past the approach was ad-hoc, and nowhere near a top priority for the department. That is changing. We are now building the most coherent, focused and ambitious approach to economic development that DFID has ever had. This represents a *radical shift* in the way that DFID works. It's a pragmatic shift to be managed carefully, *but it's arguably revolutionary.* And make no mistake: DFID's role in the developing world is steadily and surely changing for good.[1]

---

[1] Justine Greening, Speech, "Smart Aid: Why It's All About Jobs" (27 January 2014), available: <https://www.gov.uk/government/speeches/smart-aid-why-its-all-about-jobs> (accessed 6 March 2015). Emphasis added. As we will see, while DFID is currently accelerating, deepening and normatively (re-)centring economic growth, Greening's speech rather exaggerates the change. I suggest this is in order to try and distance DFID under the coalition government from DFID under New Labour, and to try and persuade

The "traditional" bilateral and multilateral donors are responding, individually and collectively, to a series of game-changing trends in international development. These include the growing voice of the South as both providers and recipients of development assistance; increasingly complex geographies of poverty and wealth, including a growing share of the world's poor in "middle income" countries; the widening marketplace for public, private and blended development finance; and the enormous domestic and international reverberations of the "global" and Euro-zone financial crises.[2] One way of framing this is to suggest that these donors are experiencing three interconnected "crises": ontological (a challenge to their "traditional" monopoly of donor identity), ideational (the erosion of their normative/agenda-setting dominance) and material (the relative and absolute rise of the South).[3] The last few years have seen the re-absorption of a number of bilateral development agencies into Ministries of Foreign Affairs and/or increased subordination to Trade Ministries (e.g. Australia, Canada, New Zealand, The Netherlands); questions over the definition and future of "foreign aid"; and some erosion of individual and collective Organisation for Economic Cooperation and Development – Development Assistance Committee (OECD-DAC) dominance in the international development architecture.[4] Crises are simultaneously opportunities, of course, and some outcomes may well be desirable and progressive—there are many elements of the pluralising architecture and the idea of moving "beyond aid" to welcome;[5] while emerging collaborations with the "rising powers" will, ideally,

---

sceptical publics and politicians of the supposed 'reinvention' of aid to support the UK economy. As one anonymous reviewer of this article rightly suggested, an analysis of the narrative framing being deployed in these speeches and documents would be extremely revealing (the construction of "frontier markets", mentioned later, is another example: see A.L. Tsing, "Natural Resources and Capitalist Frontiers", *Economic and Political Weekly*, Vol. 38, No. 48 (2003), pp. 5100–5106). Unfortunately space precludes such an analysis here.

[2] N. Woods, "Whose Aid? Whose Influence? China, Emerging Donors and the Silent Revolution in Development Assistance", *International Affairs*, Vol. 84, No. 6 (2008), pp. 1205–1221; E. Mawdsley, *From Recipients to Donors: The Emerging Powers and the Changing Development Landscape* (London: Zed Books, 2012); R. Kanbur and A. Sumner, "Poor Countries or Poor People? Development Assistance and the New Geography of Global Poverty", *Journal of International Development*, Vol. 24, No. 6 (2012), pp. 686–695; J. Sidaway, "Geographies of Development: New Maps, New Visions?", *The Professional Geographer*, Vol. 64, No. 2 (2012), pp. 1–14; W. Hynes and S. Scott, "The Evolution of Official Development Assistance: Achievements, Criticisms and Way Forward", *IIIS Discussion Paper No. 437* (October 2013).

[3] The two Asian OECD-DAC members, Japan (joined 1961) and Korea (joined 2010), on the other hand, are in some ways looking closer to the norm rather than outliers. The crises listed above have affected them differently, but arguably with positive ontological and ideational outcomes (S.-M. Kim, "Critical Geopolitics and Contemporary Development: South Korea's Place in the Changing Landscape of Foreign Aid", PhD thesis, University of Cambridge, 2015; J. Sato, "The Benefits of Unification Failure: Re-examining the Evolution of Economic Cooperation in Japan", *JICA Research Institute Working Paper No. 87*, February 2015). Needless to say, the rest of the OECD-DAC donors comprise a very diverse group, notwithstanding some of the shared trends identified in this article.

[4] S. Chaturvedi, T. Fues and E. Sidiropoulos, *Development Cooperation and Emerging Powers: New Partners or Old Patterns?* (London: Zed Books, 2012); Thomas Fues, "DCF and the International Development System", Academic Council on the United Nations System, *Quarterly Newsletter* (2/2014), pp. 6–9.

[5] H. Kharas, K. Makino and W. Jung (eds.), *Catalysing Development: A New Vision for Aid* (Washington, DC: Brookings Institution, 2011); O. Barder and A. Evans, "Evidence Submitted to the International Development Committee" (2014), available: <http://www.globaldashboard.org/wp-content/uploads/IDC-Beyond-Aid.pdf> (accessed 6 March 2015); H. Janus, S. Klingebiel and S. Paulo, "Beyond Aid: A Conceptual Perspective of the Transformation of Development Cooperation", *Journal of International Development*, Vol. 27, No. 2 (2014), pp. 155–169; International Development Committee, "The Future of UK Development Cooperation: Beyond Aid" (2015), available: <http://www.parliament.uk/

lead to mutual learning and improved development outcomes.[6] However, crises are also particular moments of opportunity for powerful vested interests.[7] This article focuses on the latter possibility, by making the case that the DFID's strong turn to a private sector-led economic growth agenda — and more particularly, one that appears to increasingly validate large-scale corporations, consultancies and the financial sector — risks enabling yet more assertive strategies of capital accumulation and profit making that, in the name of "development", overwhelmingly benefit wealthier actors in the UK and abroad. Observing the way in which "international development" (in part) serves donor commercial interests is hardly new,[8] but the article's originality lies in examining how this longstanding tension or critique is playing out in the current, rather different, development era. While the article focuses on the bilateral members of the OECD-DAC, and more specifically DFID, related issues and trends can also be observed in many multilaterals.[9]

The article contributes to a growing number of analyses that examine the strategic responses of the "mainstream" development community to the unprecedented challenges, opportunities and uncertainties of the present time.[10] This turbulence follows a period of relative agreement (notwithstanding many contestations and critiques) that emerged in the mid-1990s associated with the shift away from structural adjustment towards a post-Washington Consensus around poverty reduction, institutions and social development.[11] This paradigm found expression in the Millennium Development Goals (MDGs) and the aid effectiveness regime, which was launched with the 2005 Paris Declaration.[12] However, around the mid-2000s there were signs of a return to a stronger focus on "growth", something that has accelerated sharply following the global financial and Eurozone crises and the election of a number of right-wing governments in Western countries

---

business/committees/committees-a-z/commons-select/international-development-committee/news/bey ond-aid-report-published/> (accessed 6 March 2015).

[6] F. Zimmermann and K. Smith, "More Actors, More Money, More Ideas for International Development Co-operation", *Journal of International Development*, Vol. 23, No. 5 (2011), pp. 722–738; A. Shankland and J. Constantine, "From Geopolitics to Knowledge Politics: The Rising Powers and the Global Partnership for Effective Development Cooperation", Keynote presentation at "The Rising Powers and the Post-2015 Development Agenda", Rising Powers Study Group/Development Studies Association Workshop, London, 30 October 2014.

[7] N. Klein, *The Shock Doctrine: The Rise of Disaster Capitalism* (New York: Metropolitan Books, 2007); P. Mirowski, *Never Let a Serious Crisis Go to Waste: How Neoliberalism Survived the Financial Meltdown* (London: Verso Books, 2013).

[8] For example, R. Abrahamson and P. Williams, "Ethics and Foreign Policy: The Antimonies of New Labour's Third Way in Sub-Saharan Africa", *Political Studies*, Vol. 49, No. 2 (2001), pp. 249–264; D. Sogge, *Give and Take: What's the Matter with Foreign Aid?* (New York and London: Zed Books, 2002).

[9] N. Alexander, "The World Bank: In the Vanguard of an Infrastructure Boom", Bretton Woods Project, At Issue, February 2015.

[10] For instance, A. Abdenur and J. Fonseca, "The North's Growing Role in South-South Cooperation: Keeping the Foothold", *Third World Quarterly*, Vol. 34, No. 8 (2013), pp. 1475–1491; J. Vestergaard and R. Wade, "Out of the Woods: Gridlock in the IMF and the World Bank Puts Multilateralism at Risk", *Danish Institute for International Studies Report 2014:06*, Vol. 40, No. 5 (2014), pp. 865–877.

[11] OECD-DAC, *Shaping the 21st Century: The Contribution of Development Co-operation* (Paris: OECD, 1996); R. Eyben, "The Road Not Taken: International Aid's Choice of Copenhagen over Beijing", *Third World Quarterly*, Vol. 27, No. 6 (2006), pp. 595–608; D. Hulme and S. Fukuda-Parr, "International Norm Dynamics and the 'End of Poverty': Understanding the Millennium Development Goals", *Brooks World Poverty Institute Working Paper No. 96* (2009).

[12] T. Killick, "Policy Autonomy and the History of British Aid to Africa", *Development Policy Review*, Vol. 23, No. 6 (2005), pp. 665–681, doi: 10.1111/j.1467-7679.2005.00307.x.

(see below). Symbolic dates and events are always a double-edged sword, in danger of concealing as much as they capture, but the 2011 Fourth High Level Forum on Aid Effectiveness (the Busan Conference) can be seen as an emblematic marker of the momentous changes taking place in the ideology and governance of international development.[13] This most recent transition differs from previous paradigm shifts in two important ways. First, it has not been driven primarily by the North or the Northern-led "international" development organisations, but in various ways by a rebalancing of power to the South.[14] Second, the international development community is even more fluid and diverse than before. A successor regime that achieves even the partial claims to coherence, consensus and compliance of the previous "aid effectiveness agenda"[15] may or may not emerge through the auspices of the Sustainable Development Goals (SDGs) or initiatives like the Global Partnership for Effective Cooperation. Present-day patterns of competition, collaboration and convergence between state and non-state development actors of all hues are complex and shifting, and are by no means reducible to North-South interests and identities alone.[16]

The focus of this article is the UK's Department for International Development (DFID) under the post-2010 Conservative-led coalition government. It does not offer a comprehensive analysis of the multiple ways in which DFID is seeking to strategically respond to the challenges, opportunities and uncertainties of the current period. Rather, as the opening quote from Justine Greening suggests, it examines DFID's re-centring of economic growth in particular ways. This is traced through changing discursive strategies, institutional restructuring, new programmes and partnerships, and sectoral re-allocation of Overseas Development Assistance (ODA). The article is based on transcripts of speeches given by senior DFID figures, official reports and statistics, presentations to the UK Parliament's International Development Committee, and the reports of the recently created Independent Commission on Aid Impact (ICAI),[17] which was established by the coalition government in 2011. A centrepiece statement of purpose is the "Economic Development for Shared Prosperity and Poverty Reduction: A Strategic Framework", which was launched in January 2014 (hereafter DFID 2014).[18] The analysis

---

[13] R. Eyben and L. Savage, "Emerging and Submerging Powers: Imagined Geographies in the New Development Partnership at the Busan High Fourth High Level Forum", *The Journal of Development Studies*, Vol. 49, No. 4 (2013), pp. 457–469; E. Mawdsley, L. Savage and S.-M. Kim, "A 'Post-Aid World'? Paradigm Shift in Foreign Aid and Development Cooperation at the 2011 Busan High Level Forum", *Geographical Journal*, Vol. 180, No. 1 (2014), pp. 27–38.

[14] Eyben and Savage, *op. cit.*

[15] *Ibid.*

[16] For instance, D. Curtis, "China and the Insecurity of Development in the Democratic Republic of the Congo (DRC)", *International Peacekeeping*, Vol. 20, No. 5 (2013), pp. 551–569; Thomas Fues and Jiang Ye, "A Strong Voice for Global Sustainable Development: How China Can Play a Leading Role in the Post-2015 Agenda", in Thomas Fues and Jiang Ye (eds.), *United Nations Post-2015 Agenda for Global Development: Perspectives from China and Europe* (Bonn: German Development Institute /DIE, 2014), pp. 11–22; P. Kragelund, "Towards Convergence and Cooperation in the Global Development Finance Regime: Closing Africa's Policy Space", *Cambridge Review of International Affairs* (2015), doi: 10.1080/09557571.2014.974141.

[17] Notably, Independent Commission on Aid Impact, "DFID's Private Sector Development Work", ICAI Report 35 (May 2014).

[18] DFID, "Economic Development for Shared Prosperity and Poverty Reduction: A Strategic Framework" (2014), available: <https://www.gov.uk/government/uploads/system/uploads/attachment_data/file/276859/Econ-development-strategic-framework_.pdf> (accessed 10 March 2015).

is augmented by a number of interviews with DFID officials and academic and non-governmental organisation (NGO) development experts, all of whom requested anonymity.

The Poverty/Growth Relationship under Changing Normative Regimes

Economic growth has always been on the agenda for DFID and its predecessors. For the duration of the most recent "aid effectiveness" regime (from the late 1990s to c.2011), for example, DFID promoted and financed economic growth for the UK and its partner countries in multiple ways, ranging from small-scale micro-finance schemes to substantial commercial investments through the Common-wealth Development Corporation.[19] But in contrast to earlier eras, during this period economic growth was conceptually and discursively (if by no means always in reality) subordinated to the central analytic of *poverty reduction*.[20] Poverty reduction acted as the overarching discursive framework within which other supporting objectives—economic growth but also good governance, social welfare, sustainable development, gender empowerment and inclusive finance— were (supposedly) organised. DFID was a leading norm entrepreneur in promoting and consolidating the poverty reduction agenda,[21] something that was accompanied by a programmatic focus on the "soft wiring" of development. This was a sector-wide shift. For example, in 1990, 82% of total DAC ODA was directed towards agriculture, industry, economic infrastructure and the private sector, but by 2004, health, education and governance alone accounted for 51% of total DAC aid.[22] The poverty reduction agenda was of course firmly embedded in neoliberal ideology: just like previous market-led growth strategies, it relied on a residual rather than relational construction of "poverty" that evacuated the concept of power, inequality and the structural conditions that produce poverty.[23]

At the present juncture, however, *economic growth* is being ideationally and insti-tutionally reinstated as the central and prior condition for "development". This is not just deepening the existing poverty reduction-era focus on "bottom billion capitalism" (including land titling, markets for the poor, microfinance, supporting Small and Medium Enterprises [SMEs] and so on),[24] but extending towards new and expanding goals of large-scale public–private partnerships, donor support for major commercial investments, private equity initiatives and deepening finan-cialisation.[25] Poverty reduction will not disappear as a goal or discourse, but its

[19] DFID, *The Engine of Development: The Private Sector and Prosperity for Poor People* (London: DFID, 2011), available: <https://www.gov.uk/government/uploads/system/uploads/attachment_data/file/67490/Private-sector-approach-paper-May2011.pdf> (accessed 16 April 2015).

[20] OECD-DAC, *op. cit.*; Killick, *op. cit.*; Eyben, "The Road Not Taken", *op. cit.*; R. Eyben, "'Power' in 'Empowerment': A Case Study of Constructing a Text against the Mainstream", *European Journal of Development Research* (2014), doi: 10.1057/ejdr.2014.66; Hulme and Fukuda-Parr, *op. cit.*

[21] Killick, *op. cit.*

[22] J. Harrigan, "The Doubling of Aid to Sub-Saharan Africa: Promises and Problems", *Journal of Con-temporary African Studies*, Vol. 25, No. 3 (2007), pp. 369–389; M. Saidi and C. Wolf, "Recalibrating Devel-opment Cooperation: How Can African Countries Benefit from Emerging Partners?", *OECD Development Centre Working Paper No. 302* (2011).

[23] Eyben, "The Road Not Taken", *op. cit.*; T. Pogge, *Politics as Usual: What Lies behind the Pro-Poor Rheto-ric* (Cambridge: Polity Press, 2010).

[24] DFID, *The Engine of Development, op. cit.*

[25] Alexander, *op. cit.*; DFID, "Economic Development for Shared Prosperity", *op. cit.*

place in the sequencing and focus of many development actors is changing. Inextricably linked to the current formulation of growth is the repositioning of "the private sector" not only as the object of development, or as a broader vehicle of change, but as an active partner in development.[26] In some regards, we could say that the OECD-DAC donors are moving closer to the norms and modalities of the South, particularly in terms of putting growth and productivity higher up development partnership agendas, encouraging (and financing) a more substantial role for national firms, and moving towards various forms of "blended" finance instruments: public and private loans and grants, equity and finance and so on.[27] DFID is investing directly in infrastructure (for example, through some projects funded by the Private Infrastructure Development Group; see below), but also actively shaping the business, trade, investment and finance environment through new and expanding programmes to support corporations, foreign direct investment (FDI), financial and legal services and capital market promotion.[28] This appeals to the UK's comparative advantage in management consultancies and the financial sector, vis-à-vis rising powers which tend to be more oriented to direct investments (through various forms of loans and grants) in companies building roads, rail, energy, transmission and so on.[29]

The restoration of corporate and finance-led economic growth to the heart of "development" may well bring positive and even progressive outcomes to poor people and poor countries, but it risks being subordinated to the interests of capital, and large UK corporations and the UK financial sector in particular. DFID certainly insists on the importance of "inclusive growth", ensuring benefits for women and girls, and supporting partner country firms (including SMEs), but the evidence on the robustness of the connective infrastructure between "growth" and "development" is less convincing.[30] Adequate and appropriate

---

[26] J. Nelson, "The Private Sector and Aid Effectiveness: Towards New Models of Engagement", in H. Kharas et al., *op. cit.*, pp. 83–111; DFID, *The Engine of Development, op. cit.*; B. Tomlinson (ed.), *Aid and the Private Sector: Catalysing Poverty Reduction and Development? Reality of Aid* (Philippines: IBON International, 2012); J. Di Bella et al., *The Private Sector and Development: Key Concepts* (Ottawa: North-South Institute, 2013); M. Blowfield and C.S. Dolan, "Business and a Development Agent: Evidence of Possibility and Improbability", *Third World Quarterly*, Vol. 35, No. 1 (2014), pp. 22–42; S. Kindornay and F. Reilly-King, "Promotion and Partnership: Bilateral Donor Approaches to the Private Sector" (2013), available: <http://www.oefse.at/fileadmin/content/Downloads/Publikationen/Oepol/Artikel2013/3_Kindornay_Reilly.pdf> (accessed 6 March 2015).

[27] E. Mawdsley, "A New Development Era? The Private Sector Moves to the Centre", Commissioned publication for the Norwegian Peacebuilding Resource Centre (NOREF), Oslo, Norway (2014).

[28] This opens up a very important set of debates about the "return" of the state that cannot be covered in this article. See B. Apeldoorn, N. de Graaff and H Overbeek, "The Reconfiguration of the Global State-Capital Nexus", *Globalizations*, Vol. 9, No. 4 (2012), pp. 471–486; and also E. Mawdsley, W. Murray, J. Overton, R. Scheyvens and G. Banks, "Exporting Stimulus and 'Shared Prosperity': Re-Inventing Foreign Aid for a Retroliberal Era", Working Paper (New Zealand Aid and Development Dialogues, 2015), available: <at http://nzadds.org.nz/>, for a fuller discussion specifically in relation to international development. See, for example, a speech by Justine Greening on 14 July 2014, available: <https://www.gov.uk/government/speeches/justine-greening-beyond-aid-development-priorities-from-2015>.

[29] G. Chin, "The BRICS-Led Development Bank: Purpose and Politics beyond the G20", *Global Policy*, Vol. 5, No. 3 (2014), pp. 366–373.

[30] ActionAid, "Aid to, with and through the Private Sector: Emerging Trends and Ways Forward", ActionAid Discussion Paper (April 2014); Independent Commission on Aid Impact, *op. cit.*; National Audit Office, "Department for International Development: Oversight of the Private Infrastructure Development Group" (2014), available: <http://www.nao.org.uk/report/oversight-of-the-private-infrastructure-development-group/>.

regulation, incentive structures that reward development indices (rather than growth or return on investment alone) and recognising/addressing potentially conflicting interests (e.g. between investors, employers and workers), for example, are all vital components of the transmission from "growth" to "development" (even allowing for different understandings of what "development" might mean). However, these are weakly conceptualised within current strategic statements, although specific programmes and initiatives may prove more encouraging.[31] Problematically, although not surprisingly, official DFID statements and policy documents on Private Sector Development (PSD) are almost entirely disengaged from any discussion of the contested nature of the present coalition government's domestic growth strategy. Critical analysts of the 'recovery' programmes launched in the wake of the global and Eurozone financial crises in many Western countries point to the deeply uneven treatment of and outcomes for the rich and poor. Joseph Stiglitz, for example, calculates that in the United States, 95% of the gains of the post-2008 "recovery" have gone to the top 1% of wealthy individuals, with extremely deleterious results for the economy, human development and social and political stability.[32] The UK's economic strategy under the coalition government has been bailouts and stimulus packages for the financial and corporate sectors, and austerity for the majority. The last few years have witnessed the punitive treatment of the jobless, the low-waged and the socially marginalised in the UK, against a backdrop of rising fortunes for national and transnational millionaires and billionaires. The 2014 Global Wealth Report by Credit Suisse states that the UK is the only G7 country in which inequality has increased this century, while the global distribution of income shows a continued upwards concentration of wealth.[33] Mawdsley et al.[34] suggest that UK and New Zealand aid policies are increasingly using public money to fund domestic corporate expansion: as they put it "exporting stimulus". DFID's strategic framework for private sector-led economic growth makes little or no mention of these national or global trends, or why they would be expected to be different when exported to "developing" countries.[35] Specifically, as we will see, inequality and decent work are barely mentioned in the private sector/growth frameworks.

There can be no question that economic growth is a desirable and, for the most part, a necessary condition of development. Capital investment is urgently required in many parts of the world to build essential infrastructure and supply services. The private sector is a particularly important actor in the provision of many

---

[31] DFID is making promising claims about widening the tax base in partner countries to enable more spending on services, and taking action with other development partners. See <https://www.gov.uk/government/news/uk-plans-major-boost-to-tax-collection-in-developing-countries> (accessed 28 October 2014). This is certainly an area to watch: if it is more than a gesture in the direction of improving global tax evasion and avoidance, then it will be a positive direction for DFID to take. However, DFID's very close relations with PriceWaterhouseCooper (to name just one of the big four), recently accused of "selling tax avoidance on an industrial scale" by the Public Accounts Committee, is hardly reassuring of policy coherence in this area. For example: <http://www.ft.com/cms/s/0/d2a73216-7f0a-11e4-a828-00144feabdc0.html#axzz3SwaS3gLE> (accessed 6 March 2015).

[32] J. Stiglitz, "Why Inequality Matters and What Can Be Done about It" (2014), available: <http://www.nextnewdeal.net/stiglitz-why-inequality-matters-and-what-can-be-done-about-it> (accessed 6 March 2015).

[33] S. Anand and P. Segal, "The Global Distribution of Income", *Economic Series Working Papers 714* (University of Oxford, Department of Economics, 2014).

[34] Mawdsley et al. (2015), *op. cit.*

[35] DFID, "Economic Development for Shared Prosperity", *op. cit.*

elements of a dignified life, and an essential component of a healthy economy, polity and society. There are elements of DFID's re-centring of private sector-led growth and the wider discussion of a world "beyond aid" to welcome. At present, however, the conceptual and policy links between growth and (private sector-led) development are insufficiently acknowledged or addressed within DFID's official statements and strategic frameworks. After a quick outline of DFID, these arguments will be set out in more detail below.

A Brief Background to DFID

DFID is in many ways a remarkable institution, widely admired by its peer agencies especially for its leading role over the last 15 years or so of the aid effectiveness agenda.[36] DFID was created in 1997 when New Labour came to power under the leadership of Tony Blair. Its origins lie in colonial development institutions and then a series of Overseas Development Offices and Administrations under both Conservative and Labour governments.[37] The creation of DFID as a separate department from the Foreign and Commonwealth Office (FCO), with a cabinet-level secretary of state and an expanded budget and increased staff, apparently demonstrated New Labour's insistence that it wanted a more ethical engagement in global affairs, and was seriously committed to international development and poverty reduction.[38] Julie Gallagher brilliantly unpicks the way in which the party, but more insistently Tony Blair, sought to project this moral identity.[39] All donors—North and South—construct a narrative that blends national self-interest with doing good, the only difference being how these elements are framed, balanced and projected. In the case of DFID under New Labour, there was a heavy tilt towards the high moral ground,[40] and DFID did indeed achieve some positive and progressive outcomes, notably around policy coherence for development. However, Gallagher suggests that at least in part this was aimed at offsetting domestic criticism of Blair's enthusiastic endorsement of the USA's invasions of Iraq and Afghanistan, and courting of big business and the City of London at home.[41] Ian Taylor also dissects the gap between Blair's spin and the realities of his African policies and impacts, such as significantly expanded arms sales.[42]

---

[36] O. Morrissey, "British Aid Policy Since 1997: Is DFID the Standard Bearer for Donors?", *CREDIT Research Paper No. 02/23* (University of Nottingham, 2002); Killick, *op. cit.*; A. Webster, "New Labour, New Aid? A Quantitative Examination of the Department for International Development", *International Public Policy Review*, Vol. 4, No. 1 (2008), pp. 4–28; B. Ireton, *Britain's International Development Policies: A History of DFID and Overseas Aid* (Basingstoke: Palgrave Macmillan, 2013).

[37] O. Barder, "Reforming Development Assistance: Lessons from the UK Experience", *Centre for Global Development Working Paper 70* (October 2005).

[38] Killick, *op. cit.*; T. Porteous, "British Government Policy in Sub-Saharan Africa under New Labour", *International Affairs*, Vol. 81, No. 2 (2005), pp. 281–297.

[39] J. Gallagher, "Healing the Scar: Idealising Britain in Africa, 1997–2007", *African Affairs*, Vol. 108, No. 432 (2009), pp. 435–451.

[40] For a critical discussion of how this morality translated into practice in the Great Lakes region, see Z. Marriage, "Defining Morality: DFID and the Great Lakes", *Third World Quarterly*, Vol. 27, No. 3 (2006), pp. 477–490.

[41] Gallagher, *op. cit.*

[42] I. Taylor, "Spinderella on Safari: British Policies toward Africa Under New Labour", *Global Governance: A Review of Multilateralism and International Organizations*, Vol. 18, No. 4 (October–December 2012), pp. 449–460.

DFID under New Labour coincided with the emergence and consolidation of the aid effectiveness era, and DFID was an active driver of the poverty reduction/MDG agenda.[43] Four White Papers on international development published in 1997, 2000, 2006 and 2009 capture this emerging and deepening framework, as well as shifts along the way.[44] In 2002, the International Development Act enshrined in legislation the primacy of poverty reduction, as well as a legal obligation to untie aid.[45] As noted above, economic growth initiatives were still on the agenda, but they did not take centre stage and whatever the reality, they were constructed as serving the primary goal of poverty reduction through stimulating markets, promoting financial inclusion, privatisation and investing in growth. Like many other OECD-DAC donors in this period, DFID concentrated its financial and ideational resources on the core concepts of good governance and anti-corruption, as well as social wellbeing through health, gender and education programmes. These were embedded in neoliberal philosophies of individual attainment, natural entrepreneurship and the universal benefits of market inclusion; and increasingly inflected through a national security lens associated with the "war on terror".[46] For all of the difference that the creation of DFID seemed to signal, Abrahamson and Williams' analysis of New Labour's Africa policy observes that behind the rhetoric, it demonstrated many continuities with the interests and agendas of previous Conservative governments, not least its commitment to economic and political liberalism under the ideological leadership of the International Monetary Fund (IMF) and the World Bank.[47]

In 2010 New Labour lost power to a Conservative-led coalition with the Liberal Democrats. The Conservative party had signalled some of its intentions for DFID and the international development agenda in 2009 when it published a Green Paper on "One World Conservatism" (OWC). Reflecting a new cross-party consensus on international development, they pledged to meet the aid target of 0.7% GNP. However, OWC promised a more "hard headed", value-for-money agenda, that supposedly "rebalanced" stronger national interests with "doing good" in the world.[48] Significantly, the present prime minister David Cameron is at odds with

---

[43] Killick, *op. cit.*

[44] DFID, *Eliminating World Poverty: A Challenge for the 21st Century* (1997), available: <http://webarchive.nationalarchives.gov.uk/20050404190659/http:/www.dfid.gov.uk/Pubs/files/whitepaper1997.pdf>; DFID, *Eliminating World Poverty: Making Globalisation Work for the Poor* (2000), available: <http://webarchive.nationalarchives.gov.uk/+/http:/www.dfid.gov.uk/Documents/publications/whitepaper2000.pdf>; DFID, *Eliminating World Poverty: Making Governance Work for the Poor* (2006), available: <https://www.gov.uk/government/uploads/system/uploads/attachment_data/file/272330/6876.pdf>; DFID, *Eliminating World Poverty: Building Our Common Future* (2009), available: https://www.gov.uk/government/uploads/system/uploads/attachment_data/file/229029/7656.pdf (all accessed 16 April 2015).

[45] Barder, *op. cit.*

[46] J. Hilary, "Profiting from Poverty: Privatisation Consultants, DFID and Public Services", War on Want (2004), available: <http://www.waterjustice.org/uploads/attachments/pdf67.pdf> (accessed 6 March 2015); DFID, *Private Sector Development Strategy, Prosperity for All: Making Markets Work* (London: DFID, 2008); Blowfield and Dolan, *op. cit.*

[47] Abrahamson and Williams, *op. cit.*

[48] J. Sharp, P. Campbell and E. Laurie, "The Violence of Aid? Giving, Power and Active Subjects in One World Conservatism", *Third World Quarterly,* Vol. 31, No. 7 (2010), pp. 1125–1143; J. Glennie, "From Green Paper to Government: The Coalition's Record on International Development", *Area,* Vol. 43, No. 4 (2011), pp. 508–509; D. Hall-Matthews, "Liberal Democrat Influence on Coalition International Development Policy", *Area,* Vol. 43, No. 4 (2011), pp. 511–512; E. Mawdsley "The Conservatives, the

many of his own MPs and substantial sections of the voting public on this subject. Under its post-2008 austerity drive, the coalition government instituted budget cuts across all departments other than foreign aid and the National Health Service, leading to vociferous objections, notably voiced in the right-wing tabloid newspaper, *The Daily Mail*. Pressure on all three of the main parties, and the Conservatives in particular, continues to grow with the challenge posed by the rising popularity of the UK Independence Party (UKIP), which, among other things, argues for an 85% reduction in UK foreign aid spending.[49]

Commentators offer a number of reasons to explain why Cameron has taken this political risk.[50] One is that he is hoping to emulate Blair in using international development as a means of burnishing a "moral" identity or to shed the Conservatives' image as the "nasty party", something that might be attractive to some voters. Another factor may be pressure from a strong UK development constituency, especially its articulate NGO sector. External status and soft power is also likely to be an important driver, with the UK having successfully been appointed to represent the "traditional" donors in new international forums that are negotiating the emerging development norms and architecture, such as the Global Partnership for Effective Cooperation.[51] The UK's claim to an international leadership role in this arena depends on DFID's ongoing credibility—although this may be the issue with the least public awareness and thus traction. All of these factors may have played some role in explaining why the government, and more specifically David Cameron, has—to date—stood firm on the UK's foreign aid contributions.[52] This article, however, focuses on a fourth factor: donor interests.

Donor self-interest is not inherently right or wrong: the question is whether and how donor interests compromise or synergise with the varied interests of different stakeholders in both donor and partner countries, and with global public goods and governance. Importantly, the "facts" of who actually benefits from aid are only one part of the story. A critical dimension of domestic aid politics is how contributions are perceived and framed by the public, media and politicians.[53] Can

---

Coalition and International Development", *Area*, Vol. 43, No. 4 (2011), pp. 506–507; P. Noxolo, "One World, Big Society: A Discursive Analysis of the Conservative Green Paper for International Development", *The Geographical Journal*, Vol. 178, No. 1 (2011), pp. 31–41.

[49] Matt Chorley, "'Charity Begins at Home': Ukip's Nigel Farage Calls for Foreign aid Budget to be Used to Help Flood-Hit Communities", *Daily Mail*, 6 February 2014, available: <http://www.dailymail.co.uk/news/article-2552969/Ukips-Nigel-Farage-calls-foreign-aid-budget-used-help-flood-hit-communities.html> (accessed 6 March 2015).

[50] M. Dunne, D. Hall-Matthews and S. Lightfoot, "Our Aid: UK International Development under the Coalition", *Political Insight*, Vol. 2, No. 1 (2011), pp. 29–31.

[51] See DFID press release (29 June 2012), available: <https://www.gov.uk/government/news/aid-effectiveness-mitchell-co-chairs-post-busan-panel> (accessed 6 March 2015).

[52] This may change. In July 2014 the UK Parliamentary International Development Committee announced an enquiry "Beyond Aid: The Future UK Approach to Development". One of the questions asked in the terms of reference was "whether a stand-alone Department for International Development has a long-term future?" The final report, released in January 2015, strongly advises DFID's continued independent existence, and is in many ways an impressive intervention from the All Party Parliamentary Committee on International Development. It remains to be seen whether the government elected in May 2015 will follow its proposals and guidelines. See <http://www.parliament.uk/business/committees/committees-a-z/commons-select/international-development-committee/inquiries/parliament-2010/beyond-aid-the-future-uk-approach-to-development-/> (accessed 6 March 2015).

[53] David Hudson and Jennifer van Heerde-Hudson, "'A Mile Wide and an Inch Deep': Surveys of Public Attitudes towards Development Aid", *International Journal of Development Education and Global*

David Cameron, Justine Greening and DFID communicate the idea of a turn to growth as good for the UK and good for development in a manner that is sufficiently agile and effective in persuading different constituencies—MPs, the public, the private sector, NGOs and so on—about the "value" of foreign aid? Whatever the actual changes within DFID, and with whatever consequences, stakeholder perceptions are as critical as the substance in ensuring DFID's future.

Re-centring "Economic Growth"

In March 2013, Justine Greening gave a keynote speech, also at the London Stock Exchange (LSE), in which she promised an agenda for change using the language of investment, market making and the necessity of a structural rebalancing from the public to the private sector.[54] She returned to the LSE in January 2014, and in another high-profile statement (from which the quote at the start of this article is taken), detailed the "transformational journey" that DFID had taken over the preceding year. Economic growth was not just being expanded through sector-specific programmes and spending, but it was refocusing DFID's entire mandate: "Economic growth is a priority right across the department", said Greening.[55] This includes DFID's work with other UK government departments, and how its country offices are budgeting and planning their work. The rest of this section unpicks this statement through an examination of budget share; institutional and personnel restructuring; expanding private sector partnerships; the changing content and instruments of private sector-led growth strategies; and the changing narrative around growth and development. It should be clear that this is an overview—specific programmes, funding mechanisms, partnerships and country contexts all provide more specific influences and contexts.

To start with funding allocation, DFID has committed to increase its budget for economic development to £1.8 billion by 2015/16, which is roughly double what was spent on this area in 2012/13.[56] As the total aid budget in 2013 was £11.4 billion, spending on economic development will shortly reach about one fifth of the aid budget. This figure does not include core contributions to multilateral organisations, which are also being more strongly oriented to serve growth objectives. For example, DFID is the largest contributor by some way to the Private Infrastructure Development Group (PIDG), which was established in 2002, but which has seen accelerated growth from 2010: DFID channelled £49 million to the PIDG in 2010–11, rising to £258 million in 2012–13.[57] The centrepiece 2014 Strategic Framework states that DFID will further expand existing instruments and create new channels for promoting economic growth. It is likely then that the economic growth share of the aid budget will continue to rise.

Accompanying the increase in the share of ODA going to economic growth are changes in DFID's institutional structures and personnel profile. In 2011 a Private

Learning, Vol. 4, No. 1 (2012), pp. 5–23, available: <http://ssrn.com/abstract=2015216> (accessed 6 March 2015); Taylor, *op. cit.*

[54] Justine Greening, Speech, "Investing in Growth: How DFID Works in New and Emerging Markets" (11 March 2013), available: <https://www.gov.uk/government/speeches/investing-in-growth-how-dfid-works-in-new-and-emerging-markets> (accessed 6 March 2015).

[55] Justine Greening, Speech, "Smart Aid: Why It's All About Jobs".

[56] DFID, "Economic Development for Shared Prosperity", *op. cit*

[57] National Audit Office, *op. cit.*

Sector Department was created, and in 2013 DFID announced that it was creating the new post of Director General for Economic Development with the mandate to drive forward and scale up DFID's investments in growth.[58] In high-profile speeches, the 2014 Strategic Framework document, and in evidence to the Parliamentary International Development Committee, Justine Greening and her senior staff have made it clear that DFID can expect ongoing internal restructuring.[59] In order to improve and expand DFID's growing mission to work with business, for example, the 2014 Strategic Framework promises redesigned systems, dedicated company contact points, senior sector leads, regular strategic relationship review meetings, and memoranda of cooperation around joint objectives. A 2011 DFID document on "The Engine of Development: The Private Sector and Prosperity for Poor People" asserts the goal that "private sector thinking [must] become as much part of DFID's DNA as [its] work with charities and governments".[60] DFID is looking to import more personnel and advisors from the private sector and from other government departments, rather than "traditional" aid bureaucrats. Justine Greening herself came from the Treasury, and has a background in business. Greening insists that DFID now needs improved skills in scaling up and managing existing and new financial instruments, and ensuring risk management and mitigation across its portfolio of investments.

As well as increasingly recruiting from the private sector, DFID is growing its funding and contracting and in other ways partnering with private sector entities, including pro-market think tanks and large accountancy, financial and management consultancies.[61] These lucrative partnerships are not new, of course (see Roberts on USAID and private contractors, for example),[62] but the focus on an economic growth agenda appears to be opening up further opportunities for collaboration and contracting. Criticisms include the fact that many of these organisations are ideologically committed to privatisation regardless of context or evidence; that ODA is being used to pay six-figure salaries and lavish expenses; that they are being managed at arm's length, with insufficient strategic direction or oversight by DFID; that some are financing and working through firms domiciled in tax havens; and that regulation and oversight is inadequate.[63]

Civil society organisations (CSOs) are not excluded from the growth agenda, with the 2014 Strategic Framework stating that they can make an important contribution to ensuring "equitable and inclusive growth and poverty reduction". This is the only time "equity" is referred to in the 27-page document. The roles CSOs can

---

[58] DFID press release (23 May 2014), available: <https://www.gov.uk/government/news/dfid-boosts-economic-development-expertise-with-new-appointments> (accessed 6 March 2015).

[59] See also the transcript of evidence given to the International Development Committee, House of Commons, 9 October 2013, available: <http://www.parliament.uk/documents/commons-committees/international-development/CORRECTEDTRANSCRIPTIDC091013.pdf> (accessed 6 March 2015).

[60] DFID, *The Engine of Development*, op. cit.

[61] Mark Tran, "DfID's Aid Spend on Contractors Comes under Scrutiny", *The Guardian*, 17 May 2013, available: <http://www.theguardian.com/global-development/2013/may/17/dfid-aid-contractors-scrutiny> (accessed 6 March 2015).

[62] S.M. Roberts, "Development Capital: USAID and the Rise of Development Contractors", *Annals of the Association of American Geographers*, Vol. 105, No. 5 (2014), pp. 1030–1051.

[63] N. Benton, "CDC: A Case Study in Blinkered Development" (2010), available: <https://www.opendemocracy.net/openeconomy/nic-benton/cdc-group-case-study-in-blinkered-development> (accessed 6 March 2015); Tomlinson, *op. cit.*; ActionAid, *op. cit.*; Independent Commission on Aid Impact, *op. cit.*; National Audit Office, *op. cit.*

play in fostering local markets, SMEs, microfinance, improved value chains and holding business to account, are all mentioned. However, CSOs are given clear warning. In her 2014 LSE speech, Justine Greening commended some NGOs for their work with the private sector, but went on to say:

> But I do think NGOs can and need to do more to embed this positive approach towards private sector investment and private sector engagement. I understand why it may come more naturally to campaign to get more children into school or vaccinations for babies—but being reluctant or uncomfortable about encouraging a more entrepreneurial business environment won't do these developing countries any favours ... I believe NGOs working with business needs to become the norm not the exception. And I think we all need to be on the economic development path that DFID has set out.[64]

In terms of the "substance" of this shift, DFID is expanding some existing programmes and creating others. Like other OECD-DAC donors, DFID states that it is promoting "inclusive growth". For example, DFID states that it is interested in providing finance for firms of all sizes—including British and partner country SMEs—and in 2012 it launched an Impact Investment Fund that directs capital towards pro-poor businesses and entrepreneurs. But perhaps the centrepiece of the existing mechanisms is the Commonwealth Development Corporation (CDC). The CDC started life as the Colonial Development Corporation in 1948, and since then has acted as the UK's primary Development Finance Institution (DFI).[65] Its present mandate is to provide "developmentally beneficial investment" to help stimulate the growth of businesses in Africa and South Asia.[66] The CDC has been the subject of considerable controversy for a number of reasons, including a badly handled part-privatisation, and accusations that its investments do little to enhance development, and may in some cases have undermined social and economic wellbeing. Even *The Economist* criticised its effective privatisation under Tony Blair, pointing out in 2001 that under new (private sector) management, with a remit to achieve higher returns, "the new investments are in urban services for the rich minority, and not in poor, rural areas where 85% of Africans live".[67] The CDC was the object of reforms in 2011 under the then secretary of state Andrew Mitchell, which were intended to bring it more into line with "DFID's objectives".[68] However, it remains a highly controversial instrument,[69] as do other OECD-DAC

---

[64] Justine Greening, Speech, "Smart Aid: Why It's All About Jobs", *op. cit.*

[65] M. Cowen, "Early Years of the Colonial Development Corporation: British State Enterprise Overseas during Late Colonialism", *African Affairs*, Vol. 83, No. 330 (January 1984), pp. 63–75; C.M. Rogerson, "The Geography of Development Finance in Africa: The Commonwealth Development Corporation, 1948–1991", *South African Geographical Journal*, Vol. 75, No. 2 (1993), pp. 69–77.

[66] <http://www.cdcgroup.com/> (accessed 6 March 2015).

[67] "Two Fingers to the Poor: Privatising Britain's Development Arm May Not Help Those Who Need It", *The Economist*, 14 June 2001, available: <http://www.economist.com/node/656299> (accessed 6 March 2015).

[68] "Private Sector-Led Reform 'Key to CDC's Future' says Andrew Mitchell", *The Guardian*, 19 January 2011, available: <http://www.theguardian.com/global-development/2011/jan/19/commonwealth-development-corporation-private-sector> (accessed 6 March 2015).

[69] See, for example, evidence given to the International Development Committee in December 2010 by Private Eye and a number of NGO representatives (<http://www.parliament.uk/business/committees/

Development Finance Institutions, many of which are subject to similar critiques.[70] Whether and how DFID manages to ensure that CDC pursues inclusive and sustainable growth, which has credible claims to "development" outcomes, will be a matter of growing interest and importance. Analyses of these emerging financing approaches in other OECD-DAC donors point to a number of serious concerns. These include the tendency to invest in safer, middle-income settings with the best returns rather than where the finance may be most needed; to crowd out private finance; to support donor country firms rather than recipient country firms; to support larger over smaller companies; and to inflate private and public debt. Researchers have also found that many development finance intermediaries are based in tax havens, while generous manager compensation and shareholder profit are being effectively supported through taxpayers' money.[71] Clearly, individual programmes need specific investigation, but the aggregate trend raises concerns.

DFID is also exploring new ways of working with the private sector.[72] One example is the new Trade in Global Value Chains Initiative (TGVCI), which is aimed at encouraging UK businesses to improve supplier standards.[73] Recipients of this ODA money include Tesco, Primark and Asda. Marks and Spencer, for example, is to receive ODA to develop "the leadership and management skills of farm workers in Kenya and South Africa", while Sainsbury's is receiving aid money to establish an "innovative radio show" for farmers in Kenya. Firms are eligible for grants of up to £750,000 for which they then provide match funding. The stated goal is to harness private sector expertise, to leverage private sector finance and to raise standards in value chains with benefits for all. It is too early to assess the content and outcomes of this initiative, but we might note that the 2014 Strategic Framework makes no reference to labour rights, decent work, union representation or other more structural means of promoting "inclusive" growth. TGVCI does state that it "will help projects identify the potential to adopt new practices or scale up pilot initiatives that respect and enhance *worker entitlements* as part of building a more sustainable commercial future for the company", but it remains to be seen how robust or just these "worker entitlements" are.[74]

One of the most interesting features of DFID's current direction is the prominence of the financial sector. For example, Justine Greening has created a formal partnership with the London Stock Exchange Group (LSEG). Official documents and declarations foreground the role that DFID, other government departments and UK businesses and consultancies can play in providing "high levels of technical

---

committees-a-z/commons-select/international-development-committee/news/cdc-inquiry-/>) (accessed 6 March 2015); John Hilary, "Is it Time to Cut off the Government's Development Finance Arm?", *The Guardian*, 15 September 2010, available: <http://www.theguardian.com/global-development/poverty-matters/2010/sep/15/commonwealth-development-expenses-criticism> (accessed 6 March 2015); Benton, *op. cit.*

[70] Tomlinson, *op. cit.*; Eurodad, "A Dangerous Blend? The EU's Agenda to 'Blend' Public Development Finance with Private Finance" (2013), available: http://www.eurodad.org/Entries/view/1546054/2013/11/07/A-dangerous-blend-The-EU-s-agenda-to-blend-public-development-finance-with-private-finance> (accessed 6 March 2015).

[71] Benton, *op. cit.*; Tomlinson, *op. cit.*; Eurodad, *op. cit.*

[72] Examples can be found in the 2014 UK Memorandum for the forthcoming OECD-DAC Peer Review, available: <http://www.oecd.org/dac/peer-reviews/UK%20Memo%20for%20DAC%20Peer%20Review%202014.pdf> (accessed 6 March 2015).

[73] <http://www.tgvci.com/> (accessed 6 March 2015).

[74] *Ibid.*, emphasis added.

expertise and innovation"[75] to help developing country governments and firms create attractive investment environments, develop "frontier" markets, privatise assets, create public–private partnerships and so on. One of the goals of the DFID-funded Growth Centre at the London School of Economics is to "accelerate capital market development in Africa's frontier economies". The focus on the financial sector is explained through the UK's leading position in these fields. In her 2014 LSE speech, Greening explained that:

> Wherever possible I'm determined to pull in the best UK expertise to de-risk investment and improve the business climate. … the UK's top accountancy companies will be deployed to countries like Malawi and Nepal to help raise professional standards, improve financial reporting and build investor confidence. Thanks to our world-leading insurance sector the UK is also exceptionally well placed to respond to the challenge of insuring for private sector investors in more fragile states where the political risk is higher.[76]

The first step in the DFID-LSEG partnership that Greening launched at this event was bespoke training for financial sector professionals, regulators and government officials. Present at the launch were 20 "capital market leaders" from Tanzania, who were about to embark on a course designed to help them address constraints to growth in their stock market. Greening asserted that:

> This is a win-win partnership. It means the best run stock exchange in the world, our stock exchange right here in London, will be offering their expertise to a region where capital markets are in their infancy. And it also means the LSEG will have a fantastic, positive relationship with these frontier economies as they take off.[77]

In a keynote speech intended to inspire, it is perhaps no surprise that the distinctive contributions of the City of London to the UK and global financial crises were not mentioned; nor charges of crony capitalism that have been levied at the major accountancy companies, banks, commercial law firms and transnational corporations in their relations with the political establishment.[78] But this is not something that appears anywhere in the major speeches or policy documents on deepening financialisation in Africa or elsewhere. The 2014 Strategic Framework makes one mention of protecting against financial volatility, which is to assert that DFID will work with the IMF to help stabilise poor country economies when necessary. This rather underwhelming approach does not suggest a balanced or rigorous appraisal of the risks and rewards of greater financialisation as a development strategy.[79] This must raise concerns that there are insufficient mechanisms to ensure that privatised rewards do not simply trickle (or torrent) upwards, while risks are "socialised", as they appear to have done in more "mature" financial sectors.

---

[75] DFID, "Economic Development for Shared Prosperity", *op. cit.*, p. 4.
[76] Justine Greening, Speech, "Investing in Growth", *op. cit.*
[77] *Ibid.*
[78] O. Jones, *The Establishment: And How They Get Away With It* (London: Allen Lane, 2014).
[79] Y. Akyüz, "Internationalisation of Finance and Changing Vulnerabilities in Emerging and Developing Economies", *South Centre Research Paper 60* (January 2015).

The relationship between foreign aid and international development programmes on the one hand, and capital accumulation and commercial interests on the other is, it hardly needs to be said, not new,[80] and nor is it simple or uncontested.[81] As noted above, Mawdsley et al.[82] seek to provide a fuller theoretical dissection of current donor programmes of "exporting stimulus" and the deepening financialisation of development.

Framing the Growth Agenda for Different Audiences

As noted above, all donors claim that foreign aid brings a variety of benefits to the donor as well as the recipient. This should not be contentious in and of itself. Rather, it is how and for whom this self-interest is framed, and what balance or relationship it has with the (real and perceived) benefits to partner countries and different groups and interests within them. The 2009 Conservative Green Paper makes a clear statement that it will more effectively leverage foreign aid spending to UK interests, while maintaining that this will "do good" in the world. Justine Greening frames this as "smart aid" in an attempt to persuade critics from within the party and in the public of the value of aid to the UK, while retaining its moral claims.

The investment, trade and export opportunities opening up in and beyond the BRICS (Brazil, Russia, India, China, South Africa) and MINTs (Mexico, Indonesia, Nigeria, Turkey, South Africa), and the competition they simultaneously provide, are implicitly and explicitly noted throughout DFID's current literature. In her 2014 speech, Greening stated that DFID's "frontier economy strategy is critical for safeguarding the UK's economic prospects in the long term … just as it is in helping DFID delivering on its ambition of eradicating poverty". Greening asserts: "as a British Minister I make no apology for flying the flag in these frontier markets. My Department should be there flying the flag like every other bit of government".[83] In 2013 she led the first ever DFID-led *trade* delegation, to Tanzania in this case, and has promised more to follow. However, as well as sites of opportunity, the BRICS in particular are explicitly positioned as competitors in the "global race". The way this is finessed is to urge a stronger UK business and growth agenda, which is pitched as having higher standards:

"We do developing countries no favours by leaving the economic coast clear for those with corporate governance standards that are lower than ours".[84]

Another feature of the new growth narrative is the absolute refusal to acknowledge that not all interests align around growth. Even ICAI, an officially appointed independent scrutiny panel, felt that it had to remind DFID's leadership that:

> private sector and markets are predicated on the idea of competition, which presupposes that there will sometimes be losers. … A focus on PSD [private sector development] may, from time to time, result in

---

[80] Sogge, *op. cit.*

[81] For instance, S. Kim and K. Gray, "Overseas Development Aid as Spatial Fix? Examining South Korea's Africa Policy", *Third World Quarterly*, Vol. 37, No. 2 (forthcoming, 2016).

[82] Mawdsley et al. (2015), *op. cit.*

[83] Justine Greening, Speech, "Smart Aid: Why It's All About Jobs", *op. cit.*

[84] Justine Greening, Speech, "Investing in Growth", *op. cit.*

certain groups of the poor being worse off as a result of its interventions.[85]

The ICAI report expresses concerns that DFID's strategic framing of private sector partnership disregards the inherent production of winners and losers in any development initiative. Such trade-offs are often impossible to avoid, so the essential questions are how protection and amelioration are recognised, negotiated and managed, and by whom. The ICAI feels it necessary to recommend that DFID does some more thinking about short-term detrimental impacts, and checks that poor people are not being excluded as a result of developing "effective market systems". The report cautions that:

> DFID needs to remember that the private sector is not a developmental panacea. References to "the miracles" that companies are able to perform [made in DFID 2011, for example], risks underplaying the role that donors like DFID and country governments have in ensuring that economic development provides benefits to the poorest in society.[86]

It is notable that nowhere in the 27-page Strategic Framework is there any discussion of decent work. Trades unions or informal sector working organisations are not mentioned, nor safeguards of any variety of workers of any variety. There is a single mention of creating "quality jobs" (p. 5) but no further analysis of what this might mean, or how it might be ensured. Instead DFID proposes improved access to markets, to financial services, to property and land markets, and to the job market. The latter does not mention labour terms and conditions, but enhancing labour "participation" and "mobility", and tackling discriminatory social norms. Here we can note that following a Multilateral Aid Review (MAR) in 2011, DFID decided to end funding to the International Labour Organisation (ILO). The MAR cited "significant weaknesses" and poor value for money in making this decision. However, the ILO's response revealed inconsistencies in the UK's position, and deficiencies in the evidence base for its decision.[87] While the ILO did not say so explicitly, it is hard not to see the Conservative Party's ideological hostility to decent work and safeguarding labour as the true reasoning behind this decision.

Other mainstream development actors—represented rather surprisingly by Christine Lagarde, director of the IMF—appear to be increasingly cognisant of the threats to economies and societies of greater inequality.[88] However, inequality is occasionally "name-checked" but little discussed in these DFID documents and speeches on PSD. One of the three visions for economic development spelt out at the start of DFID 2014 states that high economic growth must also be accompanied by "wider economic transformation that benefits the poor and shares prosperity

---

[85] Independent Commission on Aid Impact, *op. cit.*, p. 21.

[86] *Ibid.*, p. 33.

[87] ILO, "Response by the ILO to the UK-DFID Multilateral Aid Review Report" (2011), available: <https://www.gov.uk/government/uploads/system/uploads/attachment_data/file/264866/ILO-response.pdf.pdf> (accessed 6 March 2015).

[88] "Economic Inclusion and Financial Integrity—An Address to the Conference on Inclusive Capitalism" (27 May 2014), available: <https://www.imf.org/external/np/speeches/2014/052714.htm> (accessed 6 March 2015).

broadly", but the rest of the document does not dwell further on what "shared prosperity" and "inclusive growth" might comprise. Three "routes" or mechanisms are presented in DFID 2014 to ensure "good" growth, all of which raise large questions. The first is that higher growth will widen the tax base, which in turn will provide greater revenues for governments, which will be able to invest in health, education and other services. This is clearly highly desirable, but the outcomes are far from guaranteed, especially given broader UK commitments to the free movement of capital, low income and corporation taxes, and the very limited regulation of capital flight and/or tax havens (see also footnote 31). The second set of mechanisms is voluntary agreements with business, and encouragement that firms invest responsibly and meet social, environmental and corporate governance standards. These are, needless to say, highly contested. When they do function as claimed, they can achieve incremental improvements, but they can also act to conceal ongoing exploitation and damaging practices. Either way, they are no solution for meaningful, rights-based development transitions. The third route is to better connect individuals to markets—in land, jobs and services. While the Strategic Framework discusses overcoming socially structured lack of equality in markets (e.g. because of gender), there is no discussion of labour rights.

Conclusions

Many of the major OECD-DAC donors are in various ways and to different extents reinstating economic growth to the normative centre of international development. In this article I have suggested that the shift is being driven by the interplay of ontological, ideational and material "crises"—or perhaps opportunities—among the (so-called) "traditional" donors. Collaboration but also competition with the rising powers is openly acknowledged, while the economic impacts of the global and/or Eurozone financial crises have provided a script for political and business leaders to cut social welfare budgets, drive regressive growth strategies domestically and present a more robust assertion of foreign aid acting in "national" self-interest. The OECD-DAC is currently debating the definition of ODA, and there is some possibility that this will lead to a new paradigm of development and climate financing that is better suited to the changing global geographies of poverty, wealth and inequality than "foreign aid", and set within a more universal suite of Sustainable Development Goals.[89] However, as suggested here, these new, expanding and reformulated development financing mechanisms and growth agendas are vulnerable to donors aiming primarily at the pursuit of national commercial (and by extension, geopolitical) interests. While, among other things, this may indeed lead to higher aggregate growth in partner countries, it could do so without necessarily reducing poverty or inequality, or building more sustainable and just societies.

David Cameron, Justine Greening and DFID's senior leadership are attempting to rescript the UK's foreign aid narrative in a way that will build support (or at least temper criticism) among its domestic detractors, without losing the claim to "doing good" that motivates some of its national and international supporters. This article has set out two critiques: the first, concerning whether DFID's current private sector-led growth agenda pays sufficient attention to the relationship

---

[89] Hynes and Scott, *op. cit.*

between "growth" and "development"; and the second questioning the idea of "national" self-interest. The fruits of the coalition government's social and economic agenda in the UK are an increasingly entrenched underclass, declining public services, the erosion of "national public goods", growing regional inequality, the creation of more and more low-waged jobs, the upward class creep of precarity and of course the continuing concentration of wealth among UK and transnational elites. Without addressing the fundamental tensions within any growth agenda, and most certainly the UK's domestic one, Greening's confident assertion that "[i]t really is that simple. Growth reduces poverty through jobs"[90] seems questionable.

The article contributes to the growing literature on how the OECD-DAC donors, and the "mainstream" international development community more generally, are strategically responding to a rapidly changing external environment, and has presented the deepening private sector-led growth agenda in this light. However, we must also recognise the complex and contradictory interplay of domestic factors with international challenges and opportunities.[91] Metaphorically speaking, DFID could be said to be in the "eye of two storms". Its efforts to reassert itself within the current international development landscape are being undertaken in a setting of intra- and infra-party domestic political contest, significant media and public debate over the amount, purpose and legitimacy of aid, and the generic difficulties of institutional repurposing. Moreover, DFID is a large, complex, multi-sited institution, subject to a spectrum of (sometimes contradictory) demands, both mandated and politically contingent. Many personnel are committed to progressive social and economic goals, while also navigating professional career trajectories, and coping with institutional restructuring and staff budget pressures. DFID, like other OECD-DAC donors, does not formulate its response within a strategic *terra nullius*, but is enabled and constrained by existing institutional and regulatory structures, Whitehall competition and party political imperatives. For example, DFID is still legally obliged by the 2002 International Development Act to put poverty reduction as its primary purpose, while the 2015 All Party Parliamentary International Development Committee offers a far more progressive and rounded set of recommendations regarding the UK's place in international development than that expressed by DFID's present leadership.[92] Whether and how the private sector-led growth agenda currently championed by DFID's leadership is actually operationalised is open to further investigation.

Economic growth is certainly necessary and desired in many partner countries, and the private sector, in all of its diversity, is an essential driver and component of that growth. But at present there is evidence that the economic growth strategies of DFID or many of its peers are being insufficiently anchored to "development". There are progressive statements, and some positive programmes and initiatives, but in aggregate DFID's private sector-led growth agenda fails to address sufficiently concerns about (in)equality, decent work, private sector accountability, the unequal distribution of risks and rewards in various public–private partnerships (e.g. Private Finance Initiatives), the short-termism and predatory nature of

---

[90] Justine Greening, Speech, "Smart Aid: Why It's All About Jobs", *op. cit.*

[91] Hynes and Scott, *op. cit.*

[92] See <http://www.parliament.uk/business/committees/committees-a-z/commons-select/international-development-committee/inquiries/parliament-2010/beyond-aid-the-future-uk-approach-to-development-/ > (accessed 6 March 2015).

shareholder capitalism, conflicts of interest that are inherent and unavoidable in all development and certainly in private sector-led development, and the relationship between exposure and risk under conditions of greater financialisation. Inclusive, just, sustainable growth is not being served at home or abroad.

Acknowledgements

My thanks to Marco Vieira and other organisers of the "Emerging and Established Powers" conference in May 2014. Versions of the article have also been presented at the 2014 Devnet Conference, Otago, New Zealand (thanks to Doug Hill and all there) and SOAS. Particular thanks to two anonymous referees for their very constructive comments, and to Rosalind Eyben, Sung-Mi Kim, Danilo Marcondes, Glenn Banks, Regina Scheyvens, Warwick Murray, John Overton and Cheryl McEwan for reading and commenting on the article. All errors and interpretations remain my own. The article was written while I was a Visiting International Fellow at Massey University, New Zealand, and my thanks to everyone there for the tremendous scholarly and collegial experience.

Disclosure Statement

No potential conflict of interest was reported by the author

Emerging Brazil: The Challenges of Liberal Peace and Global Governance

Brazil has clustered with other emerging powers to advocate a reconfiguration of the international order based upon a more inclusive multilateral architecture. Brazilian foreign policy has also defended a cautious use of coercive methods and military intervention. To pursue these aims Brazil has adopted a double-track course of action: (1) intergovernmental emerging power coalitions, which strengthen the coordination of political stances and concerns in multilateral arenas; and (2) enhanced involvement and responsibility in UN-led peace operations, accompanied by a robust portfolio of bilateral and multilateral accords with developing countries. These two tracks are addressed in this article as fertile sources for the accumulation of soft power assets. It is argued, however, that it will not be easy for Brazil to expand its voice and weight in global governance bodies in the years to come as the global scenario becomes muddier in the management of conflict, intervention and severe institutional crisis. This could lead to a more frequent use of extreme solutions that would wear out soft power approaches.

In recent years emerging powers have assumed a proactive presence in several multilateral contexts aiming to promote normative and operational changes. While these nations have acted as a propulsion force in the transition towards a multipolar order, they have simultaneously sought to expand their autonomy and recognition within the international system. This has been a gradual, disordered and uneven development in world affairs. Yet the rise of a group of countries, clustered as emerging powers, has contributed to a change in the configuration of multilateral agendas dealing with global economic, political and security matters. In consequence, these actors now represent new sources of pressure, stances and resources in global economic and political settings.

Brazil has become an active player in this global process with the purpose of fostering the configuration of a multipolar world order anchored on a restructured multilateral architecture.[1] Brazilian foreign policy has reshaped its contents and reached towards innovative diplomatic procedures with special concern regarding

---

*I am thankful to Natalia Herbst for her work as research assistant.

1. See Monica Hirst and Maria Regina Soares de Lima, "Brazil as an Intermediate State and Regional Power", *International Affairs*, Vol. 82, No. 1 (2006), pp. 21–40; Andrew Hurrell, "Lula's Brazil: A Rising Power, But Going Where?", *Current History*, February 2008; M.R. Soares De Lima, "Brasil e Polos Emergentes do Poder Mundial: Rússia, Índia, China e África do Sul", in Renato Baumann (ed.), *O Brasil e os Demais BRICS: Comércio e Política* (Brasília: CEPAL/IPEA, 2010), pp. 155–178.

uneven power distribution and the dominant security approaches. In order to expand its presence and capacity to influence the current transformations faced by the international community in international security, Brazil has pursued a double-track course of action; both tracks may be considered fertile sources for the accumulation of soft power assets. On the one side, intergovernmental coalitions, such as India, Brazil and South Africa (IBSA) and Brazil, Russia, India, China and South Africa (BRICS), have become a crucial instrument to coordinate political stances and voice shared concerns regarding the conceptual, normative and procedural frameworks put forward by multilateral organisations in addressing global peace and security matters. On the other side, enhanced involvement in UN-led peace operations together with an expanded portfolio of bilateral and multilateral cooperation accords with developing countries have allowed the country to work on a Brazilian "patent" of intervention and collaboration in defence and security.

This article will briefly address both lines of action with the purpose of pointing out their recent developments and the challenges that lie ahead. Its aim will be to underscore Brazil's recent effort to contribute to an alternative frame of thinking and *modus operandi* in addressing a diversified set of hazardous political and security realities, managed and discussed in multilateral arenas. The central assertion here is that the worldviews and approaches of emerging powers have become a source of constructive criticism, which can contribute to the improvement of global governance in a multipolar world.

The Fundamentals

Brazilian foreign policy advocates the reconfiguration of the international order based upon a more inclusive multilateral architecture and the review of methods and norms in global governance arenas. While Brazil's standpoint translates past and present aspirations to achieve a new level of international acknowledgement, it is important to underline its connection to the domestic scenario of transformations underway in the last decade. The articulation between internal and external innovations has been essential for Brazilian foreign policy during the governments of Lula da Silva and Dilma Rousseff.[2]

In international security, Brazil has become especially concerned with the question of legitimacy of the use of force and coercion in international intervention as well as the humanitarian impact of military action and the importance of solutions that seek equilibrium between peace, solidarity, sovereignty and sustainable development. From a conceptual standpoint these apprehension in fact contest the implications of liberal internationalism/interventionism as well as the normative prescriptions and justifications advocated by Western powers in different global governance arenas.[3] One of the country's main concerns has been the promotion

2. See Gilberto Maringoni, Giorgio Romano Schutte and Gonzalo Berron (eds), *Uma Nova Politica Externa* (Tubarão/SC: Copiart, 2003–2013); Celso Amorim, *Conversas con jovens diplomatas* (São Paulo: Benvirá, 2012); Monica Hirst and Maria Regina Soares de Lima, "Re-thinking Global and Domestic Challenges in Brazilian Foreign Policy", in Jorge Dominguez I (ed.), *Routledge Handbook of Latin America in the World* (New York: Routledge, 2014), pp. 139–153.

3. See Schahrbanou Tadjbakhs, *Rethinking the Liberal Peace* (London: Routledge, 2011); Oliver Richmond, "Liberal Peace Transitions, a Rethink is Urgent", *Open Democracy*, 19 November 2009, available: <https://www.opendemocracy.net/oliver-p-richmond/liberal-peace-transitions-rethink-is-urgent> (accessed 4 August 2015).

of capacity-building and the strengthening of local institutions, instead of the use of military presence to control political turmoil and the escalation of violence. Brazil has pledged for caution and prudence in international intervention and has sought the expansion of representation and the improvement of rule-making in multilateral settings.

Brazilian foreign policy expresses a myriad of aspirations, considered crucial to pursue international recognition of its political stances. These aspirations include: (1) to have greater influence in the design of a reformed multilateral global architecture; (2) to expand responsibility in scenarios of post-conflict reconstruction, humanitarian crisis and natural disasters according to multilateral norms and institutions; (3) to enforce an amplified agenda of South–South cooperation initiatives; and (4) to consolidate a regional role that is bold on peace issues, stability and sustainable development. Such aims have led to an active scheme of relationships and commitments, with special mention of a deeper engagement in the UN system, active involvement in intergovernmental groups such as IBSA and BRICS, and a leading role in the build-up of regional bodies such as the Union of South American Nations (UNASUR) and the Community of Latin American and Caribbean States (CELAC).

Brazil has tried to insert itself proactively in an international order transition that advances in the direction of a multipolar configuration, in which world powers that rely on a solid pile of hard power assets acknowledge the need to share spaces of global governance with the emerging powers. The country has defended a revision of the conceptual toolkit adopted in global governance institutions as well as a revision of the format of these bodies. This effort has been accompanied by a critical appraisal of Western biased approaches in the decisions and methods of political and military intervention.[4] While pursuing an alternative view to address international security matters, Brazil has gradually contributed to the formulation of a Southern critical view of the post-Cold War liberal peace concepts and prescriptions.[5]

Brasília has become especially concerned with the orientations that tend to legitimise 21st-century US–NATO–UN orchestrated intervention; even though enacted in the name of pro-democratic values, such interventions impose major costs on civilian populations, introduce questionable destabilising methods and prolong conflict scenarios. When addressing the realities of vulnerabilities, Brazil has avoided using terms such as "failed", "fragile" or "weak" states because of their stigmatising and prejudicial character. The Brazilian government considers such labels a subtle instrument used by world powers to cast doubt on the sovereignty of these countries. Brazil has equally avoided fully endorsing the concept of "responsibility to protect" (R2P), now a widely accepted shield to legitimise international intervention and carry forward actions driven by the aim to promote the change of political regimes. Instead, Brazil has suggested that responsibilities must

---

4. For authors who have addressed the fundamentals of liberal interventionism, see John G. Ikenberry, "The Future of the Liberal World Order", *Foreign Affairs*, May–June 2011; Anne-Marie Slaughter, "Wilsonianism in the Twenty-First Century", in Thomas J. Knock, G. John Ikenberry and Tony Smith (eds), *The Crisis of American Foreign Policy: Wilsonianism in the Twenty-First Century* (Princeton, NJ: Princeton University Press, 2001), pp. 89–119; Bruce Russet, *Grasping the Democratic Peace: Principles for a Post-Cold War World* (Princeton: Princeton University Press, 1993).

5. See M. Hirst, "O Brasil Emergente e os Desafios da Governança Global: A paz Liberal em Questão", The Institute for Applied Economic Research (IPEA), July 2014.

first of all involve the protection of civil populations, proceeding with caution when intervention is to be considered. This has been the motive behind Brazil's proposition that intervention ought to be "responsible while protecting" (RWP).[6] It should be clarified that Brazil has not intended to propose a replacement, but rather to open space for a more careful application of the R2P principle. The aim in this case has been that, when necessary, R2P- guided interventions rely upon a more solid legitimate basis with clearer humanitarian concerns.[7]

According to the Brazilian perspective, the extreme poverty and the lack of institutional resources of countries subject to international intervention are often the very consequences of prior unsuccessful experiences of intervention. Brazilian diplomatic discourse has moved away from the dogma of non-intervention and has justified military presence as the correct course of action, sustained upon the principle of non-indifference.[8] This has been the case in regard to the Brazilian presence in Haiti since 2004. Nevertheless, one of Brazil's biggest concerns has been to ensure that sustainable development becomes a main priority within UN-led interventions.

Brazilian foreign policy has defended a conceptual revision of global governance institutions, which involves, but is not limited to, the reform of the UN Security Council (UNSC).[9] Brazil has been present in the UNSC as a temporary member, claiming the right to a permanent seat if and when the council is reformed.[10] As one of the most frequent elective members on the council, Brazil has attempted to combine the defence of multilateral solutions with a prudent approach towards interventionism and even more caution regarding the use of coercive methods. Yet the enhancement of UN-led military missions, as one of the post-Cold War developments, brought new challenges to Brazilian multilateralism, broadening the scope of its normative and conceptual considerations. While Western powers sought to expand the council's prerogatives to mount pressure by way of coercion and intervention, Brazil, together with other emerging powers, has advocated for the improvement of the UN institutional-juridical frameworks when dealing with severe political crisis and the escalation of violence in the name of international humanitarian law.

To summarise, while sitting in the UNSC, Brazil has underscored three sorts of concerns: (1) the inclusion of civil and political rights associated with sustainable

---

6. Xenia Avezov, "'Responsibility While Protecting': Are We Asking the Wrong Questions?", *SIPRI* (January 2013), available: <http://www.sipri.org/media/newsletter/essay/Avezov_Jan13> (accessed 28 March 2013).

7. Sharon Wiharta, Neil Melvin and Xenia Avezov, "The New Geopolitics of Peace Operations", *SIPRI* (September 2012), p. 19, available: <http://www.sipri.org/research/conflict/pko/other_publ/NGP-Policy-Report.pdf> (accessed 9 December 2014).

8. See Breno Hermann, *Soberania, não intervenção e não indiferença: reflexões sobre o discurso diplomático brasileiro* (Brasília: FUNAG, 2011).

9. Brazil has defended the expansion of permanent seats in the UNSC and presented itself as a candidate if a reform were to take place. Since 2005 Brazil has teamed up with India, Germany and Japan in the G4 to voice the urgency of a reformed UNSC. See Gelson Fonseca Jr., "Notes on the Evolution of Brazilian Multilateral Policy", *Global Governance*, Vol. 17 (2011), pp. 375–397.

10. Next to Japan, Brazil is the country that has most frequently occupied a non-permanent seat in the UNSC. Brazil has been elected five times as a non-permanent member of the council in the post-Cold War era: 1989–1990, 1993–1994, 1998–1999, 2004–2005 and 2010–2011. See Eduardo Uziel, "O Voto do Brasil e a Condição de Membro Eleito no Conselho de Segurança das Nações Unidas", *Política Externa*, October–December 2013; Antônio de Aguiar Patriota, *O conselho de segurança após a Guerra do Golfo: articulação de um novo paradigma de segurança coletiva* (Brasília: FUNAG, 1998).

development when addressing international crises; (2) the strengthening of an agenda committed to UN-led peace keeping operations; and (3) a close and permanent articulation between the UNSC and other UN bodies, with special mention of the Council for Human Rights. Likewise, Brazil strongly supported the creation of the Peacebuilding Commission and the Human Rights Council within the UN system.[11]

Brazil has put forward a foreign policy defence formula with the resolve to upgrade the country's performance in peace and security initiatives, as part of a long-term strategy in world affairs. More and more often, the Ministry of Defense (MD) has followed in the footsteps of the Ministry of Foreign Affairs (MFA) (known as the *Itamaraty*) in the expansion of the country's external presence with explicit support of its involvement in global governance arenas. The combination of traditional diplomatic expertise with new military capabilities has led to an expanded presence in global defence matters, based upon three pillars: active participation in peacekeeping operations (PKOs); a significant portfolio of bilateral cooperation agreements; and a growing presence in the global market for military equipment.[12]

Acceptance of the limitations imposed by soft power attributes has not kept Brazil from considering the use of force under certain circumstances. With a dose of lexical inventiveness, Brazilian authorities have coined the hypothesis of "hardening soft power" to face external threats, such as unilateral actions that disregard the UNSC and/or attacks on Brazil's sovereignty regarding the abundance of its natural resources.[13] A deeper link between foreign and defence policies has become an explicit part of Brazilian strategic guidelines to address regional and global security, combining cooperative initiatives with individual national-oriented developments. This approach is coherent with Brazil's strategic priorities and translates a domestic consensus regarding the country's refusal to become a nuclear power.[14] In addition, such a consensus represents a *de facto* acceptance that diplomatic performance and military presence may compensate for Brazil's lack of hard power resources.[15]

Though it may seem paradoxical, the expanded presence of the armed forces in foreign policy decision-making has contributed even more to reinforce Brazil's rejection of securitised solutions in international scenarios. In fact, there has been a correlation between closer relations between diplomacy and military presence and an increasing caution in Brazilian diplomatic positions when approaching

11. The UN Human Rights Council was created in 2006 to increase and strengthen the role of the Human Rights Committee, which was created in 1946 as one of the organisation's functional committees.

12. The MFA-MD articulation has been addressed by Monica Hirst and Reginaldo Mattar Nasser in "Brazil's Involvement in Peacekeeping Operations: The New Defence-Security-Foreign Policy Nexus", the Norwegian Peacebuilding Resource Centre (NOREF) Report, September 2014.

13. This formulation has been expressed by Defence Minister Celso Amorim in Brazil and abroad in lectures and articles. See Hirst and Soares de Lima, "Re-thinking Global and Domestic Challenges", *op. cit.*

14. Recent public opinion studies have indicated that the Brazilian public, attentive to foreign policy, supports the country's use of soft power approaches in world politics. See Amaury de Souza, *A agenda internacional do Brasil: a política externa brasileira de FHC a Lula* (Rio de Janeiro: Elsevier-CEBRI, 2009).

15. Democratisation has sealed the Brazilian commitment to non-proliferation. While the 1988 constitution underscores the assurance of the pacific use of nuclear power, since the mid-1990s Brazil has adhered to a myriad of non-proliferation regimes. In 1994, Brazil joined the Missile Technology Control Regime (MTCR); in 1997 it signed the Anti-Land Mine Treaty; the following year it signed the Nuclear Non Proliferation Treaty (NPT).

questions of conflict, the definition of threat and the pertinent use of force. Though having been defensive at first, once the Brazilian armed forces valued their presence in PKOs, Brazil has continuously expanded its contributions to UN-led peacekeeping operations.

Putting into Practice

Strengthening its presence in global governance with the purpose of accumulating soft power resources has involved different fronts of action for Brazil. A double-track strategy has been pursued to accomplish this aim.

1.   *Teamwork with IBSA/BRICS Partners*

In broadening and deepening the scope of its responsibilities and commitments in global governance, Brazil has crafted innovative forms of interstate collaboration with other emerging powers. For over a decade, the IBSA group has transformed past coincidental or episodic interstate cooperation into a forum for concrete cooperation based mainly on soft power assets. IBSA bolsters development cooperation regarding global agendas and pressures the main multilateral forums.[16] In world politics and security, this group has put special focus on matters such as the Palestine-Israeli peace process, the stability and unity of Iraq, a sustainable diplomatic solution for the Iranian nuclear programme, a consolidated peace process in Sudan and a prudent international involvement in the internal changing realities of the Arab world. With a similar profile, but more global visibility, the BRICS group, active since 2006, has expanded its profile in world economics, politics and security matters. Its motivation has been to promote a coalition among emerging powers to generate alternative pathways to dominant Western-oriented worldviews and prescriptions.[17]

While all BRICS members include UN system reform as part of their foreign policy portfolio, their stances are not the same regarding the aspects underlined for each case, particularly where the UNSC is concerned. Brazil and India are the BRICS countries with the closest affinities, as they have made explicit their candidacy for permanent seats in an expanded UNSC. China stands for this expansion and the need to make the council more representative but does not show sympathy for a new group of permanent members, while Russia has made clear the need to preserve the exclusivity of the veto prerogative of the current permanent members. South Africa also stands for an expanded council but, for historic and regional reasons, has not made explicit any ambition for a permanent seat. If BRICS members would have to assume, on individual terms, a clearer stand on this subject, Brazil, India and Russia would probably align on the hypothesis of new

16. Since 2003, IBSA has evolved into an institutional framework based on 16 working groups, a facility for the alleviation of hunger and poverty (IBSA trust fund) and the implementation of a myriad of other South–South cooperation initiatives.

17. When addressing world finance and monetary issues, BRICS coordination translates into shared stances within multilateral organisations (the International Monetary Fund, the World Bank) and G-7 governments. During its 2014 summit, BRICS stepped forward with initiatives such as the Contingent Reserve Arrangement and the New Development Bank. See Mariano Aguirre, "BRICS, a New Cooperation Model?", *Open Democracy*, (22 January 2013), available: < https://www.opendemocracy.net/mariano-aguirre/brics-new-cooperation-model> (accessed 13 October 2014).

permanent seats with no veto power, while China and South Africa would converge on the idea of an expansion of rotating seats for the developing world. This would most certainly gain the support of two-thirds of the General Assembly (GA), which is the necessary step to move ahead with the reform.

There is not a straight connection between the individual positions of the BRICS partners and their collective stances, although one can observe coincidences and growing convergences. More and more often, the BRICS countries have been building common stances in the area of multilateralism, in New York, Vienna and Geneva. Yet it must be underlined that commonalities do not translate into rigid alignments; each partner carries forward their foreign policy orientations according to their interests and dominant orientations. In addition, political coincidences regarding general world politics and security and/or specific issues (such as the conflict in Syria or the process of fragmentation in Iraq) have not been followed by concrete diplomatic initiatives on the part of the group. In this respect, it could be said that the IBSA/BRICS groups have so far preferred to function with loose strings and non-binding understandings.

Sitting together in the UNSC became an opportunity for Brazil to work as a team with its IBSA/BRICS partners on the urgent matters of world peace and security. In 2011, the chance to work together in the UNSC signified a major opportunity for both groups to share and reinforce their values and perspectives on world politics and security. Brazil and its partners were able to increase their voice in a critical appraisal of liberal peace concepts and prescriptions. When addressing the specific agenda of the council, these emerging powers would underscore their coincidences in regard to their central concerns and the possibilities of an agreed approach to deal with the realities at stake. The fundamentals in between the lines of this effort can be summarised as follows:

- The inevitable link between security and development (Afghanistan, Somalia).
- The articulation between political liberties, peaceful resolutions, national sovereignty and territorial integrity (Libya, Syria).
- The perils of the Security Council's encroachment on other UN agencies' agendas and responsibilities (e.g. addressing climate change as a security matter).
- The need to be more cautious with coercive methods (with mention of the use of sanctions) that could signify a first step towards military action.
- The need to be cautious with the use of the UN charter when addressing local crises. The prescriptions outlined in Chapters VI and VIII of the charter ought not to be overshadowed by the use of Chapter VII. (This concern should translate into an improvement in the council's capacity to monitor and account for the use of force, which it authorises by way of reports and military information.)
- The need to be cautious with the use of preventive intervention; the protection of human lives should be carried forward with responsibility.

It is worth mentioning that Brazil's efforts to use its presence in the UNSC, albeit temporary, to work on an alternative approach to addressing escalating tension was already visible in 2010. At that time, the council's spotlight was directed at Iran in the face of its resistance to accept international inspection of its nuclear programme. Brazil took the initiative together with Turkey, which also held a non-permanent seat, to propose confidence measures, perceived by both countries as acceptable to the Western powers in the UNSC, with the purpose of de-escalating tension and avoiding the application of sanctions being followed by military intervention.[18] Though not considered acceptable at the time, this was the formula adopted a few years later, when a new government was elected in Iran.

Brazil has shown concern over the flaws of UN bureaucratic coordination, the need for improvement in the links between the UNSC, the GA and the executive boards of the UN agencies. It has also stressed the importance of exchange, on a permanent basis, with the recently created Peace Building Commission (PBC), which would have to function as an advisory body to the UNSC. Furthermore, the Security Council encroachment on the prerogatives of other UN bodies, in particular the GA, has been one of the issues addressed by IBSA countries when sitting in the UNSC. In regard to the question of broader representation, transparency and legitimacy, in addition to the quest for the expansion of permanent seats, IBSA members have underscored the importance of ensuring that non-member countries be given a say at council meetings when their realities are at stake. Following the same spirit, Brazil and its partners have advocated that PKO troop commanders and police authorities of contributing countries also be heard at the council. Concerns have been expressed regarding closed door and off-the-record meetings held by the council, with explicit mention of the annual briefing offered by the president of the International Court of Justice to the UNSC.

Since 2011, the BRICS countries' common views and shared stances have been made explicit in joint declarations released during the group's yearly summits. The contrast between the size and contents of the final joint declarations of the 2010 and 2014 BRICS summits reveals the build-up of an in-depth convergence on the questions of military intervention, escalation of conflict and severe political crisis. In four years joint declarations evolved from a vague agenda involving topics of international trade, development, energy, climate change and terrorism into a compact document encompassing specific points, which cover a broad and complex evaluation of economy, politics and international security with unequivocal positions and a robust intergovernmental action plan. Nowadays BRICS goes far beyond a label; it responds to the construction of a framework of shared economic and political stands with concrete initiatives.[19]

2. *The PKO Commitment*

Brazil's presence in the UNSC has also contributed to an expanded participation by Brazil in PKOs.[20] Yet this should not be taken as a simplistic assumption, nor one in which this sort of engagement is the result of pragmatic calculations. Perceptions shared by diplomats and the military have become quite realistic regarding a renewed multilateral architecture and the chance that the council will be reformed. At present, global political developments are seen as dissociated from an

---

18. See Asli U Bâli, "Negotiating Non-proliferation: International Law and Delegation in the Iranian Nuclear Crisis", *UCLA Law Review*, Vol. 61, No. 2 (2013), pp. 13–33.

19. "Sixth Summit: Fortaleza Declaration and Action Plan", VI BRICS Summit, Fortaleza, Brazil, 15 July 2014, available: <http://brics6.itamaraty.gov.br/category-english/21-documents/223-sixth-summit-declaration-and-action-plan> (accessed 30 September 2014).

20. See Kai Michael Kenkel and Rodrigo Fracalossi De Moraes, *O Brasil e as operações de paz em um mundo globalizado* (Brasília: Ipea, 2012).

institutional process of redistribution of power. Nevertheless, the loss of momentum regarding Security Council reform has in no way diminished Brazil's involvement in PKOs.

Brazil is currently participating in nine (of a total of 17) peace missions and has registered relevant expansion of its contribution of troops.[21] In this same context, Brazil has evolved from being a selective troop provider to an ambitious innovator regarding political approach and methods of stabilisation.[22] While the Brazilian military has a history of participation in UN-led missions, the benchmark of its present commitment was set in 2004, when the Brazilian government assumed the military command of MINUSTAH (The United Nations Support Mission for Haiti). Then came participation in UNFIL (The United Nations Interim Force in Lebanon) and, most recently, the responsibilities undertaken by a Brazilian officer as Military Commander of MONUSCO (The United Nations Organization Stabilization Mission in the Democratic Republic of the Congo). In addition, police cooperation has expanded in Guinea Bissau, and in 2013 Brazil assumed the chair of the Country-Specific Configuration of the Peacebuilding Commission.

While each mission has taken place in a specific context, presenting specific incentives and difficulties, for the Brazilian Ministry of Defence all are perceived as opportunities to build operational-logistical experience and to improve the handling of rules of engagement in UN-led interventions.[23] Brazil's expanded political and military presence in global and regional scenarios has become a stimulus to strengthen defence capabilities and professionalisation. The need to rely upon a suitable toolkit, based upon their own worldviews and differing from the doctrines and operational framework formulated by others—particularly NATO—led to the establishment by the Brazilian military of a proper training centre. Different from other emerging powers, such as India, the Brazilian armed forces in the past have had little interaction with multilateral bureaucracy. Yet once the country developed the motivation and confidence to assume high-level responsibilities on the ground, its interface with the UN headquarters notably expanded. More and more often, the presence of Brazilian military in UN headquarters underpins the country's diplomatic actions in multilateral arenas involved in global security. In consequence, a proper track of interaction between the Ministry of Defence and the UN has been slowly built up, contributing to Brazil's involvement in the creation and present functioning of the Peacebuilding Commission at the UN.[24]

Undoubtedly, Brazil's presence in Haiti as leader of the military command of MINUSTAH has become crucial to lock in the process described above. UN-led responsibilities assumed by the Brazilian military in Haiti, according to the yearly mandates approved by the Security Council, encompassed a diverse spectrum of responsibilities: (1) the stabilisation of local public order; (2) active participation in the reform and expansion of native police forces; (3) elimination, disarmament and containment of local gangs; (4) protection of human rights and

---

21. Rita Santos and Teresa Almeida Cravo, "Brazil's Rising Profile in United Nations Peacekeeping Operations Since the End of the Cold War", NOREF Report, March 2014.

22. *Ibid.*

23. Hirst and Nasser, *op. cit.*

24. In May 2014 Gal. Paul Cruz, who had previously been Chief of the Military Command of MINUSTAH and Vice Chief of Staff of the Army, became the Director of Strategic Partnership at the Department of Peacekeeping Operations (DPKO).

rule of law; (5) logistic support to development cooperation and improvement of local infrastructure.

From the very beginning, Brazil expressed the intention to differentiate its presence in Haitian soil from other examples of external intervention impelled by imperialist ambitions. The decision to assume the military command of MINUSTAH in order to avoid "other" presences was connected to the idea that the UNSC ought to be the only legitimate instance for deliberating on military intervention in sovereign countries. At the time, Foreign Minister Celso Amorim stressed: "Brazil accepted to send troops and assume the military command of MINUSTAH in the first place because it is an operation decided by the Security Council, the only organ that possesses legitimacy to decide the presence of foreign troops in a sovereign country".

Brazilian diplomats and military have shared many perceptions when addressing the perils of the Haitian reality. Haiti is not considered a "failed state" and although they acknowledge its many needs and vulnerabilities, they also believe that local institutions and political culture have been preserved. Accordingly, and despite 10 years of MINUSTAH presence, the Haitian political system is seen to still function based upon high levels of power concentration in the hands of the president (and prime minister), associated with local political groups, some of which are linked to small gang organisations. In addition, this centralised institutional frame co-exists with fragments of violence, in a context of dramatic social-economic conditions.

The Brazilian presence has oscillated between a coordinated action with its South American peers and the construction of its own profile in the performance of its responsibilities in Haiti. This double facet reproduced in reality a Brazilian pattern of behaviour that was deepened during the Lula government, aiming at combining but not completely merging regional policy with global interests. After the 2010 earthquake in Haiti, Brazil took further steps with regard to its military and economic responsibilities in the country and its actions came to be more closely linked to local demands and international expectations than to South American articulations.

Following the earthquake of January 2010, the military command had to simultaneously deal with a severe humanitarian crisis and the chaotic presence of external actors, along with the prejudices and misconceptions of their governments and organisations based upon other experiences. In the face of Haiti's dramatic reconstruction needs after the earthquake, the Brazilian army expanded its military presence, especially of military engineers, to attend to the infrastructure needs of the country.[25] This augmented presence was accompanied by the expansion of bilateral and trilateral cooperation projects, coordinated with Development Assistance Committee (DAC) donors, multilateral agencies and/or Southern partners. Altogether, these tasks have contributed to change Brazil's profile in PKOs, leading to an expanded presence at the UN PKO headquarters in New York, a stronger link between the Defence and Foreign Ministries in Brasília and the strengthening of fraternal ties with the South American military who participate in MINUSTAH.

---

25. In total, Brazil has sent approximately 20,000 troops to Haiti since MINUSTAH was installed. The Brazilian military contribution to MINUSTAH started in 2004 with an envoy of 1,210 troops. In 2010 Brazil expanded its troop contributions in Haiti from 1,282 to 2,188. Since 2012 the Brazilian contribution has been downsized annually according to a withdrawal plan approved by a Security Council resolution. See Security Council Resolutions S/2004/698, S/2009/439, S/2010/200, S/RES/2070 (2012).

As already mentioned, besides Haiti, the Brazilian military has committed to presence in other UN-led missions, notably UNFIL and MONUSCO. The decision to participate in UNFIL opened up another important international horizon for Brazil's armed forces. Whereas for the Foreign Ministry this represented a step forward in engagement in the Middle East, it has also been perceived as an opportunity to promote the participation of naval forces in UN operations.

In 2010 Brazil was invited to join UNFIL, and although it was reluctant at first, it now perceives it as a stimulating challenge to expand its presence in a particularly sensitive international area. The country's responsibilities in the mission rose in 2011 when it replaced Italy in the command of UNIFIL's Maritime Task Force (MTF), a multinational force composed of nine vessels in charge of patrolling a coastal strip of 220 kilometres. The fact that this would be the first time a non-NATO member had assumed command of the MTF represented a breakthrough for the international projection of the Brazilian navy.

Brazil's participation in the UN mission in the Congo represents a delicate and peculiar experience. The appointment of a Brazilian officer as Military Commander of MONUSCO in 2013 came as a result of a personal invitation to General Santos Cruz and not as a diplomatic negotiation between the Itamaraty and the UN General Secretary, as in the cases of MINUSTAH and UNIFIL. Yet for the Ministry of Defence, the responsibilities assumed in MONUSCO by a Brazilian officer became a new source of pride and international projection. It has also been perceived as part of a virtuous sequence in which the country engages in more complex scenarios of robust missions, involving the use of force, procedures of intervention and innovative technological back-up.

On the whole, for the Brazilian armed forces, its involvement in foreign affairs presents an opportunity to reinforce its traditional values, particularly the commitment to peace. This impetus has also involved an expanded portfolio of bilateral agreements with a myriad of partners from the developing world and with industrialised countries as well.[26] These initiatives have become fertile grounds for the Brazilian military to explore comparative advantages and improve its image abroad and at home.

While the challenges mentioned above show an effort to pursue autonomy and innovation, there has been criticism regarding the question of human resources. Firstly, in comparison with other Latin American countries, Brazil is well behind Argentina, Peru and Uruguay in the participation of women and civilian personnel in UN missions. Brazilian peacekeeping is a strictly defence operation, which translates into a dominating presence of male military personnel. Secondly, Brazil's participation in PKOs depends on domestic economics. Brazilian contributions to UN PKOs are subject to the same uncertainties as all external commitments, which are nowadays affected by domestic budgetary cuts. Since the beginning of the Dilma Rousseff administration, the Ministry of Defence and Itamaraty budgets have suffered cutbacks of 24% and 15%, respectively, curtailing the president's diplomatic agenda and affecting opportunities for expanding responsibilities on all multilateral fronts.

---

26. In early 2014 the Brazilian Ministry of Defence managed 68 international accords, of which 90% were South–South cooperation initiatives. Many projects have been carried forward with partners of the Portuguese-speaking community, of the South Atlantic Peace Zone and of the India, Brazil, South Africa (IBSA) group. In addition, Brazil has negotiated defence cooperation with all South American countries and has played a central role in the creation of the Defence Council of UNASUR.

The Challenges Ahead

It will not be easy for Brazil to expand its voice and influence as an emergent power in global governance bodies in the years to come. Brazil has become gridlocked between the legitimation of the international power structure, its contestation and the claim for its reconfiguration.

According to the regional system of rotation, Brazil will probably have to wait until 2024 to sit in the UNSC again. This restriction will lead the country to concentrate its political energies in alternative arenas such as the Human Rights Council and Peacekeeping Commission and the UN General Assembly. It is likely that Brazil will keep a high profile in UN-led missions, especially in MINUSTAH and UNFIL, and eventually in other operations. These will all be important platforms for the country to open up spaces to manoeuvre and to propose solutions and methods other than the prescriptive solutions that follow the premises of Western-led interventionism.

As has been underlined, the simultaneous presence of BRICS members in the UNSC during 2011 contributed in an important way to allow the group to articulate common stances regarding global security issues and realities. Since then, these commonalities have been underlined in the BRICS summit final declarations in which the group has agreed its stances on the complexities of current international intervention. The inclusion of many of the topics addressed in the council (Afghanistan, Syria, Libya, Palestine, Somalia, and Sudan, among others) reveals the aim to coordinate foreign policy orientations in global security. The question is how to ensure that this process be continued and expanded beyond a symbolic level when access to the inner circles of world politics is unbalanced. Clearly, consensual statements do not have the same impact and do not imply the same degree of responsibility in world politics as voting preferences in the Security Council.

At the same time, the global scenario is in no way static, and is likely to become muddier in the management of conflict, intervention and severe institutional crisis. Since 2011, the sequence of crises in Libya, Syria, Ukraine and Gaza has posed new dilemmas for emerging powers, and the differences in power assets limit their capacity to work together. There is a clear difference between abstaining and vetoing, yet the IBSA group—non-permanent members of the council—cannot veto, but only abstain. The tricky aspect of this difference is that for Brazil, India and South Africa, abstaining has been considered by Western powers as equally obstructive. Hence, less access to power has not translated into less pressure and/or discredit. On the very contrary, Brazilian foreign policy has been openly criticised within Western diplomatic circles for sustaining a sovereign-oriented stance on the NATO-led intervention taking place in Syria, Afghanistan and Iraq. Brazil's presidential speech at the opening of the 2014 General Assembly, stressing its reservations about the recent expansion of military actions against Islamic terrorist groups, and in defence of a peace-oriented approach, again raised a wave of criticism in the international and national media.[27] In fact, the present complexities in world security lead to extreme solutions that constrain and tend to wear off the country's soft power assets.

---

27. Dilma Rousseff, "Statement by H.E. Dilma Rousseff, President of the Federative Republic of Brazil, at the Opening of the General Debate of the 69th Session of the United Nations General Assembly", New York, 24 September 2014, available: <http://www.un.org/en/ga/69/meetings/gadebate/> (accessed 14 February 2015).

Within the BRICS block, the recent China–Russia articulation in the UNSC to prevent Western powers giving a permanent green light for the use of intervention and coercive measures, have created new challenges for Brazil, India and South Africa.[28] These three countries have no other choice than to accept a secondary role, imposed by the multilateral rules of the game. On the other hand, it is not clear whether these IBSA partners will coincide with China and Russia in all contexts. Differences have already surfaced in the General Assembly when resolution voting on the situations in Syria and Ukraine took place in 2012 and 2013. What would have happened if Brazil had been sitting in the UNSC in 2012, when China and Russia vetoed the intervention in Syria? Brazil and its IBSA partners would probably have abstained. In 2012, China and Russia stood together in the Security Council and in the GA against pressure for intervention in Syria advocated by the US, the UK and France. It is worth mentioning that the IBSA group, no longer sitting together in the council, did abstain in the GA on the resolution referring to the Syrian situation. The following year, Brazil, India and South Africa also abstained in the GA when the resolution on the territorial integrity of Ukraine was voted on.[29]

Restraints also are perceived in Brazil's expanded responsibilities in PKOs. Brazil, along with other emerging powers, has become more exposed to the contradictions that inevitably come along with an expanded profile in multilateral military intervention.[30] Despite signalling a willingness to play a more active and distinct role in international security and peace issues, participation in peacekeeping operations in the last decade has faced a myriad of challenges. Working intensely on an alternative approach to Western-biased military intervention has not prevented Brazil from sliding into inexorable PKO power dilemmas. The Brazilian military in Haiti faces challenges of fatigue in the management of a withdrawal strategy for MINUSTAH forces. At present, the course of action to be pursued in Haiti to carry forward a withdrawal process, beyond a simple quantitative cutback, has become a matter of discussion between the UN, the main Latin American troop contributors, the major donors and Haitian authorities. The idea has been to initiate an assisted transition, similar to those experienced in Sierra Leone and Liberia. One of the main points addressed when redesigning MINUSTAH has been the need to frame its responsibilities exclusively under Chapter VI of the UN charter, which implies also replacing the numerous blue helmets based in different parts of the island with an effective police force in charge of Haitian public security needs. In Haiti, the local pressure to accelerate this process has generated new tensions, making it more difficult to ensure that stability becomes sustainable in the country's reconstruction. Haiti is far from meeting the expectations of the international community on its economic and social transformations, worsened by the presence of a renewed generation of violent gangs. In addition,

---

28. See Peter Ferdinand, "The Positions of Russia and China at the UN Security Council in the Light of Recent Crisis", Briefing Paper for the Directorate-General for External Policies of the Union, European Parliament (March 2012), available: <http://www.europarl.europa.eu/activities/committees/studies.do?> (accessed 13 October 2014); Peter Ferdinand, "Rising Powers at the UN: An Analysis of the Voting Behaviour of BRICS States in the General Assembly", *Third World Quarterly*, Vol. 35, No. 3 (2014), pp. 376–391.

29. United Nations General Assembly, 67th Session (2012–2013), A/67/L.63; and 68th Session (2013–2014), A/68/PV.71, available: <http://www.un.org/en/ga/documents/voting.asp> (accessed 9 December 2014).

30. See Xenia Avezov, *op. cit.*

Brazil has for the first time been absorbing the indirect consequences of its performance as an occupation force. A recent development in the Brazilian military command of MINUSTAH has been the growing influx of Haitian immigrants to Brazil, which has been a source of xenophobia in parts of the country not prepared to deal with this sort of challenge, a *de facto* post-colonial challenge. Furthermore, it would be expected that Brazil, while diminishing its military presence on Haitian soil, would reinforce its commitments to assist the country with cooperation for development initiatives. Yet the recent national budget cutbacks in Brazil have affected the activities of the Brazilian Agency for Cooperation (ABC), which inevitably constrains Brazil's performance as an emerging donor.

To conclude, while Brazil has taken major steps to improve its international stature, the country still has to deal with uncertainties. The endurance of its expanded presence and responsibilities in global governance now faces a growing tension between internal political restrictions and external constraints. On the one side, recent international developments indicate that military actions and coercive diplomacy have downplayed the space for political mediation and peaceful resolutions, which inevitably reduces the space for manoeuvre of emerging powers. On the other side, domestic factors in Brazil, such as the present economic restrictions and the degree of polarisation between political forces exacerbated during the 2014 elections, tend to reduce Brazilian foreign policy initiatives. The present government has signalled that it intends to focus upon the internal front. At the same time, the Brazilian democratisation process has advanced the institutional frame, voices and interests of a myriad of actors now involved in the country's international affairs. A polarised political environment combined with an austere foreign policy will certainly amplify divergence at home and could open a Pandora's Box regarding Brazil's insertion into the 21st-century world as an emergent power.

Three Emerging Security Challenges for the UK

PAGE WILSON

In light of the planned 2015 Strategic Defence and Security Review, it is timely to consider afresh the global security landscape and the UK's place within it. What does "security" mean in this context, and what challenges does the UK face? Following a discussion of the meaning of "security", the article will identify three broad themes from which security challenges for the UK emerge. These are: (1) cyberspace and the digital age; (2) change and the current international system; and (3) inequality within the UK. By examining recent developments in each of these areas, it will be argued that there are good reasons for these challenges to remain important in thinking about British security over the medium to longer term.

In 2010, the newly elected British government completed a Strategic Defence and Security Review (SDSR), the first comprehensive reassessment of the country's security-related goals, resources and activities in 12 years. Both the SDSR and its accompanying National Security Strategy (NSS) announced the government's commitment to produce a new SDSR and NSS every five years.[1] This commitment to a regular SDSR cycle has been reaffirmed subsequently by the Prime Minister.[2] As the timetable for the next SDSR and NSS rapidly approaches, therefore, it is an appropriate moment to reconsider the global security landscape and the UK's place within it.

Following a discussion of what "security" means in this context, the article will identify three broad issue-areas from which security challenges for the UK emerge. These are: (1) cyberspace and the digital age; (2) change and the current international system; and (3) levels of inequality within the UK. By examining recent developments in each of these areas, it will be argued that there are good reasons for these challenges to remain important in thinking about British security over the medium to longer term.

---

1. HM Government, "A Strong Britain in an Age of Uncertainty: The National Security Strategy" (October 2010), p. 11, available: <https://www.gov.uk/government/uploads/system/uploads/attachment_data/file/61936/national-security-strategy.pdf> (accessed 6 January 2015); and HM Government, "Securing Britain in an Age of Uncertainty: The Strategic Defence and Security Review" (October 2010), p. 9, available: <https://www.gov.uk/government/uploads/system/uploads/attachment_data/file/62482/strategic-defence-security-review.pdf> (accessed 6 January 2015).

2. See, for example, Nicholas de Larrinaga, "Farnborough 2014: Cameron Details Defence Priorities for 2015 SDSR", *IHS Jane's Defence Weekly*, 15 July 2014, available: <http://www.janes.com/article/40776/farnborough-2014-cameron-details-defence-priorities-for-2015-sdsr> (accessed 6 January 2015).

Defining Security

What security means in the post-Cold War era, who or what is the referent object of security and how best to achieve security are questions at the heart of debates in the theory and practice of international relations. It is commonly asserted that the lack of superpower conflict, plus the intensification of globalisation, have forced a shift in the meaning of security from a state-centric, military-focused notion to a much wider concept incorporating transnational issues and new levels of analysis below, above and beyond the state.[3] However, apart from this truism, the concept of security has been notoriously difficult to pin down; instead, many different versions of "security" have emerged and flourished, attracting their own groups of proponents and opponents.[4] This process is now so prolific that it has provoked at least one school of thought to adopt as one of its central research inquiries the way in which political issues become "securitized".[5]

Reflecting this conceptual and practical complexity in "an age of uncertainty", neither the SDSR nor the NSS defines security. While they identify and prioritise a range of concerns, and set out in wide terms how the government intends to address these concerns, the absence from these documents of more specific answers to the very basic questions generated by the notion of security in the 21st century makes it very difficult to assess the extent to which the SDSR and NSS are achieving what the government intends them to achieve. The problem is well summed up by the UK's domestic intelligence service (MI5), which also provides the closest, official approximation of a definition of security:

> The term "national security" is not specifically defined by UK or European law. It has been the policy of successive Governments and the practice of Parliament not to define the term, in order to retain the flexibility necessary to ensure that the use of the term can adapt to changing circumstances.

> As a matter of Government policy, the term "national security" is taken to refer to the security and well-being of the United Kingdom as a whole. The "nation" in this sense is not confined to the UK as a geographical or political entity but extends to its citizens, wherever they may be, and its system of government.[6]

---

3. On the reconceptualisation of security in the post-Cold War era, see, for instance, Roland Dannreuther, *International Security: The Contemporary Agenda* (Cambridge: Polity Press, 2013); Barry Buzan, "Rethinking Security after the Cold War", *Cooperation and Conflict*, Vol. 32, No. 1 (1997), pp. 5–28; Barry Buzan and Lene Hansen, *The Evolution of International Security Studies* (Cambridge, UK: Cambridge University Press, 2009); Victor D. Cha, "Globalization and the Study of International Security", *Journal of Peace Research*, Vol. 37, No. 3 (2000), pp. 391–403; Gary King and Christopher J.L. Murray, "Rethinking Human Security", *Political Science Quarterly*, Vol. 116, No. 4 (2001), pp. 585–610; and J. Ann Tickner, *Gendering World Politics: Issues and Approaches in the Post-Cold War Era* (New York: Columbia University Press, 2001).

4. See, for example, the literature that has cropped up around the notions of human security, food security, energy security, environmental security and health security These supplement ongoing work on conventional concepts of national and military security.

5. Namely, the Copenhagen School; see Barry Buzan, Ole Waever and Jaap de Wilde, *Security: A New Framework for Analysis* (Boulder, CO: Lynne Reiner Publishers, 1998) and more recently the special issue of *Security Dialogue* (Vol. 42, No. 4–5, August–October 2011) on the politics of securitisation, available: <http://sdi.sagepub.com/content/42/4-5.toc> (accessed 6 January 2015).

6. Security Service MI5, "Protecting National Security" (2014), available: <https://www.mi5.gov.uk/home/about-us/what-we-do/protecting-national-security.html> (accessed 24 November 2014).

British "national security", then, is unlimited in reach, incorporating not just Britain's far-flung overseas territories, but also anywhere Britons are present, whether in another sovereign state, a failed state, a conflict zone, foreign territorial waters, the high seas or foreign or international airspace. In addition to British nationals, both individually and collectively, this definition includes the British state itself and its commitment to parliamentary democracy. By inference, the definition is likely to extend also to the security of foreign nationals resident or present in the UK ("the UK as a whole"), though this is not specifically mentioned. In terms of substance, "national security" goes beyond basic physical survival, and incorporates "well-being"—a much higher, yet at the same time more ambiguous standard.

This expansive, official notion of "security" has been further confirmed by the Prime Minister in evidence to the Joint Committee on the National Security Strategy:

> You have to take a wide definition [of security] because our nation's security relies on having strong defences so that we can protect ourselves, but it also means considering every risk to our security: from floods, pandemic diseases, new threats such as volcanic eruptions or space weather—all these things ... Security, in the end, is the ability to protect your country, your people and your interests so that they can grow and prosper, and in delivering security you have to deal with every threat, from the biggest to the most unlikely. The point of having this big army in Whitehall is to make sure that we cover all those threats ... [7]

The Prime Minister went on to recognise that, as a result of this approach, major issues not falling within the traditional security sphere—such as tax avoidance by multinational companies—can now be considered a security threat.[8] On questioning, the Prime Minister also indirectly acknowledged the inherent difficulties associated with such an all-inclusive definition of security.[9]

A flexible, yet more exacting notion of security is formulated by Ayoob.[10] He argues that "security or insecurity is defined in relation to vulnerabilities, both internal and external, that threaten to, or have the potential to, bring down or

---

7. "National Security Strategy Evidence from the Prime Minister" (HC1040), Transcript of Oral Evidence Taken before the Joint Committee on the National Security Strategy on 30 January 2014, pp. 7–8, available: <http://www.parliament.uk/documents/joint-committees/national-security-strategy/PM%20session/JCNSS14-01-30TranscriptCameronC.pdf> (accessed 24 November 2014).

8. *Ibid.*, p. 8. The Prime Minister stated: "At the heart of our national security strategy is restoring Britain's economic strength ... If we say that at the heart of our national security is strengthening our economy, if we cannot properly raise taxes from businesses because the technology has changed and they are not playing by the rules, that would, I suppose, be a threat to your security".

9. *Ibid.*, p. 8. The following exchange between the Prime Minister (PM) and Lord Waldegrave of North Hill (LW) is quoted below:

> LW: I am trying to probe what is not security.
> PM: I can see that. You have to have a hierarchy. I am afraid that we have a terrible list of acronyms in the national risk assessment and the national resilience planning assumptions, but the attempt is to try to delineate risks to security, have them all dealt with in one part of Whitehall and make sure that we have a strategy for dealing with all of them.

10. Mohammed Ayoob, "Defining Security: A Subaltern Realist Perspective", in Keith Krause and Michael C. Williams (eds.), *Critical Security Studies: Concepts and Cases* (London: UCL Press, 1997), pp. 121–148.

significantly weaken state structures, both territorial and institutional, and regimes".[11] Where a state lies on the continuum of vulnerability/invulnerability in relation to a particular security issue is determined according to factors such as "legitimacy, integration or societal cohesion, and policy capacity", which Ayoob considers equally important, if not more important, than a state's control over the means of coercion.[12]

Unlike the official notion of security discussed above, however, Ayoob limits security to the level of the state, which includes its territory, its institutions and "those who profess to represent the state territorially and institutionally".[13] For him, security is expressly political, and so risks such as environmental damage or food shortages only become *security* problems when they reach a political threshold—namely, they jeopardise the "survivability of state boundaries, state institutions or governing elites or dramatically weaken the capacity of states and regimes to act effectively in the realm of politics, both domestic and international".[14] Consequently, Ayoob's definition of security retains significant versatility while delineating the notion in a meaningful way for conceptual and practical purposes. The extent to which the emerging challenges discussed in this article comprise *security* challenges based on the two different definitions of security introduced in this section will be explored in further detail below.

Cyberspace and the Digital Age

Certain issues surrounding cyberspace and the digital age clearly fall within the government's notion of security, as demonstrated by the sustained attention they received in the SDSR and NSS. The latter listed "hostile attacks upon UK cyber space and large scale cyber crime" as one of four tier one security risks.[15] This was followed up in 2011 by a stand-alone Cyber Security Strategy (CSS) for the UK. In the latter document, cyberspace was defined as:

> an interactive domain made up of digital networks that is used to store, modify and communicate information. It includes the internet, but also the other information systems that support our businesses, infrastructure and services.[16]

The emphasis of the CSS is on risks or threats with the greatest public visibility, namely the negative economic effects caused to individuals and corporations by crime and fraud committed via the "fifth domain".[17] This includes not just direct monetary losses from theft, but also the indirect damage such acts cause to the UK's reputation as a safe place to do business. Other than economically motivated

---

11. *Ibid.*, p. 130.
12. *Ibid.*, p. 130.
13. *Ibid.*, p. 130.
14. *Ibid.*, p. 130.
15. HM Government, "A Strong Britain", *op. cit.*, p. 27.
16. HM Government, "The UK Cyber Security Strategy: Protecting and Promoting the UK in a Digital World" (November 2011), p. 11, available: <https://www.gov.uk/government/uploads/system/uploads/attachment_data/file/60961/uk-cyber-security-strategy-final.pdf> (accessed 6 January 2015).
17. The phrase is taken from "Cyberwar: War in the Fifth Domain", *The Economist*, 1 July 2010, available: <http://www.economist.com/node/16478792> (accessed 6 January 2015).

acts, the UK does acknowledge in general terms "high level threats" in cyberspace and the role of the Ministry of Defence (MOD) and Government Communications Headquarters (GCHQ) in countering them, although these challenges get comparatively little attention in the policy documents. The CSS pledged £650 million over four years to develop the UK's cyber response.[18]

This level of political and economic commitment to promote cyber security might suggest that cyberspace issues are no longer *emerging* security challenges, but have in fact already fully emerged and taken their place at the forefront of government thinking about security. However, the enormous and relatively new impact of the information revolution, plus the speed and scale of ongoing technological change, mean that the nature of this challenge will continue to metamorphose in fresh and unexpected ways. In this sense, the challenge remains "emerging".

Two challenges presented by cyberspace and the arrival of the digital age are particularly deserving of attention in the context of British security.

Stuxnet and the Rise in Destructive Attacks

The advent of Stuxnet—a computer worm that destroyed nuclear centrifuges in Iran's uranium enrichment facility at Natanz in 2010—marked a watershed in cyber security. Previously, malware had served various purposes, including discovering secret information for economic, political or personal gains; creating a nuisance or embarrassment, sometimes linked with wider political or economic aims; or symbolising an important personal and technical achievement on the part of the attacker. By contrast, the sole purpose of Stuxnet appeared to be to destroy an offline, real-life target. Stuxnet was widely attributed to the US and Israeli governments,[19] though crucially they have never confirmed this.

Since Stuxnet, there have been destructive attacks in Qatar, South Korea and Saudi Arabia, affecting, or in some cases "wiping" thousands of computers at any one time. The scale and nature of such attacks have suggested that the purpose behind them is complete demolition of the target company or state. The US's National Security Agency (NSA) has claimed such attacks are increasing, and individuals are expressing greater interest in such capabilities with a view to using them.[20] The head of the Secret Intelligence Service (SIS) has also identified "states out there … trying to do us harm through cyber attacks" among the

---

18. HM Government, "The UK Cyber Security Strategy", *op. cit.*, p. 5.

19. See, for example, "Falkenrath Says Stuxnet Virus May Have Origin in Israel", *The Washington Post*, 24 September 2010, available: <http://www.washingtonpost.com/wp-dyn/content/video/2010/09/24/VI2010092401641.html> (accessed 7 January 2015); "Edward Snowden Interview: The NSA and Its Willing Helpers", *Der Spiegel*, 8 July 2013, available: <http://www.spiegel.de/international/world/interview-with-whistleblower-edward-snowden-on-global-spying-a-910006.html> (accessed 7 January 2015); and David E. Sanger, "Obama Order Sped Up Wave of Cyberattacks Against Iran", *The New York Times*, 1 June 2012, available: <http://www.nytimes.com/2012/06/01/world/middleeast/obama-ordered-wave-of-cyberattacks-against-iran.html?pagewanted=1&_r=2> (accessed 7 January 2015).

20. Richard Ledgett, "The NSA Responds to Edward Snowden's TED Talk" (March 2014), available: <http://www.ted.com/talks/richard_ledgett_the_nsa_responds_to_edward_snowden_s_ted_talk> (accessed 6 January 2015).

main threats facing Britain.[21] In addition, the head of GCHQ has highlighted "the engagement by some states, perhaps less sophisticated states in terms of their strategic weaponry, using cyber as an over the horizon means of projecting disruption".[22]

The question is whether Stuxnet has signalled the beginning of unrestrained attacks among states in cyberspace, an occurrence which some commentators describe as "cyberwar".[23] While views are divided about this term, it has nevertheless given rise to a secondary debate concerning the use and significance of "cyber offense"[24] and "cyber defence" capabilities. The NSA is heavily biased in favour of cyber defence, though it acknowledges that the NSA's "mission" covers both possibilities.[25] Traditionally, the US has considered its own secrets of more value than anyone else's, and so has poured most of its energy into protecting them. However, to the extent that Stuxnet and/or subsequent attacks represent or induce a shift in US priorities towards "cyber offense" capabilities, this holds serious security implications for key defence and intelligence allies such as the UK.

In September 2013, in the first official recognition of cyber offense activities by any state, the Defence Secretary publicly acknowledged that the UK will build a cyber offensive capability, arguing for it on the basis of deterrence.[26] Arguments supporting the application of strategies of deterrence in the cyber realm emphasise the networked, interdependent and globalised nature of interstate relations today, meaning a potential state cyber attacker is likely to lose as much, if not more, than its intended target.[27] In addition, it is argued, strong defensive and resilience measures, plus a host of offensive capabilities—including cyber, economic, military

---

21. Intelligence and Security Committee of Parliament, Uncorrected Transcript of Evidence Given by Sir Iain Lobban, Mr Andrew Parker and Sir John Sawers (7 November 2013), p. 2, available: <http://isc.independent.gov.uk/news-archive/7november2013-1> (accessed 4 May 2015).

22. *Ibid.*, pp. 12–13. In the same statement to the Committee, the GCHQ chief also highlighted "the growth in a diverse set of very capable non-state actors". As regards the nature of the cyber threat generally, he described it as "multifaceted", including "hostile intelligence services … highly organised groups stealing industrial secrets, academic secrets. Terrorists. Hacktivists, criminal … increasingly sophisticated criminal actors" (p. 12).

23. See J.P. Farwell and R. Rohozinski, "Stuxnet and the Future of Cyberwar", *Survival*, Vol. 53, No. 1 (2011), pp. 23–40; J.R. Lindsay, "Stuxnet and the Limits of Cyber Warfare", *Security Studies*, Vol. 22, No. 3 (2013), pp. 365–404; John Richardson, "Stuxnet as Cyberwarfare: Applying the Law of War to the Virtual Battlefield", *The John Marshall Journal of Computer and Information Law* (Fall 2011), available: <http://repository.jmls.edu/jitpl/vol29/iss1/1/> (accessed 7 January 2015); and Jeremy Richmond, "Evolving Battlefields: Does Stuxnet Demonstrate a Need for Modifications to the Law of Armed Conflict?", *Fordham International Law Journal*, Vol. 35 (2011–2012), pp. 842–893.

24. The term "cyber *offense*" is deliberately used here to refer to offensive cyber capabilities—in particular, the state's ability to launch a digital, pre-emptive strike on another state or group for military, political and/or economic reasons. It is not to be confused with "cyber *offence*" which in a UK context usually refers to a traditional criminal act committed via online means—for example, theft from an individual's online bank account, or child exploitation via chat rooms/social media.

25. Ledgett, *op. cit.*

26. British Forces News, "MOD: IT Experts Wanted for Cyber Defence 30.09.13" (2 October 2013), available: <http://www.youtube.com/watch?v=CsVqnEtrJxY> (accessed 4 May 2015). The full quote from the Defence Secretary is as follows: "The threat is real. But simply building cyber defences is not enough. As in other domains of warfare, we also have to deter. So I can announce today that Britain will build a dedicated capability to counterattack in cyberspace and if necessary to strike in cyberspace as part of our full spectrum military capability". See also James Blitz, "UK Becomes First State to Admit to Offensive Cyber Attack Capability", *The Financial Times*, 29 September 2013, available: <http://www.ft.com/intl/cms/s/0/9ac6ede6-28fd-11e3-ab62-00144feab7de.html#axzz3O3N21UuG> (accessed 6 January 2015).

and political instruments—reduce the likelihood and extent of damage inflicted on the target state, and promise a comprehensive retaliation, thereby significantly diminishing the risk-to-reward ratio in the eyes of the attacker.[28] Moreover, where attribution of the attack is possible or credible suspicions raised, the damage to reputation a potential state attacker is likely to suffer may also bolster deterrence.[29]

On the other hand, some have argued that a move towards a more enthusiastic "cyber offense" posture is very dangerous, given the potential for a "cyber security dilemma" to result.[30] Others argue that conventional theories of deterrence do not work in the cyber domain, but instead result in escalation, or are otherwise problematic.[31] Yet others have criticised the announcement for legitimising the capabilities of adversaries, undermining the UK's "moral high ground" on the issue and leaving the UK open to accusations of "militarising" cyberspace.[32] Thus, the risk is that the UK's announcement may provoke other states to acquire, with greater urgency and interest than before, their own cyber weapons, thereby increasing their opportunities for effective attack against British cyberspace and government systems. Given widespread government reliance on computer systems and networks for the day-to-day running of virtually every area of policy, the impact of such an attack would certainly meet the threshold for a security challenge set down by Ayoob. How destructive attacks evolve and whether or not cyberdeterrence works are likely to remain key security questions for the UK in the foreseeable future.

Leaks, Secrecy and Government Transparency

Leaks of thousands of classified documents *en masse*—only made possible by the arrival of the digital age—have also been identified as a security challenge by government officials. In response to the Snowden leak of June 2013, all three heads of the security services have openly acknowledged that damage has been caused by the disclosed information. The head of GCHQ has stated that the "fragile mosaic" of "strategic capabilities that allows us to discover, process, investigate and then to take action that uncovers terrorist cells … is in a far, far weaker place than it was [before the leak]", as terrorist groups shift away from communication methods they now consider vulnerable, towards others they perceive as unexploitable.[33] The SIS chief has claimed that "our adversaries are rubbing their

27. Joseph S. Nye, Jr., "Cyber Power" (Cambridge, MA: Harvard Kennedy School/Belfer Center for Science and International Affairs, May 2010), pp. 16–17, available: <http://www.dtic.mil/dtic/tr/fulltext/u2/a522626.pdf> (accessed 6 January 2015).

28. Richard L. Kugler, "Deterrence of Cyber Attacks", in Franklin D. Kramer *et al.* (eds.), *Cyberpower and National Security* (Washington, DC: Centre for Technology and National Security Policy, National Defense University, 2009), pp. 309–342, available: <http://ctnsp.dodlive.mil/files/2014/03/Cyberpower-I-Chap-13.pdf> (accessed 6 January 2015).

29. Nye, *op. cit.*, p. 17.

30. See, for example, Thomas Rid's view in Richard Norton-Taylor, "Britain Plans Cyber Strike Force—With Help from GCHQ", *The Guardian*, 30 September 2013, available: <http://www.theguardian.com/uk-news/defence-and-security-blog/2013/sep/30/cyber-gchq-defence> (accessed 13 August 2014).

31. Martin C. Libicki, *Cyberdeterrence and Cyberwar* (Santa Monica, CA: RAND, 2009). Richard J Harknett, John P Callaghan and Rudi Kauffman argue that cyberdeterrence is unachievable: "Leaving Deterrence Behind: War-Fighting and National Cybersecurity", *Journal of Homeland Security and Emergency Management*, Vol. 7, No. 1 (2010), pp. 1–24.

32. See, for example, Shashank Joshi's perspective in Norton-Taylor, *op. cit.*

hands with glee. Al-Qaeda is lapping it up ... and our own security has suffered as a consequence" of the Snowden leak.[34] In a reference to the contents of the Snowden leak, the head of MI5 has said:

> It causes enormous damage to make public the reach and limits of GCHQ techniques. Such information hands the advantage to the terrorists. It is the gift they need to evade us and strike at will. Unfashionable as it might seem, that is why we must keep secrets secret, and why not doing so causes such harm.[35]

Few would disagree that there are important and legitimate reasons to keep specific information and techniques belonging to the intelligence community secret. However, the real questions are just how far this veil of secrecy can and should apply in a parliamentary democracy. Balancing and rebalancing secrecy and transparency is a task the government and the intelligence services have carried out behind closed doors since long before the internet became a widespread feature of daily life.[36] Yet in an era when the speed, nature and pervasiveness of technological development is enabling the collection and public dissemination of great swathes of information in a way previously impossible, these types of issues once again come to the fore.

It is the step change in the underlying technology itself—plus the change in public attitudes and expectations it generates—which trigger the need for reassessment of the secrecy–transparency balance, not leaks. Separate from the security value or otherwise of their contents, leaks only keep up pressure for the right balance between secrecy and transparency to be seen to be achieved within the public domain. On this point, it is relevant to note that it has long been the practice of the heads of the three security services to make public appearances and speeches only rarely. However, recently they appeared before the first ever open evidence session of Parliament's Intelligence and Security Committee (ISC). This session took place five months after the Snowden leak; the ISC has been in operation for 20 years.[37] Moreover, at this session, at least one way in which a blanket policy of secrecy can actually harm the interests of the security services was acknowledged by the head of SIS.[38]

---

33. Intelligence and Security Committee, "Uncorrected Transcript", *op. cit.*, p. 17.

34. *Ibid.*, p. 18.

35. Address by the Director General of the Security Service, Andrew Parker, to the Royal United Services Institute (RUSI), Whitehall, 8 October 2013. Transcript available: <https://www.rusi.org/events/past/ref:E5254359BB8F44> (accessed 6 January 2015).

36. One example is the decision to put MI5, SIS and GCHQ on a statutory footing—with the effect of publicly confirming their existence for the first time—decades after they were created. The Security Service Act of 1989 recognised MI5 and the Intelligence Services Act of 1994 recognised SIS and GCHQ. Another example includes the decision in 1993 to publish for the first time the name and a photo of the Director General of MI5.

37. Intelligence and Security Committee of Parliament, "About the Committee", available: <http://isc.independent.gov.uk> (accessed 6 January 2015).

38. See Intelligence and Security Committee, "Uncorrected Transcript", *op. cit.*, p. 7, footnote 40, where, in response to questioning about reports of large payments to foreign prisoners "held under questionable circumstances", the head of SIS stated: " ... on many of these cases we had a strong defence to these allegations that were being made against us, but the court system did not allow us to make those defences". Such restriction has now been swept away by the Justice and Security Act of 2013.

As technological developments continue apace, it can be expected that the parameters of the veil of secrecy will come under increasing challenge, and the heads of the intelligence community will be called upon more frequently to appear in public in order to explain what can and cannot be transparent and why; to educate the public about the intelligence community, and to advocate in public on behalf of that community. While perhaps not the most comfortable fit for a sector that specialises in secrets, this sort of enhanced public engagement role should be viewed as an opportunity to dispel the myths and speculation that thrive in an information vacuum, to contribute to more informed public debates and to bolster the legitimacy and ongoing operation of these key state institutions—an important aspect of Ayoob's definition of security. Such an approach would also help to de-sensationalise those leaks that do occur from time to time and reinforce how and why they pose a security challenge.

Change and the Current International System

Both the SDSR and the NSS recognised the current "rules-based international system" as a valuable aspect of the strategic context in which the UK operates. The SDSR cited a commitment to the ongoing development of this system, including support for the evolution of "major multilateral institutions and instruments" which can contribute to a stronger system "and reflect the changing balance of global power".[39] The goal is elaborated by the NSS as follows:

> ... We should aim to reinforce existing international institutions such as the UN and the emerging ones such as the G20 so as to preserve the best of the rules-based international system. We will need to change too, both to adapt to and influence developments in the structures that support our security. Our relationship with the US is and will remain central but we must expect it to evolve. NATO will formulate and apply its new strategic concept; the EU's international role will develop; and the UN Security Council may be reformed. We will continue to play an active role in shaping international law and norms.[40]

What these documents reveal is an intractable tension in the government's view of world order and the UK's place within it. On the one hand, there is tacit acknowledgement that the "rules-based international system"—namely, the system as presently configured—confers substantial privileges and preferential status to the UK, reflecting the extent to which the UK helped to draft those rules in the first place. These include a permanent seat and veto power on the UN Security Council (UNSC), legal recognition of the UK's nuclear arsenal under the Nuclear Non-Proliferation Treaty, and longstanding membership of important global organisations such as NATO, the EU, the International Monetary Fund (IMF) and the World Bank, as well as the G7 and G20. For these reasons, it is very much within the UK's interest to preserve the system for as long as possible.

On the other hand, the documents also recognise that the global power structures forming the foundation of this particular international system are shifting, and

---

39. HM Government, "Securing Britain", *op. cit.*, pp. 11, 59.
40. HM Government, "A Strong Britain", *op. cit.*, p. 15.

thus, to accommodate this shift, *the* "rules-based international system" must evolve into *a* "rules-based international system" of a different sort. As the BRIC states (Brazil, Russia, India, China) and regional leaders such as Germany and Japan grow and become more globally powerful, it is expected that the UK will become relatively weaker, and demands for the UK to relinquish the privileges it enjoys under the current system will intensify over time. What final form a new international system will take remains very much an open question, and so this challenge is still emerging. The SDSR and NSS could not simply ignore these underlying global trends. Hence, the NSS acknowledges the possibility of change within the international system, even if, in reality, *any* change is likely to mean a reduction in the UK's standing and influence. By implication, such reduction threatens to drastically weaken the UK's capacity to act effectively in the emerging international political landscape, and thus meets Ayoob's threshold for a security challenge. It is likely that this challenge will continue to be an overriding one in the intermediate term.

Despite some lukewarm acknowledgement in the NSS of the potential for systemic reform, the government's focus since then has been on securing from the emerging powers wider and deeper acceptance of the status quo. An example can be found in the Foreign and Commonwealth Office's "Brazil and the Rules-Based International Economic System" research report of April 2014, which includes some interesting policy prescriptions:[41]

> We should work with like-minded actors in Brazil and global organisations to show that an even warmer embrace to global rules would be good for Brazil ... *We should use football as a platform to enhance Brazil's engagement in the Rules Based System* ... Our willingness to engage in global rules and compete on a level playing field is also one of our strengths. We should exploit this as Brazil organises two of the greatest sporting events in the world, and all eyes will be on transparent and fair rules to win the day.[42]

The report briefly acknowledges Brazil's desire for a role and inclusion within international rule-setting in order to serve the interests of developing countries, noting that "they will give and take, but will be frustrated if others do not give in return".[43] Apart from this, however, no further mention of reform of the international system is made.

Similarly, in response to recent international security concerns, the government has chosen rather strict adherence to the letter of international law and traditional political-diplomatic approaches within the existing international system, instead of innovation. For instance, as regards the Libya crisis of 2011, the UK was active early on in pushing for adoption of UNSC Resolution 1973, which authorised the creation of a no-fly zone over Libya and protecting civilians using measures short of a foreign occupation force.[44] Once this was in place, the UK, alongside other

---

41. Available: <https://www.gov.uk/government/publications/brazil-and-the-rules-based-international-economic-system-the-beautiful-but-long-game> (accessed 1 December 2014).

42. *Ibid.*, p. 3. Emphasis in original.

43. *Ibid.*, p. 2.

44. Remarks by the UK's representative to the United Nations, Mark Lyall Grant, on the adoption of UNSC Res 1973. In United Nations, "Security Council Approves 'No-Fly Zone' over Libya, Authorising

"Permanent Five" members France and the United States,[45] played a leading role in enforcing the Resolution's mandate. In his speech to the House of Commons immediately after UNSC Res 1973, the Prime Minister highlighted the UK's decision to act in terms of the UN and international law enforcement.[46] He reiterated this point in a subsequent speech, and described it as "the right way of doing things".[47]

An unswerving commitment to upholding international rules—even in circumstances where there is a strong moral obligation to act—is also evident in relation to the UK's approach to the ongoing civil war in Syria. After voting in the UNSC on six occasions over a 22-month period in favour of diverse actions against Syria—including the threat of sanctions, an Arab League-sponsored power handover process and the deployment of an observer mission[48]—the UK put forward a draft resolution in the UNSC authorising military force in August 2013. This followed a reported use of chemical weapons, allegedly by regime forces, the same month.[49] As anticipated, the draft resolution failed, due to Russia's opposition to any military action against Syria. Moreover, the government's subsequent motion in the House of Commons in support of a humanitarian intervention in Syria to save lives and deter further uses of chemical weapons—on condition that it was supported by evidence from UN weapons inspectors—was narrowly defeated by 13 votes.[50] Under British law, the government did not need a Commons vote in favour—or indeed any Commons vote at all—in order to proceed with the proposed humanitarian intervention. However, having taken the matter to a vote and losing, politically the government had little choice but to accept the outcome. Since then, the government has confirmed that "there will be no action in Syria without a Commons vote unless there is an urgent humanitarian need to do so".[51]

Again, with action via the international security system blocked by Russia's veto in relation to the Ukraine crisis, the UK and the rest of the EU have used conventional diplomatic means to express their displeasure, including financial sanctions,

'All Necessary Measures' to Protect Civilians, by Vote of 10 in Favour with 5 Abstentions" (7 March 2011), available: <http://www.un.org/press/en/2011/sc10200.doc.htm> (accessed 1 December 2014).

45. China and Russia both abstained from the vote on UNSC Res 1973: *Ibid*.

46. He stated: " ... The choice we have made is to play our part in joint international action to enforce international law: to uphold the will of the United Nations Security Council, to respond to the calls from Arab countries and the Arab League, and to do the right thing for the people of Libya who want greater freedoms, and above all for the UK's own national interest ... ". In "Libya: David Cameron Statement on UN Resolution", BBC News, 18 March 2011, available: <http://www.bbc.co.uk/news/uk-politics-12786225> (accessed 6 January 2015).

47. Andrew Black, "David Cameron: Libya Action in 'National Interest'", BBC News, 18 March 2011, available: <http://www.bbc.com/news/uk-scotland-12761264> (accessed 6 January 2015).

48. Due to vetoes from Russia and China, only three of these six occasions resulted in resolution: see UNSC Resolutions 2042, 2043, 2059 relating to the authorisation and subsequent extension of an observer mission.

49. "Syria Chemical Attack: What We Know", BBC News, 24 September 2013, available: <http://www.bbc.com/news/world-middle-east-23927399> (accessed 7 January 2015).

50. Debate in the House of Commons, 29 August 2013, available: <http://www.publications.parliament.uk/pa/cm201314/cmhansrd/cm130829/debtext/130829-0001.htm> (accessed 6 January 2015) and "Syria Crisis: Cameron Loses Commons Vote on Syria Action", BBC News, 30 August 2013, available: <http://www.bbc.com/news/uk-politics-23892783> (accessed 4 May 2015).

51. "Cameron: IS Threat May Require Syria Intervention", BBC News, 26 September 2014, available: <http://www.bbc.com/news/uk-politics-29366007> (accessed 2 December 2014).

travel bans, asset freezes and arms restrictions.[52] Confirming the government's policy of strict observation of international norms, the Prime Minister has also condemned Russia's actions as a "flagrant breach of international law" and has explained that "this matters to people in Britain because we depend on a world where countries obey the rules".[53]

Thus, although on paper and in speeches the government has acknowledged that changes in the underlying distribution of power among states may require reforms to those institutions supporting the international system[54], in practice, the UK's efforts have focused on shoring up support for the existing system. This is especially the case as regards conventional threats to international security, where the government has been scrupulous in following the rules of an international system which so enshrines the UK's global prominence and interests. Although the UK may go some way in convincing emerging states as to the merits of the current international system, they are unlikely to be fully persuaded, precisely because of the in-built protections and privileges that system offers certain states such as the UK. For this reason, the aspirations of the emerging powers as regards the structures of the international system are likely to continue in tension with the interests of the established powers for some time to come. Striking a balance between the growing demands of the emerging powers and the stabilising influence and longevity of the international system created in the image of the established powers will remain a key security challenge in relation to which the UK, as one of the most privileged states in the system, has an important contribution to make.

Inequality within the UK

Unlike the preceding two security challenges, inequality is not mentioned in either the SDSR or the NSS. Nonetheless, both vertical inequality (that is, the social and economic gap between individuals or households) and horizontal inequality (namely, the social and economic gap between different culturally defined groups)[55] have been relevant as drivers of insecurity within the UK, and this is unlikely to disappear, given the dramatic increase in income inequality since the 1980s.[56] If, as the official view maintains, security includes protection of the people "so that they can grow and prosper", and also concerns "the well-being of the United Kingdom as a whole", it is difficult to fathom how large gaps in

---

52. See UK Trade and Investment, "Doing Business in Russia and Ukraine: Sanctions Latest" (11 August 2014), available: <https://www.gov.uk/government/news/doing-business-in-russia-and-ukraine-sanctions-latest> (accessed 6 January 2015).

53. Prime Minister's Office, "EU Meeting on Ukraine: David Cameron's Speech" (6 March 2014), available: <https://www.gov.uk/government/speeches/eu-meeting-on-ukraine-david-camerons-speech> (accessed 6 January 2015).

54. For instance, William Hague's "networked world" speech: Foreign and Commonwealth Office, "Britain's Foreign Policy in a Networked World" (1 July 2010), available: <https://www.gov.uk/government/speeches/britain-s-foreign-policy-in-a-networked-world-2> (accessed 4 May 2015).

55. These definitions are taken from Frances Stewart, Graham Brown and Alex Cobham, "The Implications of Horizontal and Vertical Inequalities for Tax and Expenditure Policies" (Oxford: Centre for Research on Inequality, Human Security and Ethnicity, 2009), p. 3, available: <http://r4d.dfid.gov.uk/pdf/outputs/inequality/wp65.pdf> (accessed 6 January 2015).

56. The Equality Trust, "Income Inequality: Trends and Measures", *Equality Trust Research Digest*, Vol. 2 (2011), pp. 1–8, available: <https://www.equalitytrust.org.uk/sites/default/files/research-digest-trends-measures-final.pdf> (accessed 6 January 2015).

social and economic welfare within the population can be seen as anything other than security issues. While inequality in the UK *per se* may not yet meet Ayoob's threshold for a security challenge, its role as both (1) a catalyst for actions that threaten the survivability of the UK's boundaries and (2) a motivation for actions that undermine the legitimacy of the UK's governing elites and state institutions merits its inclusion here.

One does not have to go too far back in the past to find an example of how inequality has triggered major security problems for the UK. The ubiquity of anti-Catholic discrimination in Northern Ireland during the 1960s and 1970s and its role in prompting the creation of the Northern Ireland Civil Rights Association (NICRA) has been well documented elsewhere.[57] Inequality was rife in housing allocation, private and public sector recruitment, as well as political representation, and it was in response to such disadvantage that NICRA was formed and began to organise public demonstrations. An earlier group—the Campaign for Social Justice —had begun an awareness-raising drive, but this had not led to remedial action by the Stormont government. Stormont's ban on NICRA's 1968 demonstration in Derry, and the use of batons on those who sought to defy the ban, began a descent into conflict between the two communities, culminating in the 1969 deployment of British troops into Northern Ireland and the emergence of the Provisional IRA.[58] While an ethno-nationalist conflict was at the heart of "The Troubles", it was social and economic inequalities, as well as the decision by the Stormont government to ignore these and crack down on the demonstrators instead, which initially sparked the cycle of violence. Although the Good Friday Agreement of 1998 largely brought "The Troubles" to an end, a residual threat of Northern Ireland-related terrorism remains today.[59] While promoting equality of opportunity in the public sector was prioritised in the Good Friday Agreement, it is not inconceivable that if social and economic conditions deteriorate badly along community lines again, violence may return to Northern Ireland.

In addition, the UK has also seen how underlying conditions of inequality, plus a triggering event, can lead to violence. The London riots of August 2011, following the shooting of Mark Duggan by the police, is a clear example. The riots, which continued over five nights and in reality extended beyond London to Manchester and Liverpool, resulted in 5,112 individual crimes across 10 police force areas, 51% of which were committed against commercial premises, particularly electrical and clothing shops. Assaults, robberies and four murders in the London and West Midlands area also occurred.[60] Among 270 rioters interviewed as part of research

57. See, for example, David McKittrick *et al.*, *Making Sense of the Troubles* (Belfast: Blackstaff Press, 2000), who observed: "The political, legal and policing worlds were thus inextricably linked: one community governed, judged and policed the other' (p. 11). See also John Whyte, *Interpreting Northern Ireland* (Oxford: Clarendon Press, 1991), p. 64: "all authorities are agreed that discrimination still goes on. That fact alone is sufficient to embitter relations between the two communities"; and David Smith and Gerald Chambers, *Equality and Inequality in Northern Ireland* (London: Policy Studies Institute, 1987).

58. This section draws on material from the CAIN web service hosted by the University of Ulster. Available: http://cain.ulst.ac.uk/events/crights/sum.htm (accessed 6 January 2015).

59. As confirmed by the chief of MI5: Intelligence and Security Committee, "Uncorrected Transcript", *op. cit.*, p. 12.

60. See Home Office, "An Overview of Recorded Crimes and Arrests Resulting from Disorder Events in August 2011" (24 October 2011), available: <https://www.gov.uk/government/publications/an-overview-of-recorded-crimes-and-arrests-resulting-from-disorder-events-in-august-2011> (accessed 6 January 2015).

conducted by the London School of Economics (LSE), 86% identified poverty as an "important" or "very important" cause. This was closely followed by policing (85%), government policy (80%) and unemployment (79%).[61] Interestingly, by way of comparison, the shooting of Mark Duggan was identified by 75% of those rioters interviewed as an "important" or "very important" cause. Just over half of them tended to agree, or strongly agreed with the statement "I feel I am part of British society".[62] Just under half of those interviewed were students, and of the rest, 59% were unemployed.[63] The evidence collected by the LSE study also suggested that rioters were on the whole poorer than the rest of the UK, with many explaining their participation in looting in terms of opportunism: the breakdown in law and order sparked by the riots was seen as "an opportunity to acquire goods and luxury items [the interviewed rioters] could not ordinarily afford" — in other words, "a chance to obtain 'free stuff'".[64] Eighty-one per cent of the rioters interviewed believed that the riots will recur.

It has also been demonstrated how inequality within the UK can be mobilised as a political issue to motivate peaceful action which nevertheless threatens the survivability of the UK's existing boundaries. In the lead-up to the referendum on Scottish independence held in September 2014, pro-independence groups placed inequality concerns at the centre of their arguments. Hence, in February 2014, the Radical Independence Campaign (RIC) launched a new drive under the heading "Britain is for the Rich. Scotland Can Be Ours", which included a leaflet detailing 17 social and economic indicators in relation to which the UK performs comparatively worse than most other European or advanced states.[65] The indicators — which covered topics such as pay rates, fuel poverty, child poverty and child happiness — were collated from studies conducted by the Organisation for Economic Cooperation and Development (OECD), UNICEF, the House of Commons Library and the Office for National Statistics, among others. A recent RIC conference attracted more than 3,000 people.[66]

Inequality was not just the focal point of the left-wing pro-independence fringe; it also featured strongly as part of the more mainstream "Yes" campaign run by the Scottish government itself. After the desire to create a more democratic Scotland, the two other "overriding reasons" given in support of Scottish independence both referenced issues of inequality:

61. Simon Rogers, "Data Journalism Reading the Riots: What We Know. And What We Don't", *The Guardian*, 9 December 2011, available: <http://www.theguardian.com/news/datablog/2011/dec/09/data-journalism-reading-riots#zoomed-picture> (accessed 6 January 2015); and Alan Rusbridger and Judith Rees, "Reading the Riots" (2011), available: <http://eprints.lse.ac.uk/46297/1/Reading%20the%20riots (published).pdf> (accessed 6 January 2015).

62. The exact figure was 51% (Rogers, *op. cit.*). Rogers contrasts this figure with records from a citizenship survey conducted in 2008/2009 in which 92% of respondents agreed they felt part of British society.

63. Rusbridger and Rees, *op. cit.*, p. 4.

64. *Ibid.*, p. 5. The conclusion that the rioters interviewed came from poorer sections of Britain is backed up by analysis of court records and studies conducted by the Department of Education and Ministry of Justice (also at p. 5).

65. "New RIC Campaign: 'Britain is for the Rich. Scotland Can Be Ours'" (26 February 2014), available: <http://radicalindependence.org/2014/02/26/new-ric-campaign-britain-is-for-the-rich-scotland-can-be-ours/> (accessed 6 January 2015).

66. "Radical Independence Campaign Launches 'People's Vow'", BBC News, 22 November 2014, available: <http://www.bbc.com/news/uk-scotland-scotland-politics-30151363> (accessed 6 January 2015).

2. To Build a More Prosperous Country ...

... The ability to make our own decisions is the point of independence. It will provide the best conditions for sustainable economic growth, and enable us to protect living standards, reduce poverty and inequality, and build a better society.
3. To Become a Fairer Society
Within the UK, Scotland is part of an increasingly unequal society. The UK ranks 28th out of 34 nations in the OECD on a measure of overall inequality. OECD analysis shows that since 1975, income inequality among working-age people has increased faster in the UK than in any other country in the organisation. This is not the result of the policies of one government, but of almost 40 years of decisions at Westminster.
Seeking to become a more equal society is not just the right thing to do. It also makes sense for the economy. We know that the most equal societies also have the highest levels of wellbeing and are most prosperous. They are also, more often than not, nations like Scotland; the fairest and most successful countries in the world are independent European nations of similar size. We want the powers of independence so that we can build a different and better Scotland, where the many benefits of a rich and active society are cherished and where we work together to advance our nation as a whole. Progress under devolution has shown us what is possible, but it is not enough ... [67]

Further in, the document continued:

Under the Westminster system, Scotland is also locked in to one of the most unequal economic models in the developed world: since 1975 income inequality among working-age people has increased faster in the UK than in any other country in the OECD. The increasing geographical imbalance concentrates jobs, population growth and investment in London and the South East of England, but no action has been taken to address this by successive Westminster governments ...

... The gap between rich and poor, the increasing concentration of economic activity in one part of the UK and the imbalances in the structure and composition of the UK economic model all suggest that continuing as a regional economy will hamper job creation in Scotland and reduce economic resilience and security in the long term. The Scottish Government believes that Scotland needs to become independent to address these issues ... [68]

While the referendum returned a result against Scottish independence, both the closeness of the outcome (55.3% to 44.7%) and the pre-referendum promise of further powers for Scotland in the event of a "no" win have been interpreted by

---

67. Scottish Government, "Scotland's Future: Your Guide to an Independent Scotland. A Summary" (November 2013), available: <http://www.gov.scot/Publications/2013/11/8021/downloads> (accessed 6 January 2015), p. 14.
68. *Ibid.*, pp. 16–17.

various commentators as nonetheless signalling an end to the UK as known to date.[69] Moreover, polling data collected immediately after the referendum suggested that in the event of a "no" win, 61% of "yes" voters considered the question of Scotland's status to remain settled for only the next five to 10 years.[70] This, plus a surge in membership among the losing pro-independence parties in the wake of the referendum,[71] suggests that the referendum's outcome might be interpreted as a deferred rather than a final decision.

What these instances demonstrate is how social and economic disparities within the UK can and do feed into security problems. They show that inequality erodes societal cohesion and legitimacy internally. According to Ayoob, a state experiencing reduced and diminishing societal cohesion and legitimacy is more vulnerable, and therefore more insecure. In terms of Ayoob's political threshold for security threats,[72] the referendum on an independent Scotland in particular has highlighted the significance of inequality in ongoing debates which ultimately concern the survivability of the UK's boundaries—and therefore its security in the most narrow and traditional sense. This suggests that inequality is not just a relevant driver of insecurity in the developing world, where problems are many and the resources of governments and civil society groups to address them are most limited, but is also increasingly important as a domestic security issue in developed states.

Conclusion

In light of the anticipated defence and security review in 2015, this article has sought to provide a fresh reassessment of what is understood by "security", and to identify those issue-areas from which security challenges for the UK are likely to emerge over the lifetime of the next review. It started by comparing two different definitions of security. The first definition—the "official" view—was pieced together from government statements, and was demonstrated to be rather ambiguous and virtually all-inclusive. The second definition—outlined by Ayoob—was more precise, limiting security problems to those issues reaching a particular political threshold. Both definitions were applied to the challenges identified by the article in order to assess if and how they could be considered *security* challenges.

69. See Matthew Parris, "Whoever Wins This Vote, the Union is Dead", *The Times*, 13 September 2014, available: <http://www.thetimes.co.uk/tto/opinion/columnists/article4205276.ece> (accessed 6 January 2015); Jason Cowley, "A Shattered Union: The Final Days of the Scottish Referendum Campaign", *New Statesman*, 13 September 2014, available: <http://www.newstatesman.com/2014/09/shattered-union-final-days-scottish-referendum-campaign> (accessed 6 January 2015); Janan Ganesh, "The Union Lives On—But in its Present Design it May Well Be Dead", *The Financial Times*, 19 September 2014, available: <http://www.ft.com/intl/cms/s/2/1ee0eb08-3f3d-11e4-a861-00144feabdc0.html#axzz3KrHjThkD> (accessed 6 January 2015); and Editorial, "The Union is Broken. After Thursday, Britain Will Never Be the Same Again", *The Observer*, 13 September 2014, available: <http://www.theguardian.com/commentisfree/2014/sep/13/observer-view-scottish-referendum-union> (accessed 6 January 2015).

70. "Scottish Independence: Poll Reveals Who Voted, How and Why", *The Guardian*, 20 September 2014, available: <http://www.theguardian.com/politics/2014/sep/20/scottish-independence-lord-ashcroft-poll> (accessed 6 January 2015). 45% of 'yes' voters thought that the question should be settled for the next 5 years only, and 16% of 'yes' voters for the next 10 years.

71. See Mure Dickie, "Pro-Independence Parties See Membership Surge", *The Financial Times*, 21 September 2014, available: <http://www.ft.com/intl/cms/s/0/44179c94-41a1-11e4-b98f-00144feabdc0.html#axzz3KrHjThkD> (accessed 6 January 2015).

72. On this point, see the earlier discussion of Ayoob's work in the first section of this article.

The first issue-area identified was cyberspace, and it was argued that destructive attacks and government leaks posed serious security challenges, based on both definitions of security. As regards destructive attacks, it was not just their propensity for widespread damage of critical national infrastructure which made them a security challenge but also the fact that, thus far, they have provoked a response from the UK based on cyberdeterrence, a strategy that might actually intensify rather than reduce the problem. The value of leaked secret information was also found to pose a security challenge. The ability of leaks to draw attention to, and place pressure on, the balance between secrecy and transparency was also identified as an ongoing challenge for the workings and the aims of the intelligence community.

The way in which the power structures underpinning the international system are changing was another issue-area of concern in the context of British security. Once again, this issue satisfied the tests for a security challenge set down by both the government and Ayoob. While the UK has acknowledged the underlying factors pushing for changes to the international system, its actions so far have promoted and reinforced the status quo from which it benefits greatly. To the extent that the existing international security system fails to address pressing matters such as the civil war in Syria and the Ukraine crisis, the UK and other privileged powers will be under increasing pressure to find solutions beyond the strict letter of international law that alleviate the mass suffering of civilians.

The third issue-area identified as a source of security challenge was inequality within the UK. Although not mentioned in the 2010 SDSR or NSS, it was demonstrated how inequality fits within the government's subsequent statements on security. While inequality in the UK fell short of directly satisfying Ayoob's definition of a security problem, the three examples discussed—Northern Ireland in the 1960s and 1970s, the London riots of 2011 and the referendum on an independent Scotland in 2014—all showed how inequality has driven actions that challenge British security in Ayoob's sense. Given the political ramifications for the government of mentioning inequality within a domestic security context, it is likely that this issue will prove the most difficult to address. Nevertheless, as argued here, reducing inequality remains an extremely important goal, not just for ethical or economic reasons, but also on security grounds.

Disclosure statement

No potential conflict of interest was reported by the author.

Regionalism as an Instrument: Assessing Brazil's Relations with its Neighbourhood

ELENA LAZAROU and BRUNO THEODORO LUCIANO

This article aims to understand the basic characteristics of regionalism in Brazilian foreign policy. For this purpose, it goes over the recent history of Brazilian involvement in regional trade and security arrangements in South America. It also examines the manner in which economic uncertainties, brought about by the 2008–2009 global financial crisis, affected Brazilian foreign policy towards its region. Based on this historical analysis, it defines five key aspects that characterise Brazilian behaviour in the region, namely: post-democratisation regionalism; presidential regionalism; reactive regionalism; concentric/multilevel regionalism; and instrumental regionalism.

1. Introduction

Brazil's approach towards cooperation and integration in its neighbourhood is a challenging case for the study of regionalism in South America. In the post-Cold War era regionalism has become increasingly important for the Brazilian foreign policy agenda with the aim to consolidate Brazil's position in the region. Yet, in theory and practice, doubts arise about the nature of regional leadership that Brazil is willing and able to exercise, the motivation behind its regional project and, generally, the ideological and practical limitations to South American regionalism, particularly in the light of the most recent financial crisis.

With this in mind, this article uses a historical analysis of Brazilian involvement in regional trade and security arrangements in South America in order to derive conclusions regarding the nature of regionalism in contemporary Brazilian foreign policy. More specifically, it examines the period since the early 1990s, in which regionalism in South America has been pursued more consistently as part of wider processes of national, regional and global economic transformations.[1] It then proceeds to analyse the effects of major global and regional developments, particularly the 2008 financial crisis, on South American regionalism. It proposes that financial uncertainties, among other factors, have led to a retreat from security-oriented regional projects and to a focus on trade and development, particularly during the first three years of Dilma Rousseff's government (2011–2014). It concludes by deriving from the analysis five basic characteristics of the use of regionalism in contemporary Brazilian foreign policy and proposing that the latter serves

---

1. Laura Gomez Mera, "How 'New' is the 'New Regionalism' in the Americas? The Case of MERCO-SUR", *Journal of International Relations and Development*, Vol. 11 (2008), pp. 279–308.

more as an instrument (tool) to promote Brazil's global aspirations and preferences, rather than a norm-driven goal (end). This also explains the limited dynamics for the promotion of deeper integration in the region.

The historical analysis in the article roughly coincides with the administrations of three different Brazilian presidents: the Social Democratic Party's (PSDB) Fernando Henrique Cardoso (1995–2002), Luiz Inácio (Lula) da Silva (2003–2010) and the first years of current president Dilma Rousseff (2011–2014), both from the Workers Party (PT). Rather than compare approaches towards the region under different presidents, the aim of the article is to identify overarching trends in foreign policy towards the region in post-Cold War Brazil, and produce a list of defining characteristics of the use of regional integration in contemporary Brazilian foreign policy.

2. Brazil and South American Integration

Ideas regarding the integration of the South American sub-continent are not a novelty of the 1990s. In Latin American contemporary history attempts to integrate the region after the Second World War abound. The majority of those projects, such as the Secretariat of Central American Common Market (1960) and the Andean Pact (1969), were ideationally based on recommendations of the United Nations Economic Commission for Latin America and the Caribbean (CEPAL), and specifically its mentor Raúl Prebisch, who viewed regional integration as a path towards the region's autonomous development and industrialisation. During the same period, Brazilian foreign policy also articulated concerns about the region. Notably, in 1958, President Juscelino Kubitschek launched the Pan-American Operation (OPA), which demanded from the US government more assistance and funding for Latin American development within the international context of Cold War bipolarity. Both CEPAL and OPA would later influence the creation of the Latin American Free Trade Association (LAFTA) in 1960.[2]

LAFTA's failure to integrate the region, due to the heterogeneity of economic interests involved and to the economic recession of the 1980s, hindered any further substantive advance in regional cooperation. Only in the mid-1980s did the process of democratisation in Argentina and Brazil lead to rapprochement and ultimately to the signature of bilateral economic agreements between the two South American countries.[3]

During this period, the ideal of Latin American integration, incorporated in the Brazilian National Constitution of 1988, was replaced by a South American project, with a particular focus on fostering a special relationship with Argentina. This shift by the Brazilian Foreign Ministry (Itamaraty) was based on the belief that integration with South America, Brazil's immediate neighbourhood, served as a more useful concept of identity for national interests.[4] The strengthening of Mexico's ties with the United States through the North American Free Trade Agreement (NAFTA), and the strong US presence in Central America and the Caribbean, made Latin America a region far more difficult for Brazil to influence.

---

2. Amado Cervo and Clodoaldo Bueno, *História da Política Exterior* (Brasília: UnB, 2008).

3. Alcides Costa Vaz, *Cooperação, integração e processo negociador* (Brasilia: IBRI, 2002).

4. Matias Spektor, "Brazil: The Underlying Ideas of Regional Policies", in Daniel Flemes (ed.), *Regional Leadership in the Global System: Ideas, Interests and Strategies of Regional Powers* (Aldershot: Ashgate, 2010), pp. 191–204.

In 1991 Paraguay and Uruguay joined Argentina and Brazil in the creation of the Common Market of the South (MERCOSUR). According to the Treaty of Asunción, MERCOSUR's aim was to consolidate a Free Trade Area and a common Custom Union among member states, thus expressing the principles of open regionalism: regional trade liberalisation, as an instrument to enhance competitiveness in the international trade environment.

MERCOSUR was created with a loose institutional design and a significant inter-governmental character. Due to the strong presidential and executive-branch political traditions in member states, there was no intention to create any supranational institution that would limit member state sovereignty. Decision making remained with the representatives of national executives, particularly the ministries of foreign affairs and economy. This *inter-presidential* character has remained a standard feature in all Latin and South American regional projects henceforth.[5] The political impulse for integration would stem from the figures of the presidents themselves. However, concern regarding the need to internalise norms and decisions as well as to guarantee representative legitimacy led the member states to the creation of a parliamentary dimension for MERCOSUR. The Joint Parliamentary Commission, as it was named, was composed of members of the national congresses and was responsible for bringing the legislative bodies to the negotiation process, with consultation roles.[6]

The creation of MERCOSUR led to a significant increase in intra-regional trade. This was especially true of the period between 1991 and 1997,[7] when Brazilian exports to other MERCOSUR countries grew from US$2.3 billion to US$9 billion, while in the same period imports increased from US$2.2 billion to US$9.4 billion. However, the Argentinian crisis at the end of the twentieth century[8] caused a severe reversal of this trend: intra-MERCOSUR trade fell from US$18 billion in 1998 to US$8.9 billion in 2002, recovering 1998 levels only in 2005.[9] This economic setback, however, did not undermine the priority given to MERCOSUR by the Brazilian government under Fernando Henrique Cardoso (FHC). The joint negative position of the MERCOSUR countries regarding the US proposal of a Free Trade Area of the Americas (FTAA) was critical in empowering Brazil in the negotiations with the USA, which eventually were not concluded.

In this disadvantageous scenario, paradoxically, FHC's foreign policy sought to deepen cooperation and integration with South America.[10] Under the Brazilian initiative, the first South American Presidential Summit took place in Brasília in

5. Andrés Malamud, "Presidentialism and Mercosur: A Hidden Cause for a Successful Experience", in Laursen Finn (ed .), *Comparative Regional Integration: Theoretical Perspectives* (Aldershot: Ashgate, 2003), pp. 53–73.

6. Maria Claudia Drummond, "The Brazilian Parliamentary Delegation to MERCOSUR: Its Functions in the Brazilian National Congress", Paper presented at Joint IPSA-ECPR Conference, São Paulo, 16 February 2011.

7. Paulo Fagundes Vizentini, "De FHC a Lula: uma década de política externa (1995–2005)", *Civitas – Revista de Ciências Sociais*, Vol. 5, No. 2 (2005), pp. 381–397.

8. A macroeconomic crisis faced by Argentina during Fernando de la Rua's government (1999–2001). The dollarised currency was devaluated and debt default was declared. In the space of 12 days, the country had five presidents, causing economic and social instability.

9. Ministry of Industry, Trade and Development, "Estatísticas de Comércio Exterior", available: <http://mdic.gov.br//sitio/interna/interna.php?area=5&menu=2081> (accessed 26 September 2014).

10. Tullo Vigevani, Marcelo F. Oliveira and Rodrigo Cintra, "Política externa no período FHC: a busca de autonomia pela integração", *Tempo Social* (November 2003), pp. 31–61.

2000. The summit's agenda included trade liberalisation (e.g. the FTAA and demonstrated possibility of a MERCOSUR-based Andean Community Association), regional stability and security (inauguration of Plan Colombia). However, the main and concrete outcome of the Presidential Summit was in the area of infrastructure, with the launching of the Initiative for the Integration of the Regional Infrastructure of South America (IIRSA).

Alongside infrastructure, democratic stabilisation became another key aim of Brazil's promotion of regional integration. MERCOSUR's reaction to Paraguay's institutional crises in 1996, 1999 and 2001 is a good example of the aim to defend democratic government stabilisation in the region.[11] This principle was subsequently reproduced in the Ushuaia Protocol of 1998, which reaffirmed the commitment of member states to democracy. Brazil's own commitment to the principle was also demonstrated when both Cardoso and president-elect Lula da Silva had a significant influence on the stabilisation of Venezuela in 2002, after the *coup d'état* attempt against President Hugo Chávez by opposition forces.

To summarise, Brazil's policy towards its region under FHC reinforced the centrality of MERCOSUR and South America in Brazilian foreign affairs, thus building upon an approach that had been inaugurated by the Sarney government and maintained in Itamar Franco's government.

The assumption of the presidency by Lula da Silva (2003–2010) gave renewed vigour to the region as a priority. The very concept of regional integration was transformed and amplified, incorporating issues other and beyond trade, thus replacing the "(neo)liberal" notion of integration with a "progressive" approach. The latter emphasised the expansion of the scope to include social and citizenship concerns.[12] New elements of the regional vision under this approach would include the incorporation of representative channels to citizens, non-governmental organisations (NGOs) and sub-national actors (such as federal states, departments, provinces and municipalities), discussion on the democratic deficit of regional institutions, the reduction of economic and structural asymmetries among member states, the enhancement of a regional dispute resolution system and the constitution of a regional common identity. This approach to the region was adopted by the newly elected Brazilian Workers' Party (PT), and shared by ideologically aligned political parties of other MERCOSUR and South American countries.

Two initiatives must be highlighted in the evaluation of the Lula government's policy towards the region: the deepening of MERCOSUR and the development of the Union of South American Nations (UNASUR). In 2003 Presidents Lula da Silva and Kirchner, from Brazil and Argentina respectively, proposed the relaunch of MERCOSUR in what came to be known as the Buenos Aires Consensus. As mentioned above, this came after a period of deep economic crisis and stagnation from 1999 to 2001. In recognition of the need for a paradigmatic change, the two presidents inaugurated a new "progressive" agenda in regional and bilateral relations. In the following years, several additions were made to the MERCOSUR institutional framework. Among them were the Permanent Review Court in 2004,

---

11. President Juan Carlos Wasmosy suffered an attempted *coup d'état* in 1996. President Raúl Cubas Grau faced an impeachment process in 1999, leading to his resignation and exile in Brazil. His successor, President Macchi, also witnessed *coup d'état* and impeachment attempts, in 2000 and 2001 respectively.

12. Miriam Saraiva, "Procesos de integración de América del Sur y el papel de Brasil: los casos del Mercosur y la Unasur", *Revista CIDOB d'afersinternacionals*, No. 97–98 (April 2012), pp. 87–100.

the MERCOSUR Parliament (Parlasur) in 2006, the Consultative Forum of Municipalities, Federal States, Provinces and Departments of MERCOSUR (FCCR) in 2007, and the Fund for Structural Convergence of MERCOSUR (FOCEM) in 2005. These were established to guarantee the incorporation of social and political actors, of a common legal framework and of an asymmetries reduction programme to the regional mechanisms. FOCEM, which is supported by member state contributions—70% of which are from Brazil—to the structural development of the least developed ones, can also be seen as a first step towards Brazil becoming the paymaster of regional integration.[13]

These new institutions maintained the strong intergovernmental and inter-presidential nature of South American integration, while the representative institutions continued to have mere consultative competences, but were rarely consulted.[14]

Lula's approach towards the region was consistent with two key traditional principles of Brazilian foreign policy—autonomy and development—which are somewhat contradictory to visions of deep integration and to the pooling of sovereignty "à la EU".[15] The safeguarding of autonomy has fundamentally limited the inclusion of supranational elements in regional integration initiatives, reinforcing the executive and presidential character of this process. The historical concern about national development avoids dealing with inter-state asymmetries inasmuch as strong internal inequalities remain a priority on the national level and demand solutions. The equal budget contribution per country to the MERCOSUR Administrative Secretary, for example, has never taken into consideration the huge economic disparities among member states.[16]

Consistent with the above, trade is perceived as a tool towards national development. Under Lula, trade in South America was given high importance and MERCOSUR itself served as a tool for its achievement. Between 2003 and 2010 Brazilian trade in South America grew from US$121 billion to US$383 billion (with a slight decrease in 2008/2009 due to the financial crisis). It is important to note that Brazilian exports to the region are predominantly manufactured products (82% in 2012, according to the Industry Federation of São Paulo State—FIESP).[17]

The second notable regional initiative under the Lula administration was the creation of the post of General Sub-Secretary for South America in the Itamaraty and the establishment of a South American Community of Nations (SACN) in 2004,[18] renamed UNASUR with the Brasilia Declaration of 2008. UNASUR brought

---

13. Miriam Saraiva, "Brazilian Foreign Policy towards South America during the Lula Administration: Caught between South America and Mercosur", *Revista Brasileira de Política Internacional*, No. 53, Special Edition (2010), pp. 151–168.

14. Malamud, "Presidentialism and Mercosur", *op. cit.*

15. Marcelo P. Mariano and Haroldo Ramanzini Jr., "Uma Análise das Limitações Estruturais do Mercosul a partir das Posições da Política Externa Brasileira", Paper presented at the XXVIII Congresso Internacional da Associação de Estudos Latino-Americanos, Rio de Janeiro, 11–14 June 2009.

16. Samuel P. Guimarães, "Relatório ao Conselho de Ministros" (Montevideo: Mercosul, 2012).

17. Federação das Indústrias do Estado de São Paulo, *Proposta de Agenda de Integração Externa* (June 2013), available: <http://www.fiesp.com.br/indices-pesquisas-e-publicacoes/propostas-de-integracao-externa-da-industria>.

18. Danilo Marcondes Souza Neto, "A politica externa brasileira nos oito anos do governo Lula: Legados e lições para a inserção do Brasil no mundo", in Marilene de Paula (ed.), *Nunca antes na história desse país … ? Um balanço das Políticas do Governo Lula* (Rio de Janeiro: Heinrich BollStiftung, 2011), pp. 99–115.

together, for the first time, the 12 South American independent countries in a sub-continental regional intergovernmental organisation.

While further economic regional integration was a long-term goal of UNASUR, it did not replace previous economic integration projects on the continent. Rather, it focused on issues of regional security, stability, energy and infrastructure. Not least due to Brazilian aspirations, UNASUR also included a high instance of political dialogue on security and defence affairs, the South American Defence Council (SADC).[19] The SADC aimed to promote joint defence policies, joint training and exchanges of military personnel, and political coordination among South American ministries of defence.[20] In its first steps, the SADC dealt with the mediation of conflict between Colombia and Ecuador and the neutralisation of separatist movements in Bolivia.

According to Lima,[21] UNASUR represents a post-liberal regional integration model, based on social issues, productivity, energy and logistics integration. Institutionally, this is embodied by the Council of Infrastructure and Planning of UNASUR (COSIPLAN), which replaced IIRSA, the infrastructure initiative established prior to UNASUR.

Notably, UNASUR developed a strong external and interregional dimension as a potential space for development with other emerging regions. Examples include the creation of the Summit of South American–Arab countries (ASPA) and the Africa–South America Summit (ASA).[22] Both the dialogue format as well as the geographic focus of these summits was consistent with the aspirations of Lula's foreign policy: global powermanship through South–South relations and cooperation with other emerging and non-traditional partners/regions.[23]

A final significant novelty in Brazil's approach to the region during the 2000s—and arguably a claim to Brazilian regional leadership—is the presence of Brazilian public and private agencies in South America.

> As Brazil's cooperation with other countries from the region has grown, certain agencies, such as the Ministries of Health, Science &Technology and Education, have been more involved in formulating the country's international cooperation policy, while the Brazilian Development Bank, BNDES, has started lending more abroad.[24]

BNDES, among other national agencies, became an instrument for regional integration under the Lula administration through trade and physical infrastructure development. BNDES was crucial in supporting Brazilian investments abroad and in helping to diversify export markets in the region.[25] This phenomenon occurred simultaneously with the emergence of Brazil as an actor in international

---

19. Monica Hirst, Maria Regina Lima and Leticia Pinheiro, "A política externa brasileira em tempos de novos horizontes e desafios", Nueva Sociedad, Special Edition (December 2010), pp. 22–41.

20. *Ibid.*

21. Maria Regina Soares de Lima, "Tradição e inovação na política externa", *Working Paper 3* (Sao Paulo: Plataforma Democrática, 2010).

22. Souza Neto, *op. cit.*

23. Lima, "Tradição e inovação na política externa", *op. cit.*; Saraiva, *op. cit*; Souza Neto, *op. cit.*

24. Saraiva, "Brazilian Foreign Policy", *op. cit.*, p. 155.

25. Maria Regina Soares de Lima, "As Américas na Política Externa do Governo Lula", *Anuario Social y Político de América Latina y el Caribe*, No. 6, Nueva Sociedad, Caracas (2003), pp. 49–54.

cooperation for development—including in Latin America—labelled as South–South cooperation.

It could be argued that the progress made in political, defence and developmental issues has been as—if not more—relevant than regional trade developments in the past decade. While the MERCOSUR negotiations agenda has stalled since the conclusion of free trade agreements with South American countries, Brazilian diplomacy has had a fundamental role in the establishment of UNASUR and the SADC.

While rich in discursive aspirations, the new institutions created have maintained a loose institutional design, with little prospect of deeper integration. Thus, the model of regionalism adopted gives exclusive power to member state presidents. To what extent this is consistent with Brazil's vision of the region is a key question in understanding its approach to regionalism as well as its willingness to act as a regional leader and paymaster.[26]

Indeed, the issue of Brazilian leadership in the region became an issue of intense academic inquiry in the analysis of Brazilian foreign policy under Lula. Existing definitions of leadership refer to material and ideational resources, specific foreign policy interests and strategies, as well as the reaction of secondary powers and external powers as elements that define a state's potential to exercise leadership.[27] On this basis, it could be argued that Brazil holds the material and ideational resources to exercise such a role in the region.[28] Yet it has also been posited that the Brazilian perception of regional leadership diverges significantly from the classical power- and hegemony-based approaches and leans towards a vision of "consensual hegemony",[29] through the promotion of political dialogue and economic interactions. A final concern to be factored into the discussion on leadership is the reluctance of the country to shoulder the costs of leadership, including the deepening of regional integration, and to assume regional responsibilities while domestic social and economic challenges remained unresolved.[30]

3. Changes and Continuities in Brazil's Regional Policy after the 2008 Financial Crisis

The consequences of the global financial crisis of 2008 were not limited to the developed world. Although world media and opinion makers discussed the relatively weak effects of the crisis on emerging markets, global instability did affect and—in the shorter or longer term—interrupt the recent history of economic boom in Asian, African and Latin American countries in variable ways. Figure 1 illustrates the economic disturbance experienced by some South American countries during the crisis and its aftermath, as well as the differences in their recovery in the following years, compared to US and world GDP growth.

26. Lima, "Tradição e inovação na política externa", *op. cit.*

27. Daniel Flemes and Thorsten Wojczewski, "Contested Leadership in International Relations: Power Politics in South America, South Asia and Sub-Saharan Africa", GIGA Research Program: Power, Norms and Governance in International Relations, GIGA Working Paper No. 121, (2010).

28. *Idem.*

29. Sean W. Burges, "Consensual Hegemony: Theorizing Brazilian Foreign Policy after the Cold War", *International Relations*, Vol. 22 (2008), pp. 65–84.

30. Andrés Malamud, "A Leader without Followers? The Growing Divergence between the Regional and Global Performance of Brazilian Foreign Policy", *Latin American Politics and Society,* Vol. 53, No. 3 (2011), pp. 1–24.

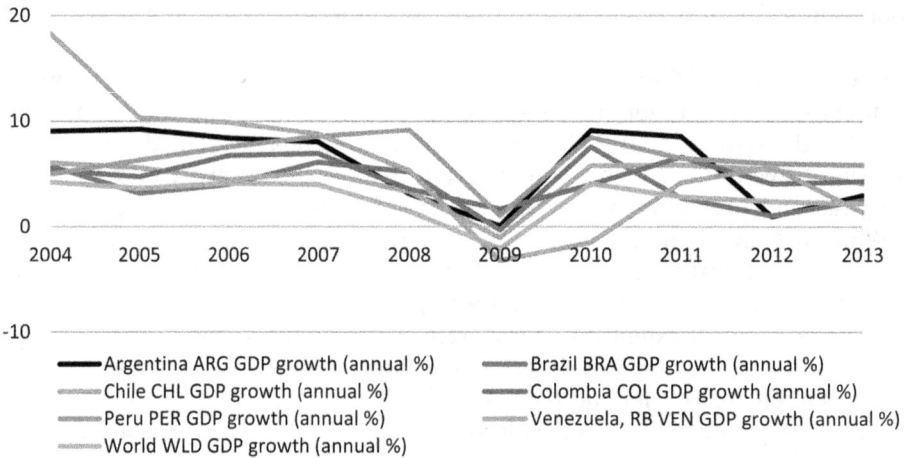

Figure 1. GDP Growth of Selected Countries (Annual %).
Source: World Bank. Available: <http://data.worldbank.org/indicator/NY.GDP.MKTP.KD.ZG/countries/1W-AR-CL-BR-PE-CO-VE?display=graph> (accessed 12 May 2014).

The rapid recovery experienced by Brazil and other emerging markets after the financial crisis, especially in 2010 (the last year of the Lula administration), stood in contrast to the harsh and slow recovery (boosted by several growth investment packages) of the USA and Northern Europe. Following an immediate GDP decline of 0.3% in 2009, Brazil grew by 7.5% in 2010, according to World Bank data.

Yet, as indicated above, during the following years, Brazilian economic growth slowed down to 2.7% and 0.9%, in 2011 and 2012 respectively, leading to strong doubts regarding the country's economic model and its inclusion in the group of rising economic powers. At the same time, the transition from President Lula to Dilma Rousseff gradually began to transform Brazil's profile in the international arena. In contrast to Lula's populist aura, Rousseff has been characterised as a more pragmatic and technical politician and one with less charisma.[31]

Nevertheless, foreign policy exhibited relative continuity during Rousseff's first years. The appointment of Antonio Patriota as Minister of Foreign Affairs and the maintenance of Marco Aurelio Garcia as Special Advisor to the Presidency indicated that the foundations of Lula's foreign policy would be preserved in Rousseff's administration.[32] Emphasis would be given to maintaining a strong Brazilian diplomatic presence worldwide, while, as some analysts were quick to point out, some topics dear to the new president—namely human rights protection and rapprochement with the United States—would be further cultivated.[33]

The post-crisis scenario and unfavourable international context, however, brought about new challenges and restrictions to the conduct of Brazilian foreign policy, particularly after the considerable national economic slowdown of 2012. As growth contracted, internal economic policies were prioritised in the new

---

31. Observatório dos Países de Língua Oficial Portuguesa, OPLOP, "Brasil: A Política Externa do Governo Dilma: Perspectivas E Pressões Iniciais", *Boletim OPLOP*, No. 8 (2011), p. 1.

32. *Ibid.*

33. BRICS Policy Center Monitor, "As Mudanças na Política Externa do Governo Dilma e a Multipolaridade Benigna" (Rio de Janeiro: BRICS Policy Center, May 2011).

administration.[34] While Lula and his Foreign Minister Celso Amorim's diplomacy had capitalised on the Brazilian economic and social successes to promote external activism, Rousseff and Patriota became increasingly focused on minimising the collateral damage from the economic crisis inside and outside Brazil.[35]

Within this context, the new administration remained committed to a strong Brazilian presence in the region. This was symbolically celebrated by the president's first official visit to Argentina. However, Dilma's foreign policy in the region gradually shifted back to trade and development issues rather than regional security ones which had gained ground in the Lula years. The effects of the financial crisis and the deadlock of the Doha round in the World Trade Organisation (WTO) boosted the pursuit of bilateral or bi-regional liberalisation agreements globally. Trade liberalisation was seen as a possible instrument for crisis recovery through more participation in international trade, led by the idea that "liberalisations at a time of external (but not internal) crisis can bring additional growth benefits by alleviating the constraints imposed by the crisis".[36]

Under the pressure of the Eurozone crisis, in 2010 the EU and MERCOSUR relaunched negotiations for an FTA, which had commenced in 1999 but had been interrupted since 2004. A bi-regional agreement gradually began to be favoured by the Brazilian industrial sector as a better option than isolation, as liberalisation expanded globally and Brazil began to feel "left out".

The creation of the Pacific Alliance, which brought together four Latin American Pacific countries—Mexico, Colombia, Peru and Chile—re-emphasised the importance of free trade and liberalisation principles in regional cooperation, in contrast to the "post-liberal" or "progressive" model of regional integration represented by MERCOSUR and UNASUR. The Alliance, still in its embryonic stage, advocates that regional trade liberalisation can serve as a platform for international insertion. Contrary to most MERCOSUR countries, which have exhibited low economic growth in recent years, its member states have grown above the world and Latin American average, as can be seen in Figure 1. The trend reversal became increasingly obvious regionally and globally:

> The most recent reaction to the ideological radicalisation of Latin American regionalism has come from the Pacific Arc, as Chile, Colombia, Peru and Mexico have signed a treaty that—once again—puts the economy first, as they vow to foster free trade.[37]

Finally, although geographically distant from the South American sub-continent, the negotiations of a Transatlantic Trade and Investment Partnership (TTIP)

34. Rubens Barbosa, "Política externa de dois governos", 8th Getulio Vargas Foundation Economy Forum (2011), available: <http://cemacro.fgv.br/sites/cemacro.fgv.br/files/Rubens%20Barbosa%20-%20Pol%C3%ADtica%20externa%20de%20dois%20governos.pdf > (accessed 14 May 2014).

35. Opera Mundi, "Em 'áreas de influência', Brasil reforça foco em integração e cooperação" (2013), available: <http://operamundi.uol.com.br/conteudo/noticias/26346/opera+mundi+faz+especial+sobre+diplomacia+de+dilma.shtml> (accessed 14 May 2014).

36. Rodney Falvey, Neil Foster and David Greenaway, "Trade Liberalisation, Economic Crises and Growth", Globalisation and Development Centre, *Working Paper 44* (2010), available: <http://epublications.bond.edu.au/gdc/44> (accessed 14 May 2014).

37. Andrés Malamud and Gianluca Gardini, "Has Regionalism Peaked? The Latin American Quagmire and Its Lessons", *The International Spectator: Italian Journal of International Affairs*, Vol. 47, No. 1 (2012), pp. 116–133, at p. 120.

between the United States and the European Union, launched in 2013, significantly affected the behaviour of the region's countries, which became threatened by the possibility of a substantial trade shift from South American states to the North–North relationship. In this sense, "a transatlantic deal would also inject a new dynamic into the world trading system that would likely change the way some large emerging markets look at trade liberalisation".[38]

Besides trade issues, infrastructure and development projects rather than grand strategies gained priority in Brazilian policy towards South America after 2010.[39] While Rousseff's foreign policy did not invest in regional security arrangements, Brazil did assume a pivotal role in the few but relevant crises that emerged with regards to the preservation of democracy in the region. During the deposition of Paraguayan president Fernando Lugo in 2012, Brazilian diplomacy pushed for a joint position of all South American presidents to condemn the coup through MERCOSUR and UNASUR, as well as to politically suspend Paraguay from both regional organisations.[40] The immediate reaction of South American leaders expressed solidarity, but also reinforced the strong regional commitment to the defence of democratic and institutional stability as incorporated in the Ushuaia II Protocol in MERCOSUR (2011) and reproduced as a UNASUR protocol.

During Paraguay's suspension, in 2012, MERCOSUR concluded the controversial approval of Venezuela as a fifth member, which had been pending the Paraguayan Senate's approval. Later in the same year, Bolivia signed an accession protocol, mapping its course towards becoming MERCOSUR's sixth full member, pending ratification from all member states. These two cases raise the question of whether MERCOSUR is moving towards a more Bolivarian, post-liberal and anti-hegemonic model of integration, or whether, following the demise of Hugo Chavez, the Bolivarian countries are gradually abandoning the ideals of the Bolivarian Alliance for the Peoples of our America (ALBA) for a Brazilian-led style of regional integration.

Brazil's regional activism in the same period included the support of the new-found Community of Latin American and Caribbean States (CELAC), inaugurated in 2010. CELAC brought together the Rio Group, created in 1986 to enhance dialogue among Latin American states, with the Latin American and Caribbean Summit (CALC). Support for CELAC coincided with support for a new kind of regionalism with the ability and flexibility not only to overcome some of the region's most enduring problems (poverty, intra-regional disputes), but also to develop a common voice for the continent in key areas, which would help achieve the region's goals and increase its international influence.[41] For example, as of 2013 CELAC became the main interlocutor between Latin America and extra-regional actors such as the European Union.

CELAC was conceived as the vehicle through which Latin America would express its positions on the main debates regarding the international community, and the norms and rules that govern it, as well as those regarding transnational challenges. It also reflected the consensus regarding the need for a new model of

---

38. Fredrik Erixon, "Transatlantic Free Trade: An Agenda for Jobs, Growth and Global Trade Leadership" (Brussels: Centre for European Studies, 2012).

39. Guilherme Casaoes, "Uma política externa à altura do Brasil", *Folha de Sao Paulo*, 9th September 2013.

40. Opera Mundi, *op. cit.*

41. Pedro Fagundes, "A América dos 33: a proposta de criação da Comunidade de Estados Latino-Americanos e Caribenhos (CELAC)", *Meridiano 47*, Vol. 47, No. 116 (2010), p. 1.

integration in the region, one that would link political cooperation with the preservation of sovereignty. This second phase of the regional integration process has been referred to as "post-liberal regionalism",[42] redirecting the main goals from economic integration and market liberalisation to political alignment and global projection.[43] This new type of regionalism points to a new set of functions, such as: building consensus; raising the number of players involved in the actions promoted; promoting flexible institutional goals, which allows the participation of a diverse set of players; democratising the decisions involving international public goods; and developing new webs of linkage on specific themes.[44]

In her speech during the CELAC launch summit, the Brazilian president described CELAC as the internal recognition of the geopolitical and strategic importance of the region. During a moment in which the West—broadly defined—had lost influence globally, Latin America gained space to create new agendas for regional integration: a post-liberal or post-hegemonic regionalism.[45] From this perspective CELAC could be seen as a product of the financial crisis. Yet enthusiasm for CELAC was short-lived and mostly concentrated on the period before a significant decline in growth began to preoccupy its members, and notably Brazil.

Foreign policy analysts have not reached a consensus regarding whether Rousseff's foreign policy has been a "strategic retreat" from grand international matters[46] or a normalisation of Brazilian diplomatic action following Lula's "point outside the curve" foreign policy.[47] Yet it can be argued with certainty that the region has remained a priority for Brazil ever since the beginning of the millennium. What has shifted since the financial crisis is the focus from security and high politics to trade and development issues. This fact, however, has reduced neither Brazil's activism in the preservation of regional democratic stability nor the rhetoric regarding a post-liberal model of regionalism, even though in practice such experiments have given way to the aforementioned economic and trade concerns.

4. A Typology of Brazilian Regionalism

The above analysis is useful in order to derive some general conclusions regarding the nature of regionalism that the Brazilian leadership has pursued in modern times and particularly during the country's so-called "emergence" as a power. Below, we propose that Brazilian regionalism can be characterised as: *post-democratisation regionalism; presidential regionalism; reactive regionalism; concentric and multilevel regionalism;* and last but not least, *instrumental regionalism.*

42. Pedro da Motta Veiga and Sandra Rios, "O regionalismo pós-liberal, na América do Sul: origens, iniciativas e dilemas", *Série Comércio Internacional*, No. 82 (July 2007), pp. 5–48.

43. Andrés Serbin, "Los nuevos escenarios de la regionalización: Déficit democrático y participación de la sociedad civil en el marco del regionalismo suramericano", *Serie Documentos CRIES*, No. 17 (Bogotá: CRIES, October 2011).

44. Grace Jaramillo, "El Doble Movimiento Sudamericano: Construcción Regional y Gobernanza Global", in Josette Altmann, Francisco Aravena and Tatiana Beirute (eds.), *América Latina y el Caribe: ¿Integrados o Marginados?* (Buenos Aires: FLACSO/CAF, Editorial Teseo, 2011), pp. 59–70.

45. Miriam Saraiva, "Novas abordagens para análise dos processos de integração na América do Sul: o caso brasileiro", *Carta Internacional*, Vol. 8, No. 1 (2013), pp. 3–21.

46. Oliver Stuenkel, "Recuo ou normalização na política externa brasileira?", *Folha de S. Paulo*, 18 April 2014.

47. Dawisson Lopes, "Recuo estratégico ou normalização da curva?", *Folha de S. Paulo*, 17 March 2014.

i. *Post-democratisation Regionalism*

As the creation of MERCOSUR exemplifies, the most substantial impulse for the Brazilian pursuit of regional integration emerged from a context of re-democratisation in the region and of Argentinean–Brazilian rapprochement under Presidents Alfonsín and Sarney. During the 1990s, Brazil strongly advocated that MERCOSUR should push for democratic stability in Paraguay. The Ushuaia Protocol, which established institutional mechanisms to deal with institutional ruptures in the region, was a product of this intent and illustrated that regional integration was not only about trade, but was also a tool for the democratic stabilisation of a region marked historically by political turmoil and military coups.

In the same spirit, UNASUR was shaped with a significant democracy and regional stabilisation dimension. Through MERCOSUR and UNASUR Brazil and its fellow member states assumed positions towards the political challenges faced by Ecuador and Paraguay that aimed at safeguarding democratic institutions. Brazilian participation (diplomatic and logistic) in the negotiations between the Colombian government and the Colombian Revolutionary Armed Forces (FARC) is further evidence of Brazilian concern with the democratic stabilisation of South America.

The consolidation of national democracies and regional stabilisation has, however, not been followed by a consistent development of a regional or supranational model of democratic governance. Under the first Lula administration there were efforts to promote a higher degree of institutionalisation of MERCOSUR, through the creation of a Court, a Parliament and social and sub-national channels. The creation of a South American Parliament, which would bring a democratic dimension to UNASUR, was also envisioned. Yet these new institutions never managed to assume more than a consultative and marginal role, without greater influence on the regional decision-making process. Rather, confined by the principle of sovereignty and reluctance towards the pooling of competencies, power remained concentrated on the national/governmental level and particularly in presidential hands.[48]

This is illustrative of the Brazilian view of regional integration, which emphasises post-democratisation discourse, despite leaving a lot to be desired in terms of the democratic nature of the regional model of governance and the development of institutions guaranteeing legitimacy and representation on the regional level.

ii. *Presidential Regionalism*

In a region where presidentialism remains extremely strong, it should come as no surprise that regional strategies remain—to a large extent—"personal projects" of individual leaders. Thus, regional integration acquires an inter-presidential character, a sort of exacerbated version of intergovernmentalism where the executive marks are centred in personal and ideological preferences of South American presidents.[49] As a result of this executive dominance, Latin American regionalism has maintained state-controlled institutions, alongside an intergovernmental structure with informal and loose institutional design on the regional level.

---

48. Malamud, "Presidentialism and Mercosur", *op. cit.*
49. *Ibid.*

From a Brazilian standpoint, some of the key traditional foreign policy principles, such as universalism and autonomy, have hindered further institutionalisation of regional integration. Potential moves towards more powerful institutions on the regional level, with possible supranational bodies, would reduce Brazilian room for manoeuvre, limiting the country's—and the president's—autonomy and national sovereignty.[50] These concepts, " ... rooted in state and society, come together for the construction of a vision of regional insertion that makes the deepening of MERCOSUR difficult".[51] Brazilian diplomacy exhibits a preference for regional processes formatted by a pragmatic and flexible design, which can accommodate presidential shifts of interest and scope, without the complications of regional institutional players with autonomous legislative or executive power.

At the same time, those same principles, as well as the presidential dominance in the external agenda, have prevented Brazil from openly assuming a leadership role in regional organisations. "Although Brazil's central location, size, share of population, and GDP make it the natural candidate for leadership in South America, the combination of reluctance on its part and suspicion on its neighbours' part has kept its potential from materializing."[52] The assumption of regional paymaster and leadership responsibilities would possibly come with a high internal political cost for the country's leader.

In general, national preferences to deepen (or not) regional projects are subjected to internal political dynamics. The presidential feature of South American integration does not necessarily exclude interactions with national elites and interest groups, public or private. If, as Andrew Moravcsik argues, regional integration is not only a product of intergovernmental bargain, but also a consequence of interactions among sub-national interest groups according to their specific preferences,[53] then what has been seen in the Brazilian case is that "there was an absence of strong pressure or demands for cooperation on the part of the elites and interest groups".[54] Sub-national interest groups are generally sceptical of regional integration and are not keen to pay the costs of regional leadership.[55] This reflects on the leadership's (president's) regional strategy, but also opens up space for the presidency to shape the Brazilian approach towards the region.[56]

iii. Reactive Regionalism

In various instances, regionalism has been perceived and used by Brazilian diplomats as a form to react against unfavourable or hegemonic outsider initiatives, especially those which came from US foreign policy in the region. This was consistent with the principle of autonomy in the post-democratisation period: "The idea of

50. Daniel Flemes, "A visão Brasileira da futura ordem global", *Contexto Internacional*, Vol. 32, No. 2 (2010), pp. 403–436.

51. Tullo Vigevani and Haroldo Ramanzini Júnior, "The Grounding of Regional Integration for Brazil: Universalism, Sovereignty and Elite Perception", *Global Society*, Vol. 25, No. 4, (2011), p. 449.

52. Malamud and Gardini, *op. cit.*, p. 128.

53. Andrew Moravcsik, "Preferences and Power in the European Community: A Liberal Intergovernmentalist Approach", *Journal of Common Market Studies*, 30th Anniversary Edition, Vol. 31, No. 4, (December 1993), pp. 473–524.

54. Vigevani and Ramanzini, *op. cit.*, p. 459.

55. Flemes, "A visão Brasileira da futura ordem global", *op. cit.*

56. For more on presidential diplomacy in Brazil, see Marco Vieira, "Ideias e Instituições: Uma Reflexão sobre a PEB do Início da década de 90", *Contexto Internacional*, Vol. 23, No. 2 (2001), pp. 245–293.

autonomy in the second half of the 1980s—and to this day, for part of the state and of society—meant autonomy in relation to the outside world, the capacity to make decisions in the face of the international centres of power".[57]

This reactive regionalism can be identified, for example, in the creation of MER-COSUR as an alternative to the conclusion of the US-led FTAA in the 1990s. The establishment of a South American free trade area hindered North American ambitions for expansive negotiation. The consolidated agreements of Brazil with Argentina, Paraguay and Uruguay, under the MERCOSUR framework, helped to attract the two smaller South American countries (which were initially more inclined to accept the US terms) to the Brazilian reactive position. In this sense, " ... regionalism is not only a goal in itself but also an instrument for exerting global influence and for 'soft-balancing' the United States".[58]

The creation of UNASUR and CELAC in the 2000s came as an additional confirmation of the regional aspiration to create political channels and institutions without a US presence, in material and ideological terms. UNASUR can also be interpreted as a reaction to the established perception of the US as a regional crisis manager, transferring this identity to the collective of South American states. Latin American regionalism on the other hand, as embodied by CELAC, is to be used to create political coalitions in order to counterbalance western powers, as well as to enhance South–South cooperation among Latin American countries and between those and other emerging regions. These new regional forums are vital as instruments for the political stabilisation of the region rather than paths to a deepened and integrated project:

> Brazil has not become indifferent to the region. However, its ambitions are increasingly defensive rather than offensive. The main goal is no longer to integrate South America into a regional bloc with a single voice but to limit damages that could spill over its borders or stain its international image as regional pacifier.[59]

iv. Concentric and Multilevel Regionalism

Brazilian foreign policy towards the region has expanded to various fronts during recent years, leading to the establishment of regional initiatives with different scopes and ranges, confirming that "in the Americas, Brazil [has] pursued an incremental strategy of expanding its weight, creating different circles step by step".[60] This concentric and multilevel regional approach began with the bilateral dialogues with Argentina, and was followed by the creation of the trade-based block, MER-COSUR, in the 1990s. UNASUR followed in 2008, as a South American project focused on infrastructure, energy and security cooperation. Finally, CELAC (2010) added a comprehensive umbrella both in terms of membership and scope, by including all Latin American states and aiming to achieve coordination on the discursive and political level, albeit with uncertain results and impact. This

---

[57] Vigevani and Ramanzini, *op. cit.*, p. 451.

58. Susanne Gratius and Miriam Saraiva, "Continental Regionalism: Brazil's Prominent Role in the Americas", *CEPS Working Document 374* (February 2013), p. 1.

59. Malamud, "A Leader without Followers?", *op. cit.*, p. 19.

60. Gratius and Saraiva, *op. cit.*, p. 3.

diverging set of regional organisations, in which Brazil not only belongs but also assumes an agenda-setting voice, testifies to the fact that "conscious or not, Brazil's regional policy follows a structure of concentric circles".[61] Brazil has sponsored all these regional initiatives, and has arguably exercised a leadership role, if not continuously then at least in the facilitation of their creation and establishment (see Figure 2).

As discussed previously, a common trait in all these regional projects is their thin and loose institutional design, which allows for flexible political arrangements. While the older and smaller outfit, MERCOSUR, consists of a relatively more complex institutional structure, and a deeper and more binding commitment to integration—namely on the trade level—others, newly founded and wider, such as CELAC and UNASUR, present few formal and binding agreements among members. This would suggest that as the circle widens, so does the purpose of regionalism shift from a more neoliberal, trade and economics-based approach, to the post-liberal, ideologically oriented approach, with a stronger presidential character and reduced space for evolved regional institutions.

Yet no one dimension replaces the other, as each one of these regional projects has different aims and purposes, based on the particular group of states that it comprises. Consequently, this multilevel regionalism works in a complimentary manner, combining economic integration/trade arrangements with political cooperation, on the basis of specific interests from the sub-regions (or geopolitical circles) involved. While MERCOSUR acts as a sub-regional economic and commercial anchor, South America (as in UNASUR) "is a label for political stabilisation and cohesion and CELAC is designed as a forum (or future organisation) for regional influence and autonomy from the United States and, in political terms, a declining inter-American system based on the [Organisation of American States] OAS".[62]

The main argument against the concentric model is that it adds to the multiplicity of regional arrangements in the region to create a potential cacophony of voices rather than project a regional stance. Adding other organisations from the region (ALBA, Andean Community, Pacific Alliance, Central American Integration System, NAFTA) to the aforementioned suggests that there exists an overlap of regional arrangements, which often can cause conflicts of norms and objectives, while overshadowing and hindering the development of less numerous but deeper and more substantive integration projects. Malamud and Gardini refer to this as a peak in Latin American regionalism, which has led to empty regionalism.[63] The regional fragmentation in sub-regional or ideological coalitions as well as the focus on extra-regional actors (especially from the Asia-Pacific) are, arguably, the new trends in Latin America.

v. *Instrumental Regionalism*

Ultimately, regionalism for Brazil is "a means to an end" rather than "an end to itself". Within the region, it is a tool for guaranteeing regional stability and cooperation; outside the region, it serves as an instrument for international

---

61. *Ibid.*, p. 8.
62. *Ibid.*, p. 10.
63. Malamud and Gardini, *op. cit.*

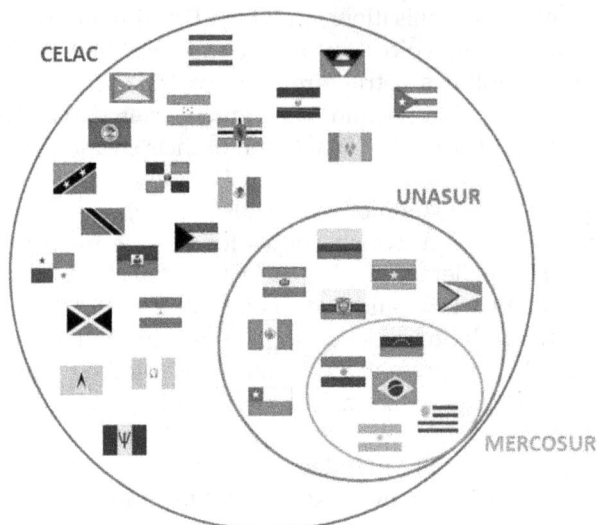

Figure 2. Concentric Circles of Latin American Integration.
Source: The authors' work, based on Susanne Gratius and Miriam Saraiva, "Continental Regionalism: Brazil's Prominent Role in the Americas", CEPS Working Document 374 (February 2013).

recognition as a regional leader, which boosts Brazil's status as an emerging power. This was particularly true of the Lula administration, whereupon " ... regional integration was considered necessary to attain regional and international credibility".[64] From the Brazilian perspective, both initiatives are complementary. Stronger ties with South American states are constructed by diplomats and policy makers, in part as a strategy to reinforce Brazilian leadership potential.[65] Yet this has created some contention in the region as "Brazil's global projection has been observed with some unease. It has not been regarded as beneficial for the region, but simply as a means for Brazil to pursue its own individual goals".[66]

A second instrumental function of regionalism for Brazil, as previously mentioned, has been as a tool for reaction towards outsider initiatives. It has served to resist the FTAA and the negotiations with the EU. "It is useful for a part of the relations with the United States; it is important in relations with the EU; it has partial importance in the case of the WTO and in some negotiations with emerging countries, particularly in cases of bloc-to-bloc dialogue."[67] For Brazil, regional cooperation is an instrument for the exertion of global influence but more importantly for balancing power—particularly vis-à-vis the United States. It is intrinsically linked to its emerging power strategy.

With regard to international security issues, South American forums have been used by Brazilian diplomats as an instrument to avoid the voicing of unilateral controversial or problematic positions. Syria, Israel and Palestine, and the Korean peninsula all produced comprehensive and soft declarations from the UNASUR

---

64. Vigevani and Ramanzini, *op. cit.*, p. 461.
65. Saraiva, "Novas abordagens", *op. cit.*
66. Gratius and Saraiva, *op. cit.*, p. 2.
67. Vigevani and Ramanzini, *op. cit.*, p. 465.

and MERCOSUR Presidential Summits.[68] For Brazil, these regional declarations served to reduce the necessity to "take sides" or be critiqued for lack of a concrete position, particularly in cases where a sole strong position might potentially injure a particular diplomatic principle or a partnership—economic or otherwise.

Other regional security initiatives, such as the SADC and the Brazilian military command of the UN Peace Operations in Haiti, have been discursively used to reinforce the Brazilian goal of attaining a permanent seat in a reformed United Nations Security Council. In this case, regional activism has helped to justify Brazilian global aspirations.

It is worth noting, however, that Brazil's global presence is in no way anchored to regional approval. In climate change and in the United Nations Security Council reform negotiations, Brazil has decoupled from concerted regional positions to sponsor individual postures, more proactive and engaged than Latin or South American ones. Brazilian proposals to the UN, such as the concept of "Responsibility while Protecting", are in the first instance launched globally, and only afterwards discussed with its neighbours.[69]

The same detachment from the region is true of Brazil's participation in forums such as the BRICS (Brazil, Russia, India, China, South Africa) and the G20: "International forums of emerging countries, such as the BRICS or IBSA [India, Brazil, South Africa], are restricted to individual countries not regions, and Brazil participates as such and not as a representative of Latin America".[70] Hence, Latin American regionalism is only one side of Brazilian international projection. Although it has been argued that South–South cooperation should be based "on a more conscious engagement with their regional partners",[71] this lack of a clear regional leadership role has not hindered the country in promoting itself internationally, and in being perceived by extra-regional actors as a regional leader, even without assuming greater costs and responsibilities within the region. Here it is worth noting that Brazil invited all South American states to participate in the last day of the VII BRICS Summit, which took place in Brazil in 2014. This action may be viewed as instrumentalisation of regionalism, as through it, Brazil manages to project an image of regional leader to other emerging powers.[72]

Under Rousseff the instrumentalisation of regional foreign policy for global aspirations has become a secondary issue, with the exception of the BRICS Summit. The unfavourable economic context has reinforced a pragmatic

68. UNASUR declaration on Syria, available: <http://www.itamaraty.gov.br/sala-de-imprensa/notas-a-imprensa/declaracao-do-conselho-de-chefes-de-estado-e-de-governo-da-unasul-sobre-a-situacao-na-republica-arabe-da-siria>; UNASUR declaration on Korean peninsula, available: <http://sedici.unlp.edu.ar/bitstream/handle/10915/44524/UNASUR_-_Declaraci%C3%B3n_de_la_UNASUR_sobre_la_situaci%C3%B3n_en_la_pen%C3%ADnsula_de_Corea__2_p._.pdf?sequence=67>; MERCOSUR declarations on Middle East situation, available: <http://www.mercosur.int/innovaportal/file/4506/1/cmc_2003_acta01-ex_declaracion_es_orientemedio.pdf>, <http://www.mercosur.int/innovaportal/file/4506/1/cmc_2006_acta01_declaracion_es_sitmediooriente.pdf> (accessed 10 July 2014).

69. Oliver Stuenkel and Marcos Tourinho, "Regulating Intervention: Brazil and the Responsibility to Protect", *Conflict, Security & Development* (2014), pp. 379–402.

70. Malamud and Gardini, *op. cit.*, p. 129.

71. Marco Vieira and Chris Alden, "India, Brazil, and South Africa (IBSA): South-South Cooperation and the Paradox of Regional Leadership", *Global Governance*, Vol. 17, No. 4 (2011), pp. 507–528.

72. Oliver Stuenkel, "BRICS Summit is Chance to Strengthen Brazil's Global and Regional Ties", available: <http://www.postwesternworld.com/2014/06/11/strengthen-brazils-regional/> (accessed 7 July 2014).

reorientation of Brazilian priorities, more focused on trade and development issues, rather than global projection and political coordination in the region. As summarised by Gratius and Saraiva:

> Lula's enthusiasm and proactive engagement for regional cooperation in a context of a booming economy and ideological affinities with the Latin American left has been replaced, under Dilma Rousseff, by a calculated mixed strategy of preserving self-interests and assuming a cautious leadership role in a less favourable economic environment.[73]

5. Conclusion

This article has covered the history of Brazil's involvement in regional cooperation/ integration initiatives in Latin America since the 1990s. It has focused particularly on the position assumed by Brazil under Presidents Cardoso, Lula and Rousseff, on the balance between trade and security-oriented visions of regional integration and on the impact of external factors, such as the 2008 global financial crisis, on Brazil's vision of the region. Based on this analysis, the article has identified five qualities of Brazilian regionalism. While oscillating between a preference for trade, political and security integration, Brazil, often influenced by the international and domestic economic environment, has consistently maintained a preference for a multilevel/ concentric model of regional organisation that is committed to democratic stability in the region, reactive to external forces of imposition, and presidential in its leadership. Finally and most importantly, Brazil has consistently used regionalism as a tool for the attainment of goals in and beyond the region, thus instrumentalising its relations with its neighbours.

As has been pointed out, Brazilians can enjoy power, prestige and influence in international relations without assuming a role of regional leader.[74] The region can serve as a platform for Brazilian international empowerment, yet the regional institutional layer cannot tighten Brazilian external choices. This explains why in Brazilian foreign policy "there is no clear specificity to the integration; it is not an end in itself".[75] By historically tracing the developments in Brazil's approach towards the region from the 1990s to today, this article has illustrated the rationale and practice of this intrumentalisation of regionalism, as well as its continuity in contemporary Brazilian foreign policy.

These observations help to qualify Brazil's relations with its region, which has become a quintessential priority of its foreign policy since the 1990s, but also to understand the continuity that has been maintained in this area of foreign policy. The typology developed may also enrich the ongoing academic discussion regarding Brazil's reluctance to assume the costs of regional leadership. Finally, it contributes to the (so far) limited analyses of the link between the global financial crisis and the approach of the Rousseff government towards the region.

---

73. Gratius and Saraiva, *op. cit.*, p. 10.
74. Matias Spektor, "Ideias de ativismo regional: a transformação das leituras brasileiras da região", *Revista Brasileira de Política Internacional*, Vol. 53, No. 1 (2010), pp. 25–44.
75. *Ibid.*, p. 454.

Acknowledgements

The authors thank Brian Malczyk (University of Toronto) for proofreading.

Disclosure statement

No potential conflict of interest was reported by the authors.

Funding

The research that went into this article was supported by the Brazilian National Council for Research (CNPq) [grant number 483426/2012-1].

Europe's British Question: The UK–EU Relationship in a Changing Europe and Multipolar World

TIM OLIVER

Britain's often uneasy relationship with the European Union has become increasingly strained, leading to speculation that Britain is—sooner or later—headed towards an in-out referendum that will result in its withdrawal. Such a development would present both Britain and the EU with unprecedented challenges. Britain's debate about its future in the EU—its "European question"—creates a "British question" for the EU, the answers to which could change the EU's unity, leadership, prosperity and security with implications for wider European politics and academic analysis of European integration. This article sets out the links between these two questions. It does so by considering what the future of UK–EU relations could mean for the regional politics of Europe in an emerging multipolar order.

Introduction

Britain has rarely played a smooth part in European integration, earning the description of "an awkward partner".[1] Some in the rest of the European Union could be forgiven for thinking that in recent years Britain has gone further, becoming a dysfunctional and destructive partner. Not a day seems to pass without Britain's domestic politics causing problems for the rest of the EU. The relationship now seems characterised by vetoes, rows, allegations of blackmail, of Britain gambling with its future, and where even a British Foreign Secretary can declare that Britain is "lighting a fire" under the EU.[2] Some of these problems stem from tensions within the Conservative Party. Yet the "European question" in British politics is not simply about the problems of one political party. Whatever the outcome of the UK's 2015 general election, the issue of Britain's EU membership looks set to remain a topic of often fraught political debate.[3] All three of the UK's main

---

1. Stephen George, *An Awkward Partner: Britain in the European Community* (Oxford: Oxford University Press, 1998).

2. See Matthias Matthijs, "David Cameron's Dangerous Game: The Folly of Flirting with an EU Exit", *Foreign Affairs*, Vol. 92 (2013), pp. 10–16; "David Cameron Blocks EU-Wide Deal to Tackle Euro Crisis", BBC News (9 December 2011), available: <http://www.bbc.co.uk/news/uk-16104275> (accessed 11 November 2014); Matthew Holehouse, "Britain is 'Lighting a Fire under the EU' Says Philip Hammond", *Daily Telegraph*, 17 October 2014, available: <http://www.telegraph.co.uk/news/politics/david-cameron/11169431/Britain-is-lighting-a-fire-under-the-European-Union-says-Philip-Hammond.html> (accessed 11 November 2014).

3. See Tim Oliver, "Will the UK's General Election Lead to an In-Out Referendum?", E!Sharp (March 2015), available: <http://esharp.eu/essay/37-will-the-uk-s-general-election-lead-to-an-in-out-referendum/>

parties are committed to holding an in-out referendum, albeit under different circumstances, with Labour and the Liberal Democrats prepared to hold an in-out referendum in the event of any new EU treaty or significant transfer of new powers.[4] That the Eurosceptic UK Independence Party (UKIP) has emerged as a political force in part explains why this has happened. But we should not overlook the internal—and in the case of Scotland's vote on independence, existential—problems the UK is going through, which have knock-on effects for the rest of Europe.[5] While a British exit (also known as a "Brexit") is not inevitable or as likely as might appear if one focuses on the UK's press coverage of EU matters, the UK's ongoing difficult relations with the rest of the EU mean that it looks set to remain an awkward partner. Even if the government elected in 2015 is not directly committed to holding a referendum, the idea and possibility will continue to hang over UK–EU relations.

So far Britain's behaviour has provoked only a few direct calls for it to leave the EU.[6] This is in part because politicians of other member states have tried to avoid involving themselves in a topic that could influence the UK's 2015 general election. However, it is also because the idea of any member state either quitting or being forced out of the EU is a taboo. Either would be an unprecedented and potentially traumatic development. Despite this, there is limited analysis of the potential implications for the EU of a withdrawal by Britain or any other member state. This compares with the plethora of books, reports, articles and speeches on what a Brexit could mean for the UK.[7] The growing possibility of a British exit, and the possibility of a Greek exit from the Eurozone (known as a "Grexit"), has led to some publications, but these remain small in number.[8] The academic, especially theoretical literature is little better. The vast literature on Europeanisation

(accessed 12 May 2015); and Mark Leonard, "The British Problem and What it Means for Europe" (London: ECFR, March 2015), available: <http://www.ecfr.eu/page/-/ECFR_128_BREXIT_%28March_-_final%29.pdf> (accessed 12 May 2015).

4. See David Cameron, "The Future of the EU and the UK's Relationship With It'", Speech, London, 23 January 2013, available: <https://www.gov.uk/government/speeches/eu-speech-at-bloomberg> (accessed 11 November 2014); *Conservative Party Manifesto 2015* (London: Conservative Party, 2015), p. 72; *Liberal Democrat Manifesto 2015* (London: Liberal Democrats, 2015), p. 149; *Labour Party Manifesto 2015* (London: Labour Party, 2015), p. 77.

5. Tim Oliver, "Scotland: Out of the UK and Into the EU? Part I - Views on Scottish Independence from Seven Member States", *IP Journal* (August 2014), available: <https://ip-journal.dgap.org/en/ip-journal/topics/scotland-out-uk-and-eu-part-i> (accessed 11 November 2014).

6. Michel Rocard, "A French Message to Britain: Get out of Europe before You Wreck It", *The Guardian*, 6 June 2014, available: <http://www.theguardian.com/commentisfree/2014/jun/06/french-message-britain-get-out-european-union> (accessed 11 November 2014).

7. A small sample of the large literature on what a Brexit could mean for the UK would include Stephen Booth and Christopher Howarth, "Trading Places: Is EU Membership Still the Best Option for UK Trade?" Open Europe (June 2012), available: <http://openeurope.org.uk/intelligence/britain-and-the-eu/eu-membership/> (accessed 12 May 2015); or the winner of the Institute of Economic Affairs (IEA)'s €100,000 "Brexit Prize", Iain Mansfield, "A Blueprint for Britain: Openness Not Isolation (London: IEA, July 2013); or David Charter, *Au Revoir Europe: What if Britain Left the EU?* (London: Biteback, 2012).

8. See Tim Oliver, "Europe without Britain: Assessing the Impact on the EU of a British Withdrawal", *Stiftung Wissenschaft und Politik (SWP) Research Paper 2013/RP 07* (September 2013), available: <http://www.swp-berlin.org/en/publications/swp-research-papers/swp-research-paper-detail/article/europe_without_britain.html> (accessed 8 April 2014); Adam Lazowski, "'Darling You Are Not Going Anywhere': The Right to Exit in EU Law", *European Law Review*, Vol. 40 (2015) (in press); "Heading for a Brexit?", *RUSI Journal*, Vol. 158, No. 4 (August 2013), p. 19.

includes only a few pieces that explore ideas and theories of European disintegration.[9] The field remains dominated by top-down theories of Europeanisation that assume continued integration. Much less research addresses how domestic politics—not least a decision by a member state to withdraw—could affect EU-level politics and the wider geopolitics of Europe.[10]

This lack of debate or analysis does not mean that a Brexit or some form of exclusion is not contemplated elsewhere in the EU.[11] But as can be seen in any review of how other EU member states view the UK–EU relationship, the question of what to do about Britain has to be seen in the wider context of an EU facing significant and potentially existential challenges ranging from the survival of the Eurozone through to the security of Eastern Europe vis-à-vis an increasingly assertive Russia. The "British question" can appear something of a distraction, one which the rest of the EU might see little incentive to agonise over. This is especially so given that Britain is not a member of the Eurozone, and seems determined to isolate itself.

Understandable though such feelings are, the "British question" is connected to broader questions about the future direction of European integration and European regional politics. Even if Britain is a declining power within the EU, thanks to a growing population it is to some extent a growing power in a wider European sense. A British withdrawal from the EU would also change the EU and European politics, adding to already transformative changes unleashed by the Eurozone's struggles. Much to the disappointment of British Eurosceptics, the EU will not disappear from British politics should it withdraw. In much the same way, "British-sceptics" in the EU will be disappointed to find that what happens in British politics will continue to matter more than they might like for the rest of Europe and the EU.

To explore how Britain's domestic debate could potentially change the path of European integration, the article examines five aspects of UK–EU relations. First, it briefly outlines some ideas and theories of European disintegration that we will return to when discussing the potential impact of a Brexit. The article then examines what Britain's "European question" is and how it shapes Britain's behaviour in Europe. The article then moves onto the "British question" facing the rest of the EU by looking at how the EU could be changed by Britain's behaviour. This opens up discussion of what the ramifications of a Brexit could be for the EU and Europe. Finally, the article turns to the wider question of the British and European security relationship in an emerging multipolar world. In analysing

---

9. See Douglas Webber, "How Likely Is It That the European Union Will Disintegrate? A Critical Analysis of Competing Theoretical Perspectives", *European Journal of International Relations*, Vol. 20, No. 2 (2014), pp. 341–36; and Hans Vollaard, "Explaining European Disintegration", *Journal of Common Market Studies*, Vol. 52, No. 5 (September 2014), pp. 1142–1159.

10. For analysis of how domestic politics can affect EU-level politics, see Simon Bulmer and Christian Lequesne, *The Member States of the European Union* (Oxford: Oxford University Press, 2012), and some discussion in Nathaniel Copsey and Tim Haughton, "Farewell Britannia? 'Issue Capture' and the Politics of Cameron's EU Referendum Pledge", *Journal of Common Market Studies*, Vol. 52, Special Supplement 1 (2014), pp. 74–89. For an analysis of how Britain has been shaped by and shaped in return the politics of the EU, see Ian Bache and Andrew Jordan (eds.), *The Europeanisation of British Politics* (Basingstoke: Palgrave Macmillan, 2006).

11. For a review of how other member states view the future of UK–EU relations, see Almut Möller and Tim Oliver (eds.), *The United Kingdom and the European Union: What Would a Brexit Mean for the EU and Other States around the World?* (Berlin: DGAP, 2014).

these issues the article draws not only on the aforementioned academic literature on Europeanisation but also the small number of reports on what a Brexit could mean for the EU. A great deal of the latter is speculative, this topic remaining an under-explored area even in the think tank community. One aim of the article therefore is to provide a synthesis of the literature that allows us to map out some of the potential scenarios for how UK–EU relations may develop.

Ideas of European Disintegration

There have been few academic attempts to analyse the way in which the EU could change direction, either disintegrating or fragmenting. In one of the few pieces of work on this topic, Douglas Webber reviewed several theories of European integration, assessing to what extent the variables that each identifies as driving forward European integration are still present, have waned or disappeared in recent years.[12] Webber defines European disintegration as meaning: "a decline in: (1) the range of common or joint policies adopted and implemented in the EU; (2) the number of EU member states; and/or (3) the formal (i.e. treaty-rooted) and actual capacity of EU organs to make and implement decisions if necessary against the will of individual members".[13] Using this, he identifies different variables that may lead to European disintegration. A realist explanation for a breakdown in European integration would point to the withdrawal of US military forces, bringing to an end the security guarantee that has sheltered European integration. Classic intergovernmentalism, based on the idea that integration is pushed forward by the preference of the main powers, would break down if the domestic politics of these powers—notably Germany and France, but also to some extent the UK—failed to align on key issues. As Weber makes clear, "[i]ntergovernmentalism implies that if a fundamental breakdown should occur in Franco-German relations, this would surely lead to European disintegration".[14] Similarly, the approach of France and Germany—and potentially the USA and the UK—is key to the approach of international relations institutionalism, which explains the EU's durability on its institutions about common interests between the member states. According to theories of historic institutionalism, the EU's survival is guaranteed by its longevity and the growing central role it plays in both the politics of Europe and of the member states. It would take a significant crisis to change this. Neo-functionalism, transactionalism and liberal intergovernmentalism theories work on the idea that the EU has already reached a constitutional and political durability thanks to growing economic interdependence. Disintegration could only follow from a decline in this interdependence. Finally, according to theories of comparative federalism, the EU is becoming—or has already become—a federal state. Any disintegration would emerge from a further transfer of powers to the EU level, provoking a backlash at the national level, which would expose the weaknesses of this federal-level political identity and structure.

Webber identifies two factors that need to be kept in mind when considering the above theories. First, many theories fail to take into account the role of domestic politics, especially growing Euroscepticism in the member states. Second,

---

12. Webber, "How Likely Is It", *op. cit.*
13. *Ibid.*, p. 342.
14. *Ibid.*, p. 345.

they overlook the powerful, potentially hegemonic role of Germany as the state central to underpinning integration. The EU and European integration have, as Webber argues, "never had to confront a crisis 'made in Germany'".[15] Germany's central position is also raised in the work of Hans Vollaard.[16] He argues that the costs of exiting the EU for some states are too high. This is especially so for those within the Euro or who have a sense of interdependence that is much stronger than for others, this particularly applying to member states who are physically surrounded by other EU member states as opposed to located on its periphery. Some states also have unique options open to them, for example links with other states around the world, which mean they can balance or seek to replace their relationship with the EU.

The Europe Question in British Politics

When in January 2013 David Cameron committed his Conservative Party to holding an in-out referendum, he argued: "It is time to settle this European question in British politics".[17] The question can appear to be a simple in-out question, and potentially one that only concerns the Conservative Party. However, closer examination of the issue throws doubts on whether the complexities of the UK–EU relationship can be reduced to a simple in-out choice or merely a Conservative Party obsession.[18] Britain has long been home to a range of ambivalent feelings about relations with the rest of Europe, and in particular the EU, that connect not only to UK–EU relations but to changes in UK politics and ideas of Britain's place in Europe and the world.

First, the European question is about identity and national interpretations of history. Britain is not the only EU member state to be home to ambivalent feelings about European integration. However, Britain's experiences seem to have created particularly strong feelings. This is in part a result of Britain's late membership of the EU, difficulties being admitted, a feeling that joining the EU was an abdication of a wider global role and giving up on a separation that has, to some extent, spared Britain some of the instability experienced elsewhere in Europe, a frustration at the failure of Britain's efforts regarding the alternative European Free Trade Area, difficult economic changes as UK trade moved towards Europe and away from former imperial markets, and a membership that began in the economic crises of the 1970s and so missed the economic growth seen in the earlier phases of European integration. Underlying all this has been a feeling that the relationship is a transactional one, a marriage of convenience with membership as a means to an end. That end has never been the EU's ideal of "ever closer union", but more of enhancing British wealth and power in the world. Seeing membership of the EU as a means to an end creates tensions because the EU has come to represent "Europe", which has for a long time served as the "other" against which British—and notably, but by no means exclusively, English—identity is cast.[19] This is so strong

---

15. *Ibid.*, p. 341.

16. Vollaard, *op. cit.*

17. Cameron, *op. cit.*

18. See Tim Oliver, "To Be or Not to Be in Europe: Is That the Question?", *International Affairs*, Vol. 91, No. 1 (2015), pp. 77–91.

19. William Wallace, "Foreign Policy and National Identity in the United Kingdom", *International Affairs*, Vol. 67, No. 1 (1991), pp. 65–80.

that the British—fed by a famously Eurosceptic media—can often overlook their European identity. Britain has not faced any catastrophic defeat or revolution that has triggered a critical juncture in its history where it has had to re-evaluate its position and identity vis-à-vis the rest of Europe. Instead, the Eurozone crisis combined with the growing appeal of emerging markets has added to a sense that the EU is the past. In a telling choice of words, former Conservative MP turned UKIP MP Douglas Carswell once told the House of Commons that "in joining Europe, we shackled ourselves to a corpse".[20]

If there is one arena where differences over UK–EU relations have played out more vividly than in any other, it is the UK's party politics. Cameron's January 2013 speech was a reflection of long-running tensions over the EU within his Conservative Party, tensions which in part brought down Mrs Thatcher, tore apart the government of John Major and plagued leaders of the party in opposition from 1997 to 2010.[21] The outcome is a party that has grown increasingly Eurosceptic. However, Conservative divisions can distract attention from tensions within other parties. The Labour Party is the only major party to have split over the issue of Europe, the Social Democratic Party splitting from Labour in 1981 over a range of differences, in particular the party's then policy of opposition to Britain's participation in European integration. Tensions could re-emerge, with Labour leader Ed Miliband under pressure to take a more Eurosceptic line to stop traditional supporters moving towards Eurosceptic parties and to reject what some on the left of the Labour Party see as the overtly neoliberal agenda of the EU.[22] Even the Liberal Democrats, a party with a commitment to the EU in its DNA, has committed itself to an in-out referendum in order to manage internal party unease over Europe.[23] The rise of UKIP, which has emerged as a fourth party in UK politics, has hit all three parties, particularly the Conservatives. UKIP's emergence is not all thanks to the issue of Europe. It has captured public disillusionment with the three main parties, unease about Britain's political economy and fears about immigration. Its power and potential might be overplayed, but it encapsulates how the issue of Europe is playing a part in the wider decline of two-party politics and the emergence of a more plural UK party system. The Northern Ireland Democratic Unionist Party, whose leader has spoken of the possibility of a coalition with the Conservative Party, supports an in-out referendum.[24] Even Nicola Sturgeon, leader of the pro-European Scottish National Party, said in October 2014 that an in-out referendum on EU membership in 2017 "now seems inevitable—almost regardless of who wins the general election

20. Douglas Carswell, Hansard (Commons), 26 October 2012, col. 1257, available: <http://www. publications.parliament.uk/pa/ cm201213/cmhansrd/cm121026/debtext/121026-0002.htm> (accessed 11 November 2014).

21. Anthony Forster, *Euroscepticism in Contemporary British Politics: Opposition to Europe in the British Conservative and Labour Parties since 1945* (London: Routledge, 2002).

22. See Kelvin Hopkins MP, *The European Union: A View from the Left,* Labour Euro-Safeguards campaign, January 2015. For further details of the Labour Euro-Safeguards campaign see <www.lesc.info> (accessed 12 May 2015).

23. George Eaton, "When Clegg Supported an EU Referendum", *New Statesman,* 22 October 2011, available: <http://www.newstatesman.com/blogs/the-staggers/2011/10/referendum-membership-lib> (accessed 11 November 2014).

24. Allegra Stratton, "Nigel Dodds Sets out DUP's Demands", BBC News (12 March 2015), available: <http://www.bbc.co.uk/news/uk-politics-31863675> (accessed 12 May 2015).

next May".[25] She potentially sees in it the chance to trigger another referendum on Scottish independence.[26] This all means that whatever the outcome of the 2015 general election, the issue of Europe looks likely to remain a lively and divisive one within the UK's party politics, with the potential for a referendum likely to hang over even a government that excludes the Conservative Party.[27]

Look beyond party politics, or the result of elections, and the issue of Europe is to be found embedded in the UK's constitutional and economic tensions. Scotland's independence referendum was the most obvious sign that the United Kingdom is going through a constitutional and identity crisis that could make or break it. The Scottish question itself is far from settled, especially with regard to potential developments in UK–EU relations.[28] Various cities, regions and centres of power across the UK are manoeuvring for change.[29] The situation in Northern Ireland, while much improved, should also not be taken for granted, especially if the UK were to vote to leave the EU.[30] The issue of sovereignty is often raised when discussing the UK's EU membership. Yet debates about sovereignty cannot be narrowed down to the UK–EU relationship given that different ideas of sovereignty exist within the UK.[31] Arguments over sovereignty also drive calls for the UK to abandon the European Convention on Human Rights—often mistakenly thought to be a part of the EU. Such calls often ignore the marginalisation this would bring to the UK and the British origins of the document. The most important political, economic and constitutional questions facing the UK revolve around the power of London.[32] The capital city is a place apart from England and the rest of the UK. It is a largely pro-European, international mega-city, where a third of the population was born outside the UK and white Britons make up only 45% of the population.[33] When it comes to participation in the EU or globalisation, London appears to be ahead in a race other parts of the UK are either falling behind in or are wary of the consequences (especially over immigration) of taking part in.[34]

---

25. "Nicola Sturgeon in Call over EU Referendum", *The Scotsman*, 29 October 2014, available: <http://www.scotsman.com/news/uk/nicola-sturgeon-in-call-over-eu-referendum-1-3587376> (accessed 12 May 2015).

26. Philip Stephens, "When Britain Leaves Europe, Scotland Will Leave Britain", *Financial Times*, 24 October 2013, available: <http://www.ft.com/cms/s/0/8eff7a1e-3bf4-11e3-9851-00144feab7de.html#axzz3Io 2ZMkLO> (accessed 11 November 2014).

27. See Oliver, "Will the UK's General Election Lead to an In-Out Referendum?" op. *cit.*

28. Stephens, *op. cit.*

29. Timothy Garton-Ash, "Let's Not Fear the F-word or the C-word: We Should Move to a Federal Britain in a Confederal Europe", *The Guardian*, 21 September 2014, available: <www.theguardian.com/commentisfree/2014/sep/21/not-fear-f-word-federal-britain-confederal-europe?index=1> (accessed 11 November 2014).

30. John Bruton, "Passport Controls on the Border at Newry Will Be a Reality if Britain Leaves EU", independent.ie (25 January 2013), available: <http://www.independent.ie/opinion/analysis/john-bruton-passport-controls-on-the-border-at-newry-will-be-a-reality-if-britain-leaves-eu-29022868.html> (accessed 11 November 2014).

31. William Wallace, "What Price Interdependence? Sovereignty and Independence in British Politics", *International Affairs*, Vol. 62, No. 3 (1986), pp. 367–389.

32. "The London Question", *New Statesman*, 28 August 2014, available: <http://www.newstatesman.com/politics/2014/08/leader-london-question> (accessed 11 November 2014).

33. Tim Oliver, "Londoners Are Not Little Englanders", LSE British Politics and Policy Blog (17 March 2014), available: <http://blogs.lse.ac.uk/politicsandpolicy/londoners-are-not-little-englanders/> (accessed 11 November 2014).

34. See Robert Preston, "Why Did UKIP Do Less Well in London?", BBC News (27 May 2014), available: <http://www.bbc.co.uk/news/business-27585765> (accessed 11 November 2014).

This creates tensions within the UK and in UK–EU relations when London domi-
nates the UK's economic, political and EU policies. Such is London's growing difference from the rest of the UK that campaigning on an anti-London ticket pays
dividends whether you are Scottish nationalists or UKIP members seeking
support elsewhere in England.

So how likely is it that if faced with an in-out choice the British people would opt
for getting out of the EU? We should be careful not to assume that such a breakdown in relations is inevitable. The rocky relationship of UK–EU relations has
seen many low points, including an in-out referendum in 1975. It remains to be
seen whether another in-out referendum will even happen. Any Labour or
Liberal Democrat commitment would only be triggered if the EU undertook a
new treaty of transfer of power. The Conservatives would need to form a majority
government in order to be sure that a referendum on their terms takes place, or to
secure a commitment to this as part of a new coalition agreement. Polling also
shows that while the British electorate are not overly enthusiastic about the EU,
their views are more complex and less harsh than is often assumed.[35] Polling
shows that support for withdrawal has not yet matched the heights it reached in
the early 1980s when one polling organisation registered 71% support for withdrawal.[36] When pushed on the issue, polling shows that a large proportion of the
public opts for the status quo of remaining within the EU, with support increasing
if this is preceded by some renegotiated relationship.[37] Nevertheless, the rise in
support for UKIP does represent a level of unease about the EU that cannot be dismissed. Some polling might have shown that the British people are likely to vote to
stay in, but there have been numerous polls indicating support for withdrawal.
Events in Scotland serve as a reminder that even though the vast majority of
polling points one way—in the case of Scotland the direction was towards remaining a part of the UK—the overall vote may be uncertain and closer than most are
comfortable with.

The British Question in European Politics

Britain's debates about its European question often focus on the negatives of Britain's EU membership. The debate therefore overlooks the fact that Britain has exercised a degree of power and influence in the EU that has passed unappreciated in
UK political debate. Britain's influence has not passed unnoticed elsewhere in the
EU. Europe's "British question" is not only about whether the UK will stay or
leave, but how to manage relations with a state that has played a large role in European integration and wider European politics. Not only has the UK successfully
secured a large number of exemptions from EU policies—the most obvious being
from the Euro, Schengen, some Justice and Home Affairs policies and a rebate
on its contributions to the EU's budget— but it has also successfully pushed
agendas such as enlargement of the EU and cooperation on foreign, security and

---

35. Copsey and Haughton, *op. cit.*

36. See Mori European Union membership trends, available: <https://www.ipsos-mori.com/
researchpublications/researcharchive/2435/European-Union-membership-trends.aspx?view=wide>
(accessed 11 November 2014).

37. "EU Referendum: Record Lead for Staying IN Europe", YouGov (17 June 2014), available: <http://
yougov.co.uk/news/2014/06/17/eu-referendum-record-lead/> (accessed 11 November 2014).

defence matters, and its "Anglo-Saxon" economic influence over the political economy of the EU was one of the reasons many feel was to blame for the 2005 French referendum rejection of the EU's constitution.[38] Indeed, Britain can be viewed as having benefitted most of all from EU membership, even in areas that give rise to much debate in the UK, such as intra-EU immigration.[39] Nevertheless, the UK's position in the EU could appear to be one of decline and marginalisation. This is not without some justification given that the UK's domestic political debate makes for an often strained UK–EU relationship. In an EU of 28 members, the UK is just one member, and could be seen as one increasingly sidelined by the attention that is focused on the leadership of Germany. British governments have long struggled in their relations with other EU states, but relations today seem to have reached new lows.[40]

As several of the theories of European disintegration touched on earlier make clear, a large member state such as the UK plays a central role in European integration, with its actions likely to influence the response of other member states. Britain's place in Europe looks set to grow, potentially counterbalancing its marginalisation within the EU. Based on current projections, Britain's population will overtake that of Germany in the 2040s. Germany has already begun to experience a decline in its population, something that has not passed unnoticed within Germany itself.[41] If the projections hold, then by 2040 the UK could have a larger population than any other EU member state. It would be behind only Russia and Turkey in a wider European context. Even the loss of 5.5 million Scots, should they hold another referendum at some point and decide to withdraw, would be made up by 10–15 years of population growth in the rest of the UK. By 2035 the population of England alone could be 62.1 million, and is expected to grow even further by 2060.[42]

Accurate population projections are notoriously difficult. A large population is also no guarantor of power. Nor does it mean that the UK's economy will become the largest or most important in Europe. However, the economies of Britain, France and Germany could become similar in size, cancelling out some of Germany's economic leadership. Germany could suffer not only thanks to population decline but also from problems in the Eurozone. It could be that Berlin's efforts to save the Eurozone have not only limited the EU's economic potential, but have overstretched Germany, leaving it destined to become a drag rather than the engine of European growth. Here it is worth recalling Webber's

---

38. "A Less 'Anglo-Saxon' EU: Sarkozy Scraps Competition Clause from New Treaty", Spiegel Online (22 June 2007), available: <http://www.spiegel.de/international/europe/a-less-anglo-saxon-eu-sarkozy-scraps-competition-clause-from-new-treaty-a-490136.html> (accessed 11 November 2014).

39. See Adrian Favell, "The UK Has Been One of the Main Beneficiaries from Free Movement of Labour in the EU", LSE British Politics and Policy Blog (3 July 2014), available: <http://blogs.lse.ac.uk/europpblog/2014/07/01/the-uk-has-been-one-of-the-main-beneficiaries-from-free-movement-of-labour-in-the-eu/> (accessed 12 May 2015).

40. Möller and Oliver, *op. cit.*

41. Suzanne Daley and Nicholas Kulish, "Germany Fights Population Drop", *New York Times*, 13 August 2013, available: <http://www.nytimes.com/2013/08/14/world/europe/germany-fights-population-drop.html?pagewanted=all&_r=0> (accessed 11 November 2014).

42. Office for National Statistics, "Summary: UK Population Projected to Reach 70 Million by Mid-2027" (26 October 2011), available: <http://www.ons.gov.uk/ons/rel/npp/national-population-projections/2010-based-projections/sum-2010-based-national-population-projections.html> (accessed 11 November 2014).

Table 1. Projected Populations 2010 and 2060.

2010	2060
Germany: 81.7 million	UK: 78.9 million
France: 64.7 million	France: 73.7 million
UK: 62 million	Germany: 66.4 million
Italy: 60.3 million	Italy: 64.9 million
Spain: 45.9 million	Spain: 52.2 million
EU: 501 million	EU: 516.9 million

Source: Eurostat, *Population Projections 2010–2060* (8 June 2011), available: <http://epp.eurostat.ec.
europa.eu/cache/ITY_PUBLIC/3-08062011-BP/EN/3-08062011-BP-EN.PDF> (accessed 11 November
2014).

warning that European integration, "has never so far had to confront a crisis 'made
in Germany'".[43]

In 2050 Britain could also still wield a more powerful military force than any
other EU member state. Britain's armed forces are of course much reduced compared to what they once were. However, the capabilities of the British military
remain considerable.[44] Britain will almost certainly remain a leading power in
NATO, committed to the regional security of Europe (even if, like the USA, it
has reduced its Cold War military commitments in places such as Germany).
Britain has committed itself to a number of bilateral defence arrangements with
other EU states such as France and the Netherlands. Despite the huge cost, the
UK still looks set, in cooperation with the USA, to replace its Trident nuclear
weapons system with an upgraded system that will be operational by the
middle of the century. Britain will also not operate alone. If there is something
"special" about the UK–US relationship, then it is cooperation on intelligence,
nuclear weapons and special forces. Despite significant strains in the relationship,
cooperation in these areas remains very close. These capabilities and relationships
also mean that the UK has, or at least feels it has compared to many other EU
member states, more options available to it when examining its future relations
with the EU and the rest of the world.

Of course, all of this could change. Germany's population decline could be
halted and reversed, its reputation for economic competitiveness and efficiency
maintained. Britain's own economic power could falter thanks to an over-reliance
on financial services and an overheated South East of England and London.
Further and deeper cuts to the British military may end what is left of UK military
capabilities with a global reach, raising doubts in the USA or elsewhere about the
viability of continued close links. Britain itself—always destined to be located
outside the geographical centre of Europe—could be an unsure power thanks
to ongoing internal problems that define its current political debates, especially
the aforementioned ones over its unity, identity and place in Europe. Current political and racial tensions surrounding immigration could grow given that Britain's
population is expected to increase in no small part thanks to immigration and

43. Webber, "How Likely is it", *op. cit.*, p. 341.

44. Andrew Dorman, "The Capabilities of Britain's Armed Forces May Not Be Diminishing as Starkly as
the Numbers Might Suggest", LSE British Politics and Policy Blog (31 January 2014), available: <http://
blogs.lse.ac.uk/politicsandpolicy/is-there-a-need-to-panic-british-defence-expenditure-today/> (accessed
11 November 2014).

high birth rates among immigrant communities. If so, then Europe could be faced with a rising power, located on the edge of Europe, one that could not only break up but be home to a political debate that is inward looking and unsure of itself.

What seems clear is that as the 2020s approach, Germany's population decline and Britain's growth will start to register as a political and strategic issue. If this is the case, then according to theories such as classic intergovernmentalism, for the EU and the UK relations between the two should matter more. It remains to be seen whether the UK and the rest of the EU will maintain the political links needed to make the most of this relationship. It is also unclear whether the EU will be able to respond in a united form. In part this is because of one of the most frustrating aspects of UK–EU relations: how contradictory, frustrating and confusing they can be. Even when relations are difficult, both sides can usually agree on some key parts of an issue. The recent appointment of Jean-Claude Juncker as the new president of the European Commission saw the UK largely alone in opposing him. Yet Britain's concerns about Juncker, if not its confrontational approach, were not without their merit and sympathy from elsewhere in the EU.[45]

Incidents such as Juncker's appointment underline how political relations, whether personal or inter-party, have rarely been harmonious. David Cameron's own decision to withdraw his Conservative Party from the European People's Party, and thus detach the Conservatives from routine links with most of Europe's centre-right parties, has left UK–EU party political relations—at least at the level of governing parties—resting largely with the Labour Party. Britain's weakness in connecting with other states in the EU becomes clear in any review of how others see the UK, with even traditionally close allies such as Sweden or the Netherlands growing distant.[46] Admittedly, if Britain remains in the EU and population projections turn out to be accurate, then in the 2040s British MEPs will begin to outnumber their German colleagues in the European Parliament, meaning that they could become the hub of many political party groupings. But this might not make up for the long-running low recruitment rates of Britons to EU institutions.[47] As discussed earlier, many theories of European integration— for example functionalism, transactionalism or liberal intergovernmentalism— rest on growing economic interdependence binding EU member states together. As we turn to below, any economic interdependence could potentially make up for strains in the UK–EU political relationship, but there are limits to how far this could bind the two together.

Brexit Stage Right?

Europe's "British question" is not then simply about the UK leaving the EU. It is about the economic and political place of the UK in a changing EU and how

---

45. "EU Diplomats Struggle to Understand Cameron's Strategy on Juncker", EurActiv.com (25 June 2014), available: <http://www.euractiv.com/sections/eu-elections-2014/eu-diplomats-struggle-understand-camerons-strategy-juncker-303045> (accessed 11 November 2014).

46. See Erik Brattberg, "Sweden" (pp. 77–78) and Rem Korteweg, "The Netherlands" (pp. 99-102), in Möller and Oliver, *op. cit.*

47. Alex Barker, "British Eurocrat: Au Revoir to All That", *FT Magazine* (23 May 2014), available: <http://www.ft.com/cms/s/2/a09b7684-db08-11e3-8273-00144feabdc0.html#axzz3IrkzafzW> (accessed 11 November 2014).

to manage relations with a large but difficult European state, whether as a member of the EU or not. Should a Brexit occur, then the initial problem for the EU would be the unprecedented experience of negotiating a withdrawal.[48] Difficult and potentially interminable Brexit negotiations would not only take place with the UK. Negotiations would also have to take place within the EU to fill the gap left by Britain. These would revolve around the never-easy tasks of negotiating changes to national voting rights, allocation of MEPs and staff, and budgets. When combined with possible changes to the Eurozone, a Brexit could add to shifts in the EU's balance of power and changes to the EU's policies and outlook. This could help push the EU towards one of the three outcomes outlined by Tom Wright in his analysis of how the EU might move forward in dealing with the Eurozone crisis: increased unity; muddling through; or disintegration.[49] Which of these the EU ends up following will largely reflect developments in the Eurozone. Nevertheless, the UK's behaviour could play an influential part because its withdrawal could change the EU's internal balance of power, with implications for wider European politics.

Increased unity within the EU could be brought about by losing a notoriously awkward member state, allowing the EU to move more easily towards "ever closer union". While countries such as France and Germany have not allowed UK objections to fundamentally delay European integration, the UK has stood as an alternative to the direction and ideas of European integration. As a result, British opt-outs, such as that over the Euro, have placed the UK in an outer tier. A British withdrawal would leave some members of the EU continuing to hold some opt-outs, for example Denmark's non-membership of the Eurozone. However, these would be smaller, and so the EU and the Eurozone would more neatly align. There could then be no repeat of the events of December 2011 when David Cameron's lone veto of a new treaty for the Eurozone led the rest of the EU to bypass the UK and establish arrangements for the Eurozone among themselves, and therefore separate from the EU treaties.

Alternatively, the EU could continue to muddle through, with Britain's absence having little or no effect. The UK's absence from the Eurozone has not meant that leadership or unity of the zone has been easy, with deep disagreements over austerity policies and the degree of supranational oversight of member states. Any muddling through following a UK exit would also be the likely result of the remaining EU members coming to terms with shifts and changes to the distribution of power within it. Germany's dominant position could be extended, reinforcing at an EU level Germany's preference for geo-economic thinking over the geopolitical.[50] The EU's centre of gravity could also shift eastwards, presenting difficulties to states such as France that worry about an EU that no longer focuses on Western Europe and in particular the Franco-German axis.

The possibility of EU disintegration as a result of the Eurozone's problems remains a possibility. Whether a British exit by itself could trigger such a collapse would depend on whatever centrifugal pressures it could unleash. If a Brexit pressured Germany to weaken its commitment to either the EU or the Eurozone,

---

48. For a discussion of the withdrawal procedure, see Adam Lazowski, *op. cit.*

49. Tom Wright, "Europe's Lost Decade", *Survival*, Vol. 55, No. 6 (2013), pp. 7–28.

50. Han Kundanani, "Germany as a Geo-economic Power", *Washington Quarterly*, Vol. 34, No. 3 (2011), pp. 31–45.

then as argued earlier by Webber, European integration could face its biggest test to date.[51] Britain might not even need to go so far as to withdraw to pose such a challenge. Demands by some in the UK for a renegotiated relationship within the EU have led to warnings from elsewhere in the EU that an "à la carte Europe" is unacceptable as it would lead other states—and in particular political groups on the far right and left—to make their own demands, in turn fragmenting the EU.

The British question also has implications for wider European unity and cooperation. The European Free Trade Area (EFTA) and/or the European Economic Area (EEA) could be transformed by changes to UK–EU relations. Further afield, losing a large, Western, Christian country would make it highly unlikely that many of the remaining states, especially France, would agree to a large Eastern European, Muslim country such as Turkey being allowed to join. But as with Norway and Switzerland, a British exit, or renegotiated relationship within the EU, could open up new models for relations that could then be extended to other states. However, this depends on the willingness of these states to give up their own individual relationships with the EU, and the willingness of Britain or the EU to share any special arrangements.

If there is one issue that fuels the UK's debate about membership of the EU, it is economics. The same applies to the EU, and especially countries such as Germany who have close relations with the UK in trade and shared approaches to political economy. Given the important part played by economic interdependence in many theories of European integration, it is in this area that we may find some pointers to how the EU and the UK–EU relationship may develop should the UK decide to withdraw. The UK's economic place in the EU is significant. Britain constitutes 14.8% of the EU's economic area, with 12.5% of its population.[52] British exports make up 19.4% of the EU's total exports (excluding intra-EU trade).[53] Britain runs a trade deficit with the rest of the EU in goods and services of around £28 billion a year (2012 figures).[54] Neither the UK nor the EU would have an interest in allowing a situation to develop in which their economic links are damaged. Nevertheless, the various proposals put forward for a new UK–EU economic relationship focus almost entirely on what might be best for Britain. Yet the final agreed arrangement will also be one shaped by what is best for the EU and Europe. Few if any member states will see anything to be gained from agreeing to a deal whereby the UK can undercut the EU by having access to the EU's single market without shouldering any of the costs of membership. The City of London, already something of a target for some within the EU, could become an even clearer target for hostile acts should the UK withdraw. In the longer term a Brexit could make the EU less inclined towards liberal, free market

51. See Webber, "How Likely Is It", *op. cit.*

52. Population figures calculated from Eurostat figures for 2011, available: <http://appsso.eurostat.ec. europa.eu/nui/show.do?dataset=demo_gind&lang=en> (accessed 12 May 2015); economic figures calculated from Eurostat figures for 2013, GDP at current prices. The UK economy is €1,940,659.6 billion of the EU's €13,086,459.2 billion economy. <http://appsso.eurostat.ec.europa.eu/nui/show.do?dataset=nama_gdp_c&lang=en> (accessed 12 May 2015).

53. "Right Speech, Right Time?" (London: Open Europe, 22 January 2012), available: <http://archive. openeurope.org.uk/Content/Documents/Pdfs/EuropeSpeech.pdf> (accessed 12 May 2015).

54. See answer from Baroness Warsi, *Hansard*, HL Deb, 14 November 2012, col. 1507, available: <http:// www.publications.parliament.uk/pa/ld201213/ldhansrd/text/121114-0001.htm#12111438000002> (accessed 12 May 2015).

economics, a concern often raised by supporters in the EU and elsewhere of Britain's continued membership.[55] Britain has been a long-standing supporter of the EU's single market and has repeatedly pushed for it to be more open and deregulated.[56] This has led to uneasy talk elsewhere in the EU of Europe being subject to an "Anglo-Saxon" agenda, or even the "Britishisation" of the EU.[57] However, Britain's role in the EU's economic thinking is already limited by its exclusion from the Eurozone. Without the UK the Eurozone and the EU could more neatly align, leaving the members of the Eurozone as the undisputed heart of the EU both politically and economically. It is also questionable to what extent countries such as Germany or even France would allow the EU, or the Eurozone, to become more inward looking and protectionist. Even the European Commission, often lambasted by British Eurosceptics as a bastion of state socialism, also often finds itself accused of pursuing harsh neoliberal trade agendas.[58] Reforms to the Eurozone might have struggled to overcome its problems, but the intention has been to ensure that the Eurozone is more open and competitive.[59] The UK is also not alone in seeing the potential and feeling the draw of emerging markets, something some British politicians accuse the EU of holding Britain back from. Germany's interests in markets such as China and Brazil dwarf those of the UK, with many other EU members also pursuing links. Pressure from the USA or China and international trade negotiations will not leave the EU many options but to continue embracing an outward-looking economic agenda.

Possible economic implications of a Brexit could first be seen with the Transatlantic Trade and Investment Partnership (TTIP), a development Britain has been at the forefront of efforts to create.[60] While a TTIP without the UK would not be impossible—indeed, the USA and the EU have warned that this could happen—Britain's close economic and political relations with the USA and rest of the EU mean it would be more difficult and a lesser deal if secured, and potentially a more difficult sell to the US Congress.[61] Given that the aim of the TTIP is to expand to include other states such as Canada, a UK outside the EU could secure some form of partnership.

---

55. See the Swedish, Japanese and US views in Möller and Oliver, *op. cit.*

56. "Review of the Balance of Competences between the United Kingdom and the European Union: The Single Market" (July 2013), available: <https://www.gov.uk/government/uploads/system/uploads/attachment_data/file/227069/2901084_SingleMarket_acc.pdf> (accessed 12 May 2015).

57. Charles Grant, "In Defence of Anglo-Saxon Capitalism", Centre for European Reform (CER) (29 September 2008), available: <http://www.cer.org.uk/insights/defence-anglo-saxon-capitalism> (accessed 12 May 2015); and Douglas Webber (ed.), *New Europe, New Germany, Old Foreign Policy?* (London: Frank Cass, 2001), p. 14.

58. Ferdi de Ville and Jan Orbie, "The European Commission's Neoliberal Trade Discourse since the Crisis: Legitimizing Continuity through Subtle Discursive Change", *British Journal of Politics and International Relations*, Vol. 16, No. 1 (February 2014), pp. 149–167.

59. Laurence Knight, "Eurozone's Long Reform Wishlist", BBC News (26 June 2012), available: <http://www.bbc.com/news/business-18560234> (accessed 12 May 2015).

60. Raf Sanchez, "Britain Leads Push to Convince Washington to Back Transatlantic Free Trade Deal", *The Telegraph*, 24 September 2014, available: <http://www.telegraph.co.uk/finance/economics/10329783/Britain-leads-push-to-convince-Washington-to-back-transatlantic-free-trade-deal.html> (accessed 12 May 2015).

61. Julian Borger, "EU Exit Would Put US Trade Deal at Risk, Britain Warned', *The Guardian*, 27 May 2013; and Tim Oliver, "The British Problem Facing a Transatlantic Trade Deal", *Huffington Post*, 25 October 2013, available: <http://www.huffingtonpost.com/tim-oliver/the-british-problem-facin_b_4164712.html> (accessed 12 May 2015).

However, what this partnership with other countries might entail is not yet clear. Nor is it clear whether the EU would allow the UK anything less than a backseat in the TTIP. For the EU the partnership would be a bilateral one between Washington and Brussels.

Europe and Britain's Global Security Questions

Even if Britain—in or outside the EU—is a rising power in Europe, the place of Britain, the EU and wider Europe will continue to face decline in a wider global sense. Given that Britain has played a prominent role in European approaches to matters of international security, what then might the changing UK–EU relationship mean for how the UK and the EU face the political and security challenges of an emerging multipolar world?

Despite its relative decline in power, Britain remains a European power with global aspirations and capabilities and can deliver on this to a certain extent. This is especially so when the UK is compared to other EU member states. Along with France, it is the only other EU state with a sizeable military that is both experienced and able to operate independently—even if in a limited sense —beyond Europe. Britain's soft power, along with other aspects of its power such as in intelligence, diplomacy and humanitarian aid, remains considerable. Britain's international aspirations have been one of the drivers behind efforts to develop the EU's own foreign, security and defence policies and capabilities.[62] This might be little appreciated in the UK itself, but one only has to look to the efforts made by successive UK governments in trying to develop European cooperation on international matters to see how Britain has sought to lead the EU on international matters in order to secure its sought-for end of Britain as an international player. This has not focused exclusively on EU cooperation. NATO, bilateral and multilateral cooperation have also been pursued. Defence and security cooperation with France in particular has been pursued, in no small part as a result of frustrations by both at the inability of EU cooperation to deliver progress with other European partners, particularly Germany.

British disengagement from the EU could therefore further complicate European defence and security cooperation. It may leave France with few options by which to pursue closer links with other EU partners, particularly the Weimar Group involving France, Germany and Poland. Britain might have been central to EU efforts in these areas, but it has also been a big obstacle as a result of domestic unease at cooperation on defence matters at the EU level. Britain's absence could therefore offer the remaining EU member states opportunities to develop new ideas on defence and security matters. However, as with previous efforts at defence cooperation, a lot would depend on Germany's response.[63] A similar problematic outlook could then face NATO, leaving doubts about the future of transatlantic relations. Britain would no doubt remain committed to NATO, facilitating a means through which high-level international security issues can be discussed in addition to any bilateral discussions. But NATO itself continues to face an uncertain

---

62. For a discussion of the UK's role in the EU's foreign, security and defence policies, see "Heading for a Brexit?", *op. cit.*

63. Ronja Kempin and Jocelyn Mawdsley, "The UK, the EU and European Security: A German Perspective", *RUSI Journal*, Vol. 158, No. 4 (August 2013), pp. 32–36.

future, with British–EU relations having the potential to further complicate efforts at maintaining or increasing European defence cooperation.

The future of Europe's place in the world, and how UK–EU relations might shape this and the future of NATO, would depend significantly on the positions taken by the USA. The US "pivot to Asia" and away from Europe is not a new development, the USA having pivoted from Europe in the early 1990s when it withdrew large numbers of its Europe-based forces following the end of the Cold War. This US disengagement could be reversed should Russian behaviour towards states in Eastern Europe become more belligerent. But any such re-engagement is unlikely to equal that of the Cold War. While talk of a US decline can be overblown, the US is not in a position to commit to European security in the way it did in the past. Indeed, the disappearance from Europe of the American security guarantee—one of particular interest to realist interpretations of European integration—is a test the EU and Europe have yet to face.[64]

Britain's behaviour—particularly a Brexit—could therefore add to strains in the transatlantic relationship, which impacts on the US security guarantee. Any desire by Britain to continue working with the USA would require it to engage in affairs beyond Europe. While it will retain an ability to do so to some extent, this would face significant difficulties if the security of Europe became a more pressing matter. In such a context it is unlikely that the USA would welcome British support of US efforts internationally instead of British engagement in European security matters. The USA could face a series of European problems from a UK exit from, or marginalisation in, the EU. Not only could a British exit reduce the UK's international standing, and thus its utility to the USA, but an EU that became more inward looking—economically and strategically—as a result of a British exit would damage US hopes of European cooperation and engagement in international matters, and increased cooperation on defence, that reduce Europe's security dependence on the USA. This does not mean that the USA would then give up on the EU or the UK. The sheer economic size of the EU—a collective GDP of $18.5 trillion compared to Britain's $2.5 trillion—means that close transatlantic relations will be crucial. Nor, despite talk of Britain as the US's "Trojan Horse" in the EU, will there be any shortage of applicants to fill the UK's place. The USA has long had close relations with a large number of EU states, even if it has sometimes abused those relationships or taken them for granted.[65]

One reason the USA is likely to maintain an interest in Europe is due to a concern that the continent could again become a divided and contested space in international relations. The USA is not alone among allies of both the UK and the rest of the EU in expressing concerns at where UK–EU relations may take the wider geopolitics of Europe.[66] Countries such as Canada, Singapore, Japan, Australia and New Zealand have, like the USA, used their links with the UK to influence

---

64. For a discussion of the possible security implications for the UK and Europe of a US withdrawal from Europe, see David Blagden, "Global Multipolarity, European Security and Implications for UK Grand Strategy: Back to the Future, Once Again", *International Affairs*, Vol. 91, No. 2 (March 2015), pp. 333–350.

65. Andrea Thomas, "US Spying on Germany Unacceptable, Says Merkel", *Wall Street Journal*, 12 July 2014, available: < http://online.wsj.com/articles/u-s-spying-on-germany-unacceptable-says-merkel-1405174452> (accessed 11 November 2014).

66. See the views from Canada, Australia and New Zealand, Singapore and Japan in Möller and Oliver, *op. cit.*

the EU and maintain an outward-looking EU agenda that is friendly and accommodating to these states and wider Western interests. But as with the USA, their
relations with the EU go beyond the UK, with many also having close relations
with other EU states. For these states the possibility of the EU fragmenting and/
or being weakened would add to the pressures already facing the West from emerging powers. A Brexit could help to create a multipolar Europe in a multipolar
world.[67] A Brexit or breakdown in UK–EU relations could see the EU surrounded
by the poles of Britain, Russia and Turkey. The outcome, should the EU remain
weak or carry on muddling through, could make more likely a scenario, as outlined
by Jan Techau, of a Europe that "is not a pillar of world affairs but a territory that
risks being pulled asunder between the United States and Asia".[68]

Conclusion

The EU faces a long list of challenges, not least of which are the Eurozone's continuing fragility and security fears surrounding the intentions of Russia towards
Eastern Europe. The "British question" can therefore be seen as an unwanted distraction. If Britain is going to be half-hearted and awkward in its relationship with
the EU, then why should the rest of the EU show anything other than half-hearted
interest in Britain? Similar feelings can be found among those in the UK who feel
that Britain would be better off if it withdrew from the predominant political
and economic organisation of the continent it is forever bound to. Neither approach
is sustainable or likely to make the most of a relationship in which the EU will
remain the most important partner for the UK in the world and an integral part
of many of the domestic debates shaping Britain.

The various theories of European integration show that the UK's behaviour—
especially a Brexit—could be an important independent variable that shapes how
the EU develops, in particular whether the EU disintegrates. A realist account
points to the strained security situation in Europe, and Britain's unwillingness or
inability to change this, as a key pressure on European integration. Cooperation
between large member states, the key component of classic intergovernmentalism,
could continue despite a Brexit if the Franco-German axis was sustained. The continued vitality of the Franco-German axis is also important for theories of international relations institutionalism, the durability of the EU's institutions being
sustained by support from the axis. It would take a collapse of the Franco-
German axis, perhaps brought on or exacerbated by a Brexit, to bring about the
type of crisis necessary to change integration as understood by the theory of historic institutionalism. Theories of neo-functionalism, transactionalism and liberal
intergovernmentalism provide perhaps the most optimistic outlook, with economic
interdependence making it too costly even for a state such as the UK to withdraw
or, should it do so, leaving it in a position where it will continue to be bound economically to the rest of the EU. For comparative federalism, Britain's increasingly
distant political relationship with the EU could limit the potential for it to

67. Ivan Krastev and Mark Leonard, "The Spectre of a Multipolar Europe", European Council on
Foreign Affairs (October 2010), available: <http://www.ecfr.eu/page/-/ECFR25_SECURITY_UPDATE_
AW_SINGLE.pdf> (accessed 11 November 2014).

68. Jan Techau, "Europe Torn Apart in the Asian Century?", Carnegie Europe (1 July 2014), available:
<http://carnegieeurope.eu/strategiceurope/?fa=56054> (accessed 11 November 2014).

disrupt the emergence of a federal state. As Webber pointed out, with all of these theories we should not overlook the wider domestic politics of other EU member states, especially growing Euroscepticism in a range of states, meaning that the UK is not the only state with a strained political relationship with the rest of the EU. And the role of Germany is key, whether as part of a Franco-German axis or in its approach to managing the security and defence challenges the EU and European integration look set to face. Ignoring the possibility of a Brexit risks ignoring a development that would play an important, perhaps transformative part in the EU's development.

A way has therefore to be found for the EU to give appropriate attention to the possibility of a Brexit. Focusing solely on the "British question" would more than likely lead to disappointment on all sides. The attention would create expectations on the part of the British that concerns about Britain's membership are the most important issue on the agenda. This is an expectation that the rest of the EU would be unable to fulfil. For the rest of the EU, focusing on Britain is likely to cause resentment across the EU about giving into—or being more willing to discuss—British demands at the expense of other agendas. Neither would be in the interests of the EU or wider European unity, especially when Europe's place in the world will face a growing number of challenges as the world enters a more multipolar era.

Acknowledgements

I am indebted to the following for their support, comments and guidance: Bastian Giegerich, Chris Chivvis, Dan Hamilton, Almut Möller, Roderick Parkes, Claudia Major, Markus Kaim, William and Helen Wallace and the two anonymous reviewers. I am grateful to Marco Vieira for giving me the opportunity to refine my arguments as a participant in the Birmingham University conference "Challenges to Engaging and Established Powers: Brazil and the UK in the Contemporary Global Order".

Brazilian Energy-Climate Policy and Politics towards Low Carbon Development

EDUARDO VIOLA and LARISSA BASSO

Climate change has proved to be one of the greatest threats to human survival on Earth. Its mitigation requires that the greatest Greenhouse Gases (GHG) emitters adopt low carbon development, reducing emissions substantially. Brazil is among them. Although deforestation is still the main source of Brazilian emissions, since 1990 emissions from energy systems and industrial processes have increased and their shares in total Brazilian emissions have been consistently larger. It is the objective of the article to analyse Brazilian energy-climate policy and politics from 1990 to 2014 in order to clarify Brazilian progress towards low carbon development and Brazilian positions in the international climate change regime.

Introduction

In the field of sustainability, achieving low carbon development is the new way forward. Low carbon development is a path that reconciles economic growth and climate stability, one of the planetary boundaries of a safe operating space for humanity. In order to be achieved, low carbon development demands stabilisation of the concentration of Greenhouse Gases (GHG) in the atmosphere. Energy is intrinsically related to low carbon development, given that it accounts for more than half of total global emissions. If the world is to control its carbon emissions, it is mandatory that the largest carbon emitters and energy users make efforts to increase energy efficiency and use alternative low carbon sources of energy.

Brazil is the fifth largest country in the world. It has a territory of more than 8 million km², and a population of around 200 million inhabitants. It plays an increasing international role, and is already the world's eighth largest economy. Economic growth was on average 3.6% a year between 1990 and 2012, compared to 2.8% during the previous decade,[1] having reduced inequality from 0.58 Gini index in 2000 to 0.54 in 2012.[2] Between 2003 and 2014, Brazil's greater international role can be noted in several different arenas, including global energy governance in the transition to low carbon development. It is the 11th greatest energy producer

The authors sincerely thank the two anonymous reviewers and Marina Kayumova for their comments, which helped improve the article.

1. GDP growth, data from World Bank, 1993 to 2002 and 2003 to 2012, available: <http://data.worldbank.org/indicator/NY.GDP.MKTP.KD.ZG?page=4> (accessed 25 January 2014).

2. From Gini 57,78 (2003) to 54,70 (World Bank, 2009), available: <http://iresearch.worldbank.org/PovcalNet/index.htm?2> (accessed 28 July 2013).

and seventh largest energy consumer;[3] it already occupies fifth place among producers of low carbon technology.[4] Brazil is an important player in the climate change regime, and is also a leader, although as well as pushing the regime forward, at other times it blocks progress. The paradoxical situation in which new positions might contradict previous ones can only be understood if Brazilian policy and politics are analysed in detail.

In order to understand Brazilian energy-climate policy and politics and Brazil's positions in the international climate change regime, the article will be divided into five parts. First, low carbon development will be defined. Then, the Brazilian GHG emissions profile and energy matrix will be checked, followed by a description of the domestic policy and politics in the field—focusing on electricity, fuel and energy efficiency—between 2003 and 2014. The description will justify Brazil's classification in the international climate change regime as a moderate conservative great climate power. The article argues that Brazil has moved towards domestic implementation and international action in favour of low carbon development, but important setbacks took place during 1990–2014, so it is perhaps premature to state that Brazil has embarked on the low carbon development paradigm.

Low Carbon Development

Sustainability has been on the international agenda since the United Nations Conference on the Human Environment (1972), when it was decided that the impact of development on the environment should be considered. In 1987, the Brundtland Report, or "Our Common Future", was released, and sustainable development was defined as "development that meets the needs of the present without compromising the ability of future generations to meet their own needs".[5] The concept of sustainable development was adopted by the United Nations Conference on Environment and Development (1992) as the leading guideline for proposals and commitments.

Green economy was first employed in a report for the UK government,[6] and the concept is intended to frame the new economic model that should follow the end of the global financial crisis. There is no official definition for green economy; the most commonly applied is "economy that results in improved human well-being and social equity, while significantly reducing environmental risks and ecological scarcities".[7] The concept was discussed during the United Nations Conference on

3. 2010 data, World Bank, available: <http://data.worldbank.org/indicator> (accessed 28 July 2013).

4. World Wild Fund and Roland Berger, "Clean Economy, Living Planet: The Race to the Top of Global Clean Energy Technology Manufacturing 2012" (2012), available: <http://www.rolandberger.com/media/publications/2012-06-06-rbsc-pub-Clean_Economy_Living_Planet.html> (accessed 10 July 2013); The Pew Charitable Trusts, "Who Is Winning the Energy Race" (2012), available: <http://www.pewenvironment.org/news-room/reports/whos-winning-the-clean-energy-race-2012-edition-85899468949> (accessed 12 July 2013).

5. World Commission on Environment and Development, "Our Common Future" (1987; annex of document A/42/427 of the Secretary-General of United Nations), available: <http://www.un-documents.net/wced-ocf.htm> (accessed 1 July 2013).

6. David W. Pearce, Anil Markandya and Edward B. Barbier, *Blueprint for a Green Economy* (New York: Earthscan, 1989).

7. United Nations Environmental Programme, "Towards a Green Economy: Pathways to Sustainable Development and Poverty Eradication" (2011), p. 2, available: <http://www.unep.org/greeneconomy/Portals/88/documents/ger/ger_final_dec_2011/Green%20EconomyReport_Final_Dec2011.pdf> (accessed 1 July 2013).

Sustainable Development (UNCSD) in 2012, but there was no agreement to make it more prescriptive. The final report of Rio+20 states that green economy is "one of the important tools available for achieving sustainable development and that it could provide options for policymaking but should not be a rigid set of rules".[8] The conference was a failure from the point of view of progress in building up global governance.[9]

Taken seriously, beyond politically correct rhetoric, the concepts of sustainable development and green economy would imply deep socioeconomic restructuring to counterbalance economic growth and environmental protection. They should give rise to an economic path that respects at least the eight identified and already quantified planetary boundaries — limits to human action before a systemic environmental disruption: (1) climate change; (2) biodiversity loss; (3) nitrogen cycle; (4) phosphorus cycle; (5) stratospheric ozone depletion; (6) ocean acidification; (7) global freshwater use; (8) change in land use.[10] Nevertheless, they are controversial and complex parameters, unable to guide effective policy-making; therefore, other parameters evolved from multilateral environmental negotiations, and low carbon development is among them. Low carbon development aims at a consistent reduction of GHG emissions per GDP unit (well beyond the "normal" reduction derived from business-as-usual economic and technological development), a clear direction in policy-making. Essentially, the low carbon development path is embedded in the commitment to reduce carbon emissions, rendering economic growth and climate constancy structurally compatible.[11]

Climate change is a complex topic, for a number of reasons: (1) it is intrinsically global, because it is centred around changes in concentration of atmospheric gases led by rising CO2 (weighting around 80%), methane and nitrous oxide levels; (2) it operates on a time scale that is beyond the human daily experience; (3) it involves intra and intergenerational equity issues; (4) it is not linear; it is not possible to identify direct cause and effect, since the causes of climate change are complex; (5) it challenges decision-making processes and institutions, which are not prepared to deal with non-linear issues.[12] Climate stability has been extremely relevant to human life since the Neolithic revolution — around 11,000 years ago — and could be classified as a key civilisational driver of contemporary society, together with the expansion and deepening of globalisation and the diffusion of democracy.[13]

---

8. United Nations Conference on Sustainable Development, "The Future We Want", United Nations General Assembly Resolution A/RES/66/288 (2012), available: <https://sustainabledevelopment.un.org/futurewewant.html> (accessed 1 May 2014).

9. Eduardo Viola and Matías Franchini, "Os limiares planetários, a Rio+20 e o papel do Brasil", *Cadernos EBAPE*, Vol. 10, No. 3 (2012), pp. 470–491.

10. Johan Rockstrom et al., "A Safe Operating Space for Humanity", *Nature*, Vol. 461 (24 September 2009), available: <http://www.nature.com/nature/journal/v461/n7263/full/461472a.html> (accessed 1 July 2013); Eduardo Viola, Matías Franchini and Thais Lemos Ribeiro, *Sistema internacional de hegemonia conservadora – governança global e democracia na era da crise climática* (São Paulo: Annablume, 2013), p. 60.

11. United Nations Department on Economic and Social Affairs, "A Guidebook to the Green Economy" (2012), p. 51, available: <http://www.uncsd2012.org/content/documents/528Green%20Economy%20Guidebook_100912_FINAL.pdf> (accessed 28 June 2013).

12. Will Steffen, "A Truly Complex and Diabolical Policy Problem", in John S. Dryzek, Richard B. Norgaard and David Schlosberg (eds.), *The Oxford Handbook of Climate Change and Society* (Oxford: Oxford University Press, 2011), pp. 22–26.

13. Viola, Franchini and Ribeiro, *Sistema internacional, op. cit.*

Climate change mitigation requires stabilising the concentration of GHG in the atmosphere, either by reducing emissions or carbon capture and storage (CCS).[14] In 1996, developed countries agreed on limited compulsory reduction emissions targets and on mechanisms for their implementation. However, at the 3rd Conference of Parties (COP 3), held in Kyoto in 1997, they failed to set compulsory commitments for reducing the rate of emissions growth from fast-growing economies; the United States therefore withdrew from the Protocol in 2001.[15] The Kyoto Protocol was in force from 2005 to 2012. By the end of the period, three key developed countries (Japan, Russia and Canada) raised arguments similar to the Americans' and also withdrew. In 2013 the Protocol was a poor caricature of the treaty signed in 1997:[16] if in 1997 65% of global GHG emissions were constrained by commitment to the Protocol, in 2013 the commitment was reduced to only 12% of the total (mostly enforced by the European Union). At COP 18 (2012), countries established 2015 as the deadline for creating a legally binding agreement to allocate emissions reductions to all countries from 2020 onwards. At COP 19 (2013), a bitter debate started between developed and developing countries on how to define the criteria for the new commitments, and it continued at COP 20 (2014). It is clear that an ambitious agreement will not be achieved unless developing countries, as well as developed ones, that account for relevant shares of current GHG emissions, agree to undertake significant mandatory emissions reduction targets for the period between 2020 and 2030.[17] In fact, eight countries are key in achieving low carbon development: three climate super powers (the USA, the EU and China) and five climate great powers (India, Russia, Japan, Brazil and South Korea).[18]

Low carbon development requires implementation of measures that interfere in core issues of the contemporary lifestyle, such as energy sources and uses, institutions, governance, economic organisation and values.[19] Therefore, it "will only be successfully achieved as a benefit contingent upon other goals which are politically attractive and relentlessly pragmatic".[20] Since CCS is still a limited option,[21] it is imperative to reduce emissions—especially carbon, i.e., to

14. United Nations, "United Nations Framework Convention on Climate Change" (1992), available: <http://unfccc.int/resource/docs/convkp/conveng.pdf> (accessed 1 July 2013).

15. Eduardo Viola, "O regime internacional de mudança climática e o Brasil", *Revista Brasileira de Ciências Sociais*, Vol. 17, No. 50 (2002), pp. 25–46, available: <http://www.scielo.br/pdf/rbcsoc/v17n50/a03v1750.pdf> (accessed 1 May 2014).

16. It is important to remember that the Kyoto Protocol was signed in 1997, but its text continued to be discussed until 2001, when the final version was issued. It took the member countries a further four years to ratify the Protocol; it entered in force in 2005.

17. Eduardo Viola, Matías Franchini and Thais Lemos Ribeiro, "Climate Governance in an International System under Conservative Hegemony: The Role of Major Powers", *Revista Brasileira de Política Internacional*, Vol. 55, special edition (2012), pp. 9–29.

18. The definitions of climate super power and climate great power must not be confused with traditional IR definitions. For an extensive analysis of this issue, see Viola, Franchini and Ribeiro, "Climate Governance", *op. cit.*

19. Steffen, *op. cit.*, p. 21; Dale Jamieson, "The Nature of the Problem", in Dryzek, Norgaard and Schlosberg, *op. cit.*, pp. 38–54.

20. Gwyn Prins et al., "The Hartwell Paper – A New Direction for Climate Policy after the Crash of 2009" (London School of Economics and University of Oxford, 2010), available: <http://eprints.lse.ac.uk/27939/1/HartwellPaper_English_version.pdf> (accessed 2 August 2013).

21. International Energy Agency, "Technology Roadmap Carbon Capture and Storage" (2013), available: <http://www.iea.org/publications/freepublications/publication/TechnologyRoadmapCarbonCaptureandStorage.pdf> (accessed 15 November 2013).

decarbonise. Energy supply and use accounts for more than 60% of the world's GHG emissions,[22] and it is likely that this share will increase even more once developing countries achieve higher levels of development. Hence, the two main drivers for global decarbonisation are increasing energy efficiency and disseminating low carbon energy sources,[23] and success will only be possible if the eight key countries —among them Brazil—are committed to these objectives.

Brazilian GHG Emissions and Climate Change Policy

Brazil is among the six greatest GHG emitters, but its emissions profile has been historically different from that of most other countries. Due to its relatively low carbon energy matrix, land use, land use change and forestry (LULUCF) have traditionally been the major drivers of Brazilian emissions. Deforestation is a relevant issue in various parts of Brazil, but has been considerably reduced. During the period in which Marina Silva (2003–08) and Carlos Minc (2008–10) were Ministers of the Environment, deforestation decreased from 27,000 km^2 in 2004 to 7,500 km^2 in 2009.[24]

The profile of Brazilian emissions has changed from 1990 to 2013, as seen in Table 1. The numbers show that, in 1990, Brazilian emissions were very different from those of other middle income countries: LULUCF accounted for 69% of the emissions, while both energy and industrial processes contributed only 13.55% of the total amount. In 2013, the share of energy and industrial processes was 35.71% (from total emissions), which was much more similar to other middle-income countries. LULUCF, however, still accounted for the largest share of Brazilian emissions. When the variation in emissions from different economic sectors is taken into account (Table 2), a clear trend emerges. Emissions from energy and industrial processes are increasing, while LULUCF emissions tend to decrease, albeit on an irregular basis. This is a very important shift, which has a direct effect on Brazilian policy-making and policy thinking. Climate change mitigation, once a by-product of deforestation policies, now requires action in other sectors.[25]

Table 2 shows that Brazilian total emissions in 2013 were 13% lower than in 1990. This is an important achievement. Still, a qualitative analysis of the emissions reductions and a comparison to the reductions undertaken by the European Union are important. Brazil reduced LULUCF emissions, which came mostly from intense deforestation; even if tackling deforestation requires serious efforts in monitoring legal compliance and sanctioning breaches, the winners of the activity are a small and disorganised group whose interests are easily dismissed by the largest share of the population. European Union emissions, however, have energy and industrial processes as the source of their largest share. As a result, European emissions can only be reduced with a true collective effort in advancing low carbon development. While the chances are high that the European effort will be sustained in time—after struggling to shift a paradigm, there is interest in advancing it—further reduction of Brazilian

---

22. Data available at <http://www.grida.no/graphicslib/detail/world-greenhouse-gas-emissions-by-sector_6658> (accessed 15 December 2013).

23. Viola, Franchini and Ribeiro, *Sistema internacional, op. cit.*, p. 143.

24. Annual averages. Data from the National Institute of Spatial Research (INPE), available: <http://www.obt.inpe.br/prodes/index.php> (accessed 15 December 2013). In the first two years of Silva's tenure (2003–04) there was a dramatic increase in deforestation.

25. Viola and Franchini, *op. cit.*

Table 1. Brazilian Emissions 1990–2013, Total and Per Economic Sector (t of GHG).

	1990	2000	2005	2010	2013
Energy	194,097,928	304,988,022	333,834,060	389,017,084	473,265,688
Agriculture and cattle grazing	286,974,002	327,805,048	392,045,485	406,453,897	416,694,029
LULUCF	1,246,826,159	1,457,940,463	1,506,174,139	598,966,415	524,467,957
Industrial processes	50,821,446	69,230,853	76,269,915	79,663,247	86,512,922
Waste	28,951,842	38,209,467	41,229,018	48,770,448	48,738,583
Total	**1,807,671,377**	**2,198,173,853**	**2,349,552,616**	**1,522,871,092**	**1,567,679,179**
% Energy in total emissions	10.74	13.87	14.21	25.54	30.19
% Agriculture in total emissions	15.88	14.91	16.69	26.69	26.58
% LULUCF in total emissions	68.97	66.33	64.10	39.33	34.60
% Industrial processes in total	2.81	3.15	3.25	5.23	5.52
% Waste in total emissions	1.60	1.74	1.75	3.20	3.11

Source: Own elaboration, based on data from *Observatorio do Clima, Sistema de Estimativa de Emissão de Gases de Efeito Estufa*, available: <http://www.seeg.eco.br/tabela-geral-de-emissoes/> (accessed 30 November 2014).

Table 2. Variation in Brazilian Emissions (%).

	1990-2013	2000-2013	2005-2013	2010-2013
Energy emissions, variation (%)	143.83	55.18	41.77	21.66
Agriculture and cattle grazing emissions, variation (%)	45.20	27.12	6.29	2.52
LULUCF emissions, variation (%)	-56.49	-62.79	-63.98	-9.43
Industrial processes emissions, variation (%)	70.23	24.96	13.43	8.60
Waste emissions, variation (%)	68.34	27.56	18.21	-0.07
Total emissions, variation (%)	**-13.28**	**-28.68**	**-33.28**	**2.94**

Source: Own elaboration, based on data from *Observatorio do Clima, Sistema de Estimativa de Emissão de Gases de Efeito Estufa*, available: <http://www.seeg.eco.br/tabela-geral-de-emissoes/> (accessed 30 November 2014).

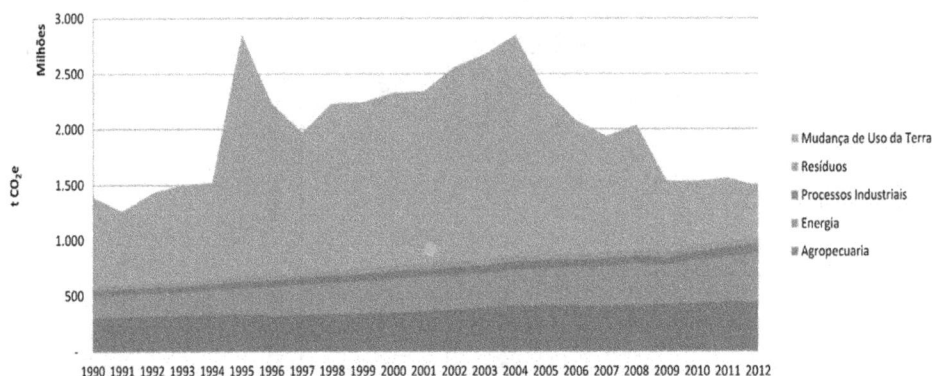

Figure 1. Brazilian GHG Emissions Profile, 1990–2012.
Source: Observatório do Clima, available: <https://s3-sa-east-1.amazonaws.com/arquivos. gvces.com.br/arquivos_gvces/arquivos/301/SEEG_DocumentoSintese.pdf> (accessed 30 November 2014).

emissions depends on important action to keep deforestation low and to push for low carbon development in other economic sectors. To date, there are no clear signs of either (Figure 1).

Domestic climate change policy discussions were very restricted (developed mostly among a small number of natural/social scientists and some non-governmental organisations [NGOs], particularly branches of international NGOs) before 2000, the year in which the Brazilian Climate Change Forum—an alliance of government, business, civil society, scientific and non-governmental sectors to discuss the issue—was created. In 2007, the drafting of a national policy in the field entered the Brazilian agenda, and the National Climate Change Plan was enacted in 2008. The Plan establishes several targets that should be achieved to mitigate climate change, including to: stimulate efficiency in all economic sectors (especially to increase energy efficiency, substitute coal with charcoal coming from planted forests, replace old fridges using hydrochlorofluorocarbon (HCFC), invest in solar water heating and urban waste recycling, phase out the use of fire for clearing sugar cane plantations, and integrate agriculture and cattle raising systems); maintain the share of renewable energy in the Brazilian electricity matrix; encourage the domestic and international use of biofuels; seek further reduction of deforestation; eliminate the net loss of forest coverage; strengthen inter-sector actions to reduce climate change vulnerability; and identify impacts of climate change on the environment and support relevant scientific research. In 2009, the Plan was included in a legal framework—the National Climate Change Law (Law No. 12187, complemented by Decree No. 7390/2010). This was a major achievement, placing Brazil among the selected group of countries that had enacted a Climate Change Law to constrain carbon emissions, and the first non-OECD (Organisation for Economic Cooperation and Development) country to do so (even some OECD countries, such as the USA, Canada and Australia, did not have one). Besides incorporating the Plan, the legal framework established that sectorial action plans should target the reduction of GHG emissions. Among the most relevant sectorial plans are plans to reduce deforestation in the Amazon and Cerrado Savannah, the low carbon agriculture plan, and plans to reduce emissions from the steel industry and energy sectors.

Due to the reduction of deforestation and the increasing relevance of energy in Brazil's carbon emissions, analysing the Brazilian energy matrix and policy transformations is key to understanding the country's trajectory in the international climate change regime.

Brazilian Energy Matrix Transformations

The Brazilian energy matrix is relatively low carbon when compared with that of most other countries. In 2012, 46% of its total primary energy production came from low carbon sources;[26] the number is high mainly due to electricity, since 76.9% of the Brazilian electricity supply comes from hydropower.[27] Nevertheless, it could do better. With its large territory located mostly in a tropical and subtropical climate, with mostly plain relief (plains and plateaus) and extent drainage basins, Brazil has enormous potential for developing renewable energy. In fact, considering the currently available technology, this potential is among the highest in the world.

Still, in recent years, low carbon sources have reduced their share in the Brazilian energy matrix. While total energy production and supply increased by approximately 40% from 2003 to 2012, energy production and supply from renewable sources increased by 37% and 36% respectively during the same period (Table 3).

The increasing share of non-renewable energy sources in the Brazilian energy matrix was one of the setbacks of the decade. The other relates to energy efficiency. In fact, due to (1) the time span required for Research and Development (R&D) in low carbon energy sources, and (2) the intrinsic need to reduce energy consumption so as to assimilate a low carbon way of living, investing in energy efficiency is the most rational choice to achieve low carbon development. Yet energy efficiency plays second fiddle in Brazil. From 1984 to 2004,[28] the amount of energy effectively employed in final use (in relation to total energy input) shifted from 46.9% to

---

26. Empresa de Pesquisa Energética, "Balanço Energético Nacional – BEN 2013" (2013), available: <https://ben.epe.gov.br/downloads/Relatorio_Final_BEN_2013.pdf> (accessed 17 December 2013), pp. 21–22.

27. *Ibid.*, p. 16.

28. Latest available data.

Table 3. Domestic Energy Production and Domestic Energy Supply, by Source 2003–2012 (103 tep (toe)).

Energy source	Energy production 2003	Energy production 2012	Variation (%)	Energy supply 2003	Energy supply 2012	Variation (%)
Oil	77,225	107,017	38.5%	80,688	111,193	37.8%
Natural gas	15,681	25,574	63%	15,512	32,598	110%
Coal + peat	1,823	2,517	38%	12,848	15,287	19%
Uranium	2,745	3,881	41.3%	3,621	4,286	18%
Total non-renewable	**97,474**	**138,989**	**42.5%**	**112,669**	**163,364**	**45%**
Hydro	26,283	35,719	36%	29,477	39,181	33%
Wood	25,965	25,735	-1%	25,973	25,735	-1%
Sugarcane	28,357	45,132	60%	27,093	43,572	60.8%
Other renewable	5,663	11,723	107%	5,663	11,754	107.5%
Total renewable	**86,268**	**118,309**	**37%**	**88,206**	**120,242**	**36%**
Total	183,742	257,298	40%	200,875	283,606	41%

Source: Own elaboration, based on data from *Balanço Energético Nacional - séries completas 1970-2012*, available: <https://ben.epe.gov.br/BENSeriesCompletas.aspx> (accessed 12 January 2014).

57.8%.[29] Many sectors' performances were even poorer—for example, from 31.4% to 37.5% in transport.[30] In comparison to the US, Brazilian truckload freights consume 85% more fuel.[31] In order to understand such setbacks, it is necessary to analyse how energy policy and politics evolved in Brazil between 2003 and 2014.

Brazilian Energy Policy and Politics

From 2003 to 2010, Brazil's economy grew at the rate of 3.5% a year, a little more than the average world economy but much less than other emerging countries. From 2011 to 2014, growth decreased to 1.7% a year, less than the average world economy and dramatically less than other emerging economies. The 2003–2010 growth had its roots in three main factors: (1) substantial change in the relative prices of industrial products and commodities, favouring the latter (and Brazil is a great exporter of commodities); (2) positive effects of the pro-market macroeconomic reforms performed in the second half of the 1990s; and (3) high rates of Foreign Direct Investment (FDI). From 2011, the lack of pension, labour, fiscal, tax and political system reforms and the intense interventionism of the federal government were felt: economic growth declined; inflation was always significantly above the target defined by the Central Bank; and FDI remained high but did not increase. The global economic crises did play a role in the big picture, but growth would not have decreased so sharply if the crises were alone in influencing Brazilian growth in the period.

29. Empresa de Pesquisa Energética, *op. cit.*, p. 193.

30. *Ibid.*, p. 193.

31. Ministério de Minas e Energy, "Plano Nacional de Eficiência Energética" (2011), available: <http://www.orcamentofederal.gov.br/projeto-esplanada-sustentavel/pasta-para-arquivar-dados-do-pes/Plano_Nacional_de_Eficiencia_Energetica.pdf> (accessed 12 February 2014).

These factors influenced energy policy and politics in Brazil. Regarding low carbon energy sources, two different factors can be observed: from 2003 to 2007, an increased share of renewable sources in the energy matrix; and from 2007 to 2014, their declining role, due to the discovery of deep offshore oil reserves and the use of oil prices as a heterodox policy tool to artificially maintain greater economic growth rates. Regarding energy efficiency, there was no consistent development of policy and politics during the decade.

Electricity

Hydropower is the main source of Brazilian electricity. From 1920 to the 1970s, relying on hydropower for electricity generation was "natural" in a country with little coal and oil reserves. After 1973, it gained strategic importance due to energy security concerns in the context of world oil crises. The country has hydropower potential among the greatest in the word, but most of its southern river basins are already greatly explored; 70% of its remaining potential is located in the Amazon basin,[32] a region with complex ecosystems and great importance for maintaining the continent's climate and biodiversity.

Most Brazilian hydropower plants were built between 1968 and 1984, when lower environmental standards were in force and both national and foreign financial resources were available. Since 1985, it has become much more difficult to license a new hydropower plant, and many of the projected ones had their construction postponed or disrupted due to further environmental demands and the fiscal crisis of the Brazilian state. After the 2001 supply crisis,[33] the federal government resumed efforts to build new plants, some of them in the Amazon region. From 2007 to 2013, the Jirau and Santo Antonio hydropower plants were built on the Madeira river; the Belo Monte hydropower plant is under construction on the Xingu river. In common, they employ run-of-the-river technology, a product of negotiations between environmentalists and defenders of development at all costs. On the one hand, run-of-the-river hydropower plants produce electricity according to the natural river flows, allowing for smaller dams to be built and reducing environmental impacts. On the other hand, because electricity demand is constant, run-of-the-river hydropower plants are less efficient from an economic point of view and must have back-up systems, so their total environmental impact depends on the chosen back-up system. Sadly, in recent years, this role has been played by fossil fuel thermal power plants. Therefore, it is not straightforward that a run-of-the-river hydropower plant in the Amazon region will have less environmental impact than a hydropower plant with a great reservoir built in the same or another region of the country.[34]

32. Eletrobras, "Potencial hidrelétrico brasileiro por bacia – Dezembro 2012" (2012), available: <http://www.eletrobras.com/elb/data/Pages/LUMIS21D128D3PTBRIE.htm> (accessed 17 January 2014). According to official data, the rivers of the Amazon basin have 34,000 MW of hydropower potential not yet explored.

33. In 2001, the Brazilian electricity supply was disrupted after an abnormally dry summer reduced water levels at key dams. The government rationed electricity, and fossil fuel thermal power plants were put into operation as back-up systems.

34. From many works on environmental impacts of dams, three international guidelines are especially recommended: World Commission on Dams, "Dams and Development: A New Framework for Decision-Making" (2000), available: <http://www.internationalrivers.org/files/attached-files/world_commission_on_dams_final_report.pdf>; International Hydropower Association, "IHA Sustainability

The controversy over the construction of the Belo Monte hydropower plant has led to several legal battles, including disputes between the Brazilian federal state and the Inter-American Commission of Human Rights and Court of Justice.[35] Public opinion is mostly against the project, not only due to the environmental impact, but also because of its impact to indigenous populations. The same controversy exists around other projects, such as those on the Tapajos river. Recently, the federal government has changed some environmental laws to facilitate the construction of hydropower plants in the Amazon region. In 2011, the limits of several national parks and national forests were modified, and areas estimated to be flooded were excluded from the obligation to be preserved,[36] and the government has postponed demarcation of indigenous lands. In 2013, there were several confrontations between the native population from the Tapajos river area and government officials.

Among the alternatives to avoid the stricter Brazilian environmental requirements is the construction of new hydropower plants in Peru to export electricity to Brazil. This has been supported by large Brazilian construction corporations, which are very powerful in defining Brazilian domestic and foreign energy policy. In 2010, Brazil and Peru signed the Energy Agreement[37] planning the construction of six hydropower plants in the Peruvian Amazon. This initiative is highly controversial: there are claims of Brazilian imperialism and opposition from Peruvian indigenous populations. The treaty is not yet in force and its ratification was delayed, although some of the projects are in advanced stages of planning.

Another solution is to develop alternative energy sources. In 2002, the Alternative Energy Sources Incentive Programme—in Portuguese, PROINFA—was enacted by the federal government, and was regulated in 2004. It mandates that 10% of Brazil's energy supply in 2020 should be produced by renewable sources, meaning small hydropower plants (with installed capacity between 1 and 30 MW and reservoirs smaller than 3 km^2), wind and biomass (solar photovoltaic was left out due to concerns over prices).[38] After 2004, these energy sources took their places in the federal government's auctions for electricity: between 2004 and 2011, small hydropower

Guidelines" (2004), available: <http://www.hydrosustainability.org/IHAHydro4Life/media/PDFs/PDF%20docs/IHA-Sustainability-Guidelines_2004.pdf>; IEA Hydropower Agreement, "Annex III – Hydropower and the Environment: Present Context and Guidelines for Future Action", available: <http://www.ieahydro.org/reports/HyA3S5V2.pdf>, revised in 2010: "Update of Recommendations for Hydropower and the Environment", available: <http://www.ieahydro.org/uploads/files/finalannexxii_task2_briefingdocument_oct2010.pdf> (all accessed 7 November 2013).

35. In 2011, the Inter-American Court of Justice, following a claim presented by NGOs that the UHE Belo Monte had several social and environmental impacts not covered by the environmental licensing in process, asked Brazil to suspend the licensing. The request came after the Brazilian government had answered several consultations of the Court on the same issue, and was not welcomed. The relationship between the country and the Court worsened; on occasion, Brazil has stated its support for the Venezuelan, Ecuadorian and Bolivian pledge to diminish the Court's powers regarding interventions in matters of human rights.

36. Law 12.678/2012, available: <http://www.planalto.gov.br/ccivil_03/_Ato2011-2014/2012/Lei/L12678.htm> (accessed 13 January 2014).

37. Agreement between the government of the Federal Republic of Brazil and the government of the Republic of Peru for the supply of electricity to Peru and exports of surplus to Brazil, available in Portuguese: <http://dai-mre.serpro.gov.br/atos-internacionais/bilaterais/2010/acordo-entre-o-governo-da-republica-federativa-do-brasil-e-o-governo-da-republica-do-peru-para-fornecimentos-de-energia-eletrica-ao-peru-e-exportacao-de-excedentes-ao-brasil> (accessed 12 January 2014).

38. The first auction including solar energy took place on 31 October 2014; solar sold 1,048 MW (installed capacity); it is expected that solar will produce at least 889.7 MW starting in 2017.

plants sold around 1,800 MW; wind sold 5,399.5 MW; and biomass was responsible for around 2,500 MW.[39] Despite their increased participation in the Brazilian electricity market, alternative renewable electricity production sources still face many challenges: (1) their share in electricity production is very small—for example, small hydropower plants account for 3.63%[40] of Brazilian electricity; (2) they face difficulties in competing with traditional sources due to the minimum cost criteria employed in the auctions; (3) they are opposed by an alliance of large hydropower technicians, Eletrobras (the state-owned corporation for operating hydropower plants and electricity transmission), bureaucratic circles and large private corporations who construct dams; (4) there is no official policy that establishes long-term incentives, quotas and minimum prices for alternative energy sources, or any legal obligation to auction alternative energy production periodically.

Nuclear power is an important low carbon energy source for a large part of the world, and could be successfully applied as a transitional source. Since it is highly effective in generating electricity, it could replace fossil fuels until technology for renewable sources is developed.[41] Brazil has two nuclear power plants (Angra 1 and Angra 2) and a third under construction (Angra 3), but public opinion does not favour nuclear energy; in fact, it has the strongest opposition in the country —even most of the academic community is against it. The lobby in favour of nuclear power (nuclear engineers, the military, diplomats) is losing power because most of them are nearing retirement. Nuclear power will never be an important source of energy in Brazil, although it will remain in place due to technological know-how, security reasons and the fact that the country has huge uranium reserves.

This scenario of slow hydropower expansion and barriers to alternative renewable sources has led to the major setback in the Brazilian electricity sector during the last decade: the increased role of fossil fuel thermal power plants. These plants—once employed in just a few locations not connected to the grid, or as back-up systems—are now constantly in use. Their impact on the Brazilian environment and economy is great. They pollute the air and the water, they contribute to the increase of carbon emissions and the electricity they generate costs more for consumers; in addition, they usually depend on imported fuel (coal or oil). Recent (2013 and 2014) cuts in the electricity supply to several regions of the country have shown that Brazil is coming to a crossroads in the sector.

Fuel

Oil remains the main source of fuel in Brazil. The Brazilian transport system is highly dependent on roads—terribly built and poorly maintained—and its fleet

39. Luiz A. Horta Nogueira and Jonas Carvalheira Costa, "Opções tecnológicas em energia: uma visão brasileira" (Fundação Brasileira para o Desenvolvimento Sustentável, 2012), available: <http://fbds.org.br/fbds/IMG/pdf/doc-531.pdf> (accessed 17 December 2013)

40. Data from <http://www.aneel.gov.br/aplicacoes/capacidadebrasil/capacidadebrasil.cfm> (accessed 12 February 2014).

41. Andre Cultrim Carvalho, "Expansão da fronteira agropecuária e a dinâmica do desmatamento florestal na Amazônia Paraense", PhD thesis, Universidade Estadual de Campinas, 2012, available: <http://www.bibliotecadigital.unicamp.br/document/?code=000862229> (accessed 2 May 2014).

employs mostly diesel as fuel. A large country with mostly plain relief, important river basins and an extensive coastline could make better use of these assets in transportation.

Brazilian diesel was traditionally low quality, due to the high level of sulphur in its mix. Biodiesel production is still in its infancy in Brazil. The National Biodiesel Programme, created in 2005, aims at increasing the uptake of biodiesel nationally. It established a minimum of 8–10% biodiesel in the diesel mix. Brazilian biodiesel comes mostly from soybeans; one of the obstacles to increasing its production is the difficulty in using other vegetable species, which are more efficient than soybeans in producing biodiesel but are mostly produced on small family farms, making it difficult to be commoditised and sold on a large scale.

Brazil is a traditional producer of ethanol from sugarcane. High prices of oil during the crises of the 1970s and energy security reasons played important roles in encouraging its use as fuel; back then, sustainability concerns were absent. In the 1990s, due to a severe crisis of supply, ethanol's role as a biofuel faded; it came back into the spotlight in 2003, after the development of flexible fuel technology.

Competition between oil/derivatives and ethanol is not a fair one. Until 2006, the domestic prices of oil/derivatives followed international ones; after that, however, due to the discovery of the deep offshore reserves—and the illusion that Brazil would rapidly become a great producer and exporter of oil—the federal government was misled in using domestic prices as a heterodox economic tool. In 2007, the Brazilian government subsidised oil prices to maintain high economic growth rates, changing the relative prices of gasoline/ethanol and undermining the competiveness of the last. After the collapse of Lehman Brothers, tax exemptions given to the automobile industry led to a dramatic increase in fuel demand, while ethanol prices were still not competitive. These heterodox policies enhanced short-term economic growth but increased long-term macroeconomic imbalance, and penalised both Petrobras—having faced huge financial losses—and the ethanol production chain.

Expectations about the deep offshore oil reserves were high until 2010. Most environmentalists avoided the criticism of "popular pre-salt", afraid of being isolated in public opinion. There was no strong environmental movement to defend low carbon energy sources rather than exploiting the new oil reserves. Nevertheless, it was a victory without a battle: while it was expected that exploitation would start soon after the discovery, disputes among state governments over the distribution of revenues from the reserves postponed the auctions of the reserves for a couple of years. During this period, the economic output of the technology (dramatically improved in the second half of the 2000s) to exploit shale gas was achieved in the US—supposedly the largest market for Brazilian deep offshore oil—and Mexico got close to ending the PEMEX monopoly over oil, facts which appealed to American companies such as Chevron and Exxon Mobile. Petrobras, whose participation in the auction was imperative due to legal requirements, lost the financial capacity to act due to the continued losses it faced by subsidising gasoline and incompetence in closing business deals (due to increased levels of corruption). In 2013, enthusiasm for deep offshore oil reached a low point and there were some small changes in the relative prices of gasoline/ethanol, though not enough to change the current situation.

From 2005 to 2007, ethanol played an important role in Brazilian diplomacy. Brazil defended the creation of a global market for biofuels, and tried to make an international commodity out of ethanol. It exported technology and established partnerships to develop ethanol markets in several countries; multinational companies—Shell, Petrobras and Chevron—bought assets from ethanol companies during this period. This position, which suited the Brazilian national interest but was dissonant from the positions of Brazil's allies in climate change negotiations, such as China, India, Indonesia and South Africa, did not last. By the time the deep offshore oil was discovered, ethanol quickly vanished from Brazilian official speeches, the same having happened to investments in ethanol companies.

It is uncertain how ethanol production will develop in the years to come. Brazilian public opinion favours biofuel, but few groups are mobilised or understand the bigger picture. A clear example is the positive connotation federal government subsidies to gasoline held for the average Brazilian population. Other important obstacles to greater ethanol production are the influence of oil and gas groups in the government and the misunderstanding that it implies a further commoditisation of the Brazilian economy. In the international market, the competition from ethanol made from corn, produced by the US, and a possible ethanol made from cellulose, developed by the US and Europe, undermines the possibilities for Brazilian ethanol to be vastly exported. If there is no change in the next few years to create strategic reserves to avoid price volatility and reliability of supply, or to invest in the production of pure ethanol vehicles, it is likely that ethanol will remain a fuel of secondary importance in Brazil.

Energy Efficiency

The topic of energy efficiency has been on the agenda since the 1990s, though in a diffuse fashion. Brazil has developed a regulatory framework and mandatory programmes for energy efficiency. The National Electrical Energy Conservation Programme (in Portuguese, PROCEL) aims at reducing the consumption of electricity; the National Programme of Rational Use of Oil and Natural Gas By-products (in Portuguese, CONPET) targets the use of oil and its derivatives; the Brazilian Labelling Programme (in Portuguese, PBE) classifies house appliances, devices and light utility vehicles according to their energy use; Law No. 9991/2000 mandates electricity companies to make a minimum investment in energy efficiency R&D. Yet public debate about energy efficiency and response to the initiatives was limited.

The picture changed during the 2001 electricity supply crisis. Electricity was rationed, and surprisingly, the Brazilian society was capable of a rapid and efficient response to electricity scarcity. Following this, the National Policy for Conservation and Rational Use of Energy (Law No. 10295/2001) was enacted, and created an interministerial committee to manage and enhance initiatives related to energy efficiency. Labelling became much more stringent, and industries were obliged to increase energy efficiency so as not to face economic losses. After the crisis, though, energy waste gradually returned to high levels.

Electricity transmission also performs very poorly. Brazilian electricity is mostly transmitted through the National Interconnected System (in Portuguese, SIN). An integrated transmission system has supply security advantages, as long as the transmission lines are well built and well maintained. Unfortunately, the main criterion in Brazil is short-term cost, not reliability and efficiency. Lines are of inferior quality and barely maintained; even cheap electronic leak detectors are not yet in place in the country. In addition, the expansion of electricity supply and grid improvements are not coupled. For instance, UHE Belo Monte's connection to the SIN will be concluded two years after it starts producing electricity; several wind farms are disconnected as well. The lack of a smart grid prevents the intelligent distribution of energy throughout Brazil and is a stumbling block to the complementarity of renewable energy sources.

Inefficiency is also a concern in the automotive industry. Since the 1950s, this has been one of the main sectors of the Brazilian economy. The federal government always encouraged car production, to be consumed domestically or exported to undemanding markets in terms of carbon emissions. The automotive industry accepts only vague energy efficiency labelling. Brazilian branches of European and US companies lobby against strict energy efficiency labelling and sell in Brazil outdated and inefficient models no longer commercialised in their home countries.[42] Most consumers do not understand the concept of energy efficiency, and still take into account only short-term costs. Even the flex-fuel technology was not developed purely due to environmental concerns, but as a means to employ a boosted ethanol production.

There are groups in favour of energy efficiency and a smart grid in Brazil, but they are not strong enough to change the situation. Given that energy access is no longer a major issue in the country—electricity is available to 100% of the Brazilian urban population and to 97% of the Brazilian rural population; Liquified Petroleum Gas (LPG) for cooking is available to 94% of the total population[43]—and given the recent supply crises,[44] quality should be a priority. However, government propaganda is always based on quantity; recent policies—reducing prices for electricity based on a distorted calculation that benefited companies that do not invest in productivity and energy efficiency—were clearly energy populist measures targeting the 2014 elections. Energy efficiency requires massive investments in long-term quality and reliability, which will never be achieved through increasing economic interventionism and reduction of macroeconomic predictability.

5. Brazil in Global Climate Governance: A Moderate Conservative Great Climate Power

The Brazilian trajectory in global climate governance during the period 2003–2014 can be divided into three phases: (1) conservatism, Amazonian forest paranoia and erratic leadership (1990–2004); (2) complex transition to a moderate reformism (2005–10); (3) back from moderate reformism to moderate conservatism (2011–14).

---

42. Japanese and Korean companies are exceptions to this rule.

43. International Energy Agency, *World Energy Outlook 2014* (2014), available: <http://www.worldenergyoutlook.org/resources/energydevelopment/energyaccessdatabase/> (accessed 30 November 2014).

44. In February 2014, due to an unusually hot summer and the increased use of cooling devices, there were several cuts in the electricity supply due to the incapacity of the system to meet the demand. Given that the summer was also unusually dry and Brazil relies on summer rains to refill UHE reservoirs, either electricity will be rationed or fossil fuel thermal power plants will be further employed over the winter.

By the time discussions over climate issues entered the international arena in 1987–88, Brazilian positioning was extremely conservative and embedded in the G-77 discourse, which defended development at all costs. This position gave way to a different approach in the mid-1990s, following Brazilian market-friendly reforms and the need to enhance the country's credibility in climate negotiations. Brazil started to admit the relevance of environmental issues, but defended the principle of common but differentiated responsibilities to address them. This move from extremely conservative to conservative positioning was consolidated during Cardoso administration (1995–2002), when Brazil aimed to be in a central international position and started leading the developing world towards more ambitious environmental measures.[45] During the Kyoto Protocol negotiations (COP 2, 1996 and COP 3, 1997), Brazil based its position on five dimensions: (1) the right to development is pivotal; (2) sustainable development is the target development pattern; (3) increased Brazilian prestige and role as a leader; (4) opposition to international regulation on forests; and (5) a radical view on common but differentiated responsibilities.[46] During these COPs, Brazilian discourse remained paradoxical. On the one hand, it proposed a fund for emerging countries' initiatives, later implemented as the Clean Development Mechanism, and accepted market mechanisms to complement the compulsory reduction emissions targets for developed countries. On the other hand, Brazil refused to accept proposals considering vegetal carbon in the carbon cycle (carbon sinks and avoided deforestation), and formed an alliance with highly carbonised energy matrix countries (China, India, South Africa and Indonesia), despite its own relatively low carbon energy matrix. Such a paradox is explained by the country's inability to deter deforestation of the Amazon at the time and fear that it would be internationally charged for it; the advantage of the energy matrix was subordinated to the disadvantage of deforestation.[47]

But there were changes. In 2001, Brazil played, together with the European Union and Japan, a leading role in finalising the Kyoto Protocol, and in 2002 tried to lead its international ratification. The shift was a result of civil society pressures, a new awareness of president Cardoso and a more environmentally friendly Minister of Foreign Affairs (Celso Lafer). At the beginning of the Lula administration (2003–04), there were some setbacks due to a nationalist and conservative Minister of Foreign Affairs (Celso Amorim). A dramatic shift in deforestation policy took place in 2005 due to the stronger influence of the Minister of Environment (Marina Silva). From 2005 to 2009, the dramatic reduction of deforestation in the Amazon destroyed the myth of inability to tackle deforestation and empowered reformist forces across the country (government, corporations, civil society and media). No country in the world has ever had such a quick transformation in its place in the global carbon cycle.

From 2006 to 2010, there were changes in the Brazilian position. In 2006, based on its reduced deforestation, Brazil abandoned its previous strong opposition to international forest regulation and accepted it, as long as international financing to tackle deforestation was not coupled with a carbon market. In 2009, the country sided with China, India and South Africa in the BASIC coalition—which considers

---

45. Viola, Franchini and Ribeiro, *Sistema internacional, op. cit.*, pp. 278–279.
46. *Ibid.*, p. 280.
47. *Ibid.*, p. 281.

itself leader of the G-77—but pledged a voluntary 36–39% reduction of its emissions by 2020, having a business-as-usual projected emissions scenario as baseline. This was a major victory for reformist forces (the scientific community, the Ministry of the Environment, branches of Brazilian and transnational corporations, civil society and media).

In 2011 and 2012, the Brazilian position regarding emissions reduction targets was more independent from the Chinese and Indian ones, and Brazil had an important role in diplomatic manoeuvres that achieved the (small) success of the COPs.[48] Nevertheless, its action during Rio+20, in which it established a broader focus for the conference—sustainability in connection with core developmental issues, which are also important but, at that moment, were used to reduce the target of deepening environmental obligations—was a major setback in international climate negotiations.

At the beginning of COP 19 (2013), Brazil unexpectedly reintroduced the "Brazilian doctrine of historical responsibilities": the carbon budget, in terms of commitment, should be measured and allocated according to accumulated historical emissions since 1850. This doctrine had been always present in the Brazilian positioning—though its centrality changed—but had been abandoned in 2009. The doctrine has six major vulnerabilities: (1) there are very good records of consumption of energy since 1850 for developed countries, but not for the rest of the world; (2) records of CO_2 emissions from LULUCF are precarious or inexistent before the last quarter of the twentieth century; (3) since 1850, dramatic changes have taken place in geopolitics, with the number of countries changing from 50 to more than 200, and old empires now dissolved (Ottoman, Europe under Nazi occupation, French and British); (4) emissions during the WWI and WWII periods were considerably higher than those of relatively peaceful periods; (5) from an ethical point of view, it is wrong to blame present generations for the behaviour of previous ones; history proves this is the recipe for perpetual conflict and war; and, even worse, (6) climate change was not scientifically known until the late 1970s, and even at that time was accepted only by a small proportion of climatologists. The Brazilian doctrine was supported by non-Annex I countries and rejected by the Annex I countries. In spite of this beginning, during the development of the COP, Brazil distanced itself from the very conservative and confrontational positioning (reinforcing common but differentiated responsibilities and requesting commitment of developed countries to a second period of compulsory emissions reduction targets before emerging economies accept binding targets themselves) of G-77, led by China and India.

At COP 20 (2014), Brazil submitted a new proposal for differentiating countries' responsibilities, called "Concentric Circles". It consists in placing countries in three different and concentric circles. In the inner circle are countries previously placed in Annex I of the Kyoto Protocol, plus any other that decides to join them; these countries must assume mandatory commitments for reducing emissions. Emerging economies will be placed in a second circle, immediately around the inner; they will pledge voluntary commitments that include all economic sectors and should reduce (1) emissions compared to business-as-usual projections, (2) absolute emissions or (3) carbon intensity of GDP. The most vulnerable and the least developed countries will compose a third concentric circle, and they will have voluntary

---

48. *Ibid.*, p. 285.

emission reduction commitments for either the whole economy or only some economic sectors. Countries placed in the second circle will decide when they are ready to move to the first one, and the same applies in relation to countries in the third circle regarding moving to the second and first. The proposal also states that substantial and new financial resources should be supplied by the countries of the first circle to foster the transition to low carbon development in the countries of the second circle—and even more resources to countries in the third circle. This proposal is in line with the recent conservatism of Brazil, but a setback if compared to the Brazilian position of 2009.

Currently, Brazil is a moderate conservative great climate power. The classification takes into account three different dimensions of power: (1) military capacity; (2) economic power; and (3) climate power, which accounts for the volume and trajectory of GHG emissions, human and technological capital to generate a considerable impact on the transition to a low carbon economy and energy behaviour, the relation between resources and energy culture—and different levels—from local to global, from public to private.[49] Throughout the evolution of the climate regime, Brazil has been a rule shaper of international climate norms, although it has blocked deeper commitments more times than it has supported them:

(1) It has led a radical interpretation of the principle of common and differentiated responsibilities that undermines global agreements.
(2) It has resisted the introduction of vegetable carbon into the regime.
(3) It has blocked the introduction of avoided deforestation in the Kyoto Protocol.
(4) It has created the doctrine of historical responsibilities.
(5) It has supported very irresponsible behaviour by China and India.
(6) It has led a simplistic and obsolete division of the world in North/South, developed/ developing countries, and has been a major promoter of the survival of the G-77, an extremely heterogeneous coalition created during the Cold War.
(7) It started promoting ethanol as a global commodity, but abandoned it when it seemed likely that it could become a major producer and exporter of oil.

Conclusion

From 1990 to 2014, three different trends can be identified in the Brazilian trajectory of global climate governance. Until 2004, Brazil had been conservative and blocked advances in the regime, due to the fear that international pressures over Amazon deforestation could disallow its ownership of the area. From 2005 to 2010, there was a complex transition to a moderate reformism, pushed forward by an alliance between the Minister of the Environment, the scientific community, civil society, low carbon corporations and the media. From 2011 to 2014, Brazil took a step back, moving from moderate reformism to moderate conservatism, due to the discovery of deep oil reserves and the use of oil prices as a heterodox policy to maintain higher rates of economic growth.

Brazil has tackled deforestation, thereby reducing GHG emissions per GDP unit and per capita; but it is too early to state that the country has embarked on low carbon development. Great challenges lie ahead. Once GHG emissions from energy, industrial processes and agriculture gain momentum in Brazil, climate policy and politics become more complex. Several sectors, with strong vested

---

49. Viola, Franchini and Ribeiro, "Climate Governance", *op. cit.*, p. 15.

interests, will need to comply with emissions reduction targets if the country is to internalise the low carbon development paradigm. In addition, structural reforms that have been postponed since the 1990s are important stumbling blocks for Brazilian economic growth and productivity and have direct negative effects in energy efficiency and in expanding the use of low carbon energy sources. These shifts are reflected in the Brazilian positions in international regimes and explain its puzzling alliances with high carbon emissions countries. Brazil, together with India and Russia, is in the "club" of the worst performing major powers in terms of the evolution of economic and labour productivity in the last three decades.

Brazilian energy-climate policy and politics will likely face important obstacles for development from 2015 onwards. On the one hand, foreign and national economic agents are almost as concerned about Brazil's current economic situation as they were before 2003. It is clear that without consistent tax, pension, labour, fiscal and political system reforms, no new system of governance will emerge and it will be difficult for Brazil's economy to reach its potential. On the other hand, the public political demonstrations of 2013 did not translate into change in the composition of the federal government that is in power from 2015. President Rousseff has made some changes in the composition of the ministries and has indicated that some economic reforms are likely to be made; however, there are no signs that decarbonisation will be a priority under the Rousseff government. In the international arena, moderate conservative positions will likely be maintained, as shown by the proposals of the Brazilian delegation at COP 20 (2014).

Global progress towards low carbon development depends on the greatest energy producers and consumers truly committing to energy efficiency and low carbon energy. Blaming present generations for the behaviour of previous ones or compelling emerging economies to adopt mandatory emissions reductions without a strong compromise from developed countries to substantially reduce theirs will not dismantle the paralysis of the international regime. Smaller countries depend on agreement between the greatest. In the end, low carbon development is not a competition for resources to allow some to live better in the future, but a compromise to guarantee the survival of as many as possible, together with many other species that have the same right to this planet as humans do.

Disclosure statement

No potential conflict of interest was reported by the authors.

The UK and Emerging Countries in the Climate Regime: Whither Leadership?

SEVASTI-ELENI VEZIRGIANNIDOU

This article discusses the UK's climate diplomacy towards emerging countries. The UK as an established power and as a member of the European Union appears keen to play a leadership role in climate cooperation, both within the EU and at the multilateral level. However, as in other areas of international politics, emerging countries are becoming increasingly important players for dealing with climate change. In this sense, leadership on the part of the UK would require some constructive engagement of these countries. The article looks at how the UK engages emerging countries, both on its own and in coordination with its EU partners. It addresses both multilateral and bilateral diplomacy efforts. It argues that although the UK is making an effort to engage emerging countries, these efforts are still at an early stage, and they also suffer from a lack of resources and strategic direction. Some policy diffusion is observed in relation to China, but this has not translated to the convergence of positions in climate negotiations. The article concludes that the possibility of influence is constrained by limited resources and the degree of coincidence of interests between the UK/EU and emerging countries.

Introduction

Like so many other areas of international politics, climate politics is increasingly characterised by multipolarity. The main Greenhouse Gas (GHG) emitters consist of both developed and developing countries. Traditional or established powers, like the United States and the European Union, have seen their share of global emissions diminish compared to that of rapidly industrialising or "emerging" countries like China and India. Specifically, China is now responsible for 28% of global GHG emissions, with the US and EU matching this level only through their combined emissions profile (16% and 11% respectively).[1] Therefore, the established powers cannot provide a solution to climate change mitigation and adaptation without the contribution of emerging powers. In the context of this special issue, this article looks at whether the UK as an established power is adjusting its diplomatic behaviour in order to respond to this increased multipolarity in the field of climate politics. Such adjustment would consist of an increased attempt to engage

---

1. Environmental Performance Index, "Who Are the Largest Emitters of Carbon Pollution?" (15 June 2014), available: <http://epi.yale.edu/the-metric/who-are-largest-emitters-carbon-pollution> (accessed 30 January 2015).

emerging powers, while continuing to work with its traditional allies (the US and Europe).

The UK is a relatively progressive climate actor, compared to most non-EU-15 countries. Although arguably not the most progressive within the EU,[2] it has gradually embraced the climate agenda and eventually set high domestic targets for emissions reductions. Its Climate Change Act (CCA) of 2008 stipulates a long-term binding commitment to reduce emissions by 50% from 1990 levels by 2025, and by 80% by 2050. It is the first country in the world to have made such a legally binding long-term commitment. The UK is also a member of the EU and coordinates both domestic climate legislation and negotiating positions with other EU member states. Climate policy is a shared competence between the EU and its member states, and therefore it is impossible to understand the UK's climate policy without reference to the EU. Shared competence means that both the member states and the EU can exercise competence in an issue area, but EU law supersedes any member state's law. Therefore, the autonomy of the UK to legis-late in climate policy is constrained by EU competence,[3] although the UK as a large member state can have influence on EU legislation in this area.

The EU is also considered a progressive climate actor when compared to other developed countries. It has long adopted the climate agenda as an important issue and has taken up (and kept) commitments for mitigation measures under the Kyoto Protocol and beyond, with its 2020 package in 2008 and most recently the 2030 commitments agreed in late 2014. Both its internal and EU commitments to climate mitigation suggest that the UK has an interest in advancing the goal of climate change mitigation and adaptation at the international level, which in turn means that it has an interest in engaging emerging countries and ensuring they become more progressive climate actors themselves. To what extent is the UK enga-ging these countries, and how successful is this engagement?

The article will assess the level of engagement with emerging countries at two distinct levels of interaction. The first part will look at multilateral climate diplo-macy, which mostly takes place within the United Nations Framework Convention on Climate Change (UNFCCC). At this level the UK mostly acts in cooperation with other EU states as prescribed by EU treaties on shared competence and exter-nal representation, so both the UK and the EU's climate diplomacy will be assessed. The second part will look at bilateral climate diplomacy towards emerging countries outside the UNFCCC. Again, both UK and EU bilateral climate diplomacy will be assessed in this section, since the UK actively participates in EU bilateral initiatives.

The analysis will draw on government and international documents and reports, as well as on secondary literature. It will mostly concentrate on the post-Kyoto

---

2. For example, Denmark and Sweden outperform the UK in the 2015 Climate Change Performance Index, but its overall score is high and its performance is among the best compared to other significant emitters. See Germanwatch and Climate Action Network, "Climate Change Performance Index 2015" (December 2014), p. 8, available: <https://germanwatch.org/en/download/10407.pdf > (accessed 1 February 2015).

3. In fact a study by Cary and Metternich found that the EU directive on renewable energy has had a significant impact in supporting the deployment of renewable energy in the UK. See Rachel Cary and Friederike Metternich, "What Has EU Climate and Energy Policy Done for the UK? A Review with 20 Climate and Energy Specialists" (Green Alliance, October 2013), available: <http://www.green-alliance.org.uk/uploadedFiles/Publications/reports/What%20has%20EU%20climate%20and%20energy%20policy%20done%20for%20the%20UK.pdf> (accessed 30 January 2015).

period of climate negotiations, as this period represents both a distinct period in UK climate politics, with the adoption of the Climate Change Act signalling a new domestic bargain on climate, and a distinct phase in the climate negotiations, where the distinction between developed and developing countries started to erode with the expectation that developing countries would start taking on some mitigation commitments.

UK and EU Multilateral Climate Diplomacy

The UK's multilateral diplomacy is mostly exercised in the context of the nego-tiations under the United Nations Framework Convention on Climate Change (UNFCCC). In this context, the UK rarely acts alone, as the EU member states regularly coordinate their negotiating positions as per the treaty provisions on shared competence and external representation. Individual EU member states also send their own delegations, but these tend to spend a lot of time coordinating positions rather than representing their own country's interests. For the UK it makes sense to act through the EU, since the UK on its own only represents 1.5% of global emissions, whereas the EU as a whole represents around 11% of emissions and as a collective is a much bigger player than any of its individual countries, including big member states like the UK.

EU climate diplomacy has two elements in which the UK has the potential to play an important role. One is the internal EU climate policy, which can make an impact on EU credibility in negotiations. The other is the EU negotiating pos-ition and strategy, which is developed through coordination between the member states. In relation to the EU's internal climate policy, the UK as a large member state has played an important role, but not always a leading or progressive role. Its record as a climate actor within the EU is quite mixed. On the positive side, the UK has undertaken a large amount of the reduction needed to achieve the EU's Kyoto targets, and having overachieved on its own target has actually provided room for some members to do less.[4] The UK has also supported rela-tively ambitious targets in the negotiations of the 2008 package of the EU's targets for 2020, and supported upgrading the EU's commitment to 30%, even after other major emitters refused to make binding commitments at the Copenha-gen Conference.[5] In the recent negotiations over the EU's 2030 targets, the UK again was one of the most progressive voices, arguing for a 40% reduction.[6] It formed a group with other progressive EU states like Germany in order to per-suade the more reluctant Eastern European states to accept the higher targets.[7] However, when it comes to individual policies, the UK has also played a laggard role. For example, it has consistently opposed and attempted to weaken binding renewable energy targets, both in the 2020[8] and 2030 package

---

4. T. Rayner and A. Jordan, "The United Kingdom: A Paradoxical Leader?", in R.K.W. Wurzel and J. Connelly (eds.), *The European Union as a Leader in International Climate Change Politics* (Abingdon: Routledge, 2011), p. 106.

5. *Ibid.*, p. 99.

6. E. Davey, "EU 2030 Climate Deal Meets UK's Core Demands of Ambitious Cuts and Choice", *The Guardian*, 23 January 2014, available: <http://www.theguardian.com/environment/2014/jan/23/eu-2030-climate-deal-emissions-uk-renewables-target> (accessed 26 September 2014).

7. *Ibid.*

8. Rayner and Jordan, *op. cit.*, p. 105.

negotiations.[9] This has been criticised by a variety of green businesses and by non-governmental organisations (NGOs).[10] In this sense, the UK's influence on EU climate target setting is not entirely on the positive side, but overall it has had a more positive than negative influence in the post-Kyoto period.

It is more difficult to determine the role of the UK in EU multilateral climate diplomacy. This is because the inner workings of determining the negotiating position and tactics are not really transparent[11], which makes it difficult to distinguish the influence of particular member states. The negotiating position is adopted by consensus, and any change in strategy or any adjustment to the position needs to be coordinated during the negotiations themselves, with any member able to veto changes.[12] In that sense, the EU position may not represent UK interests exactly, but the UK can block decisions that it considers against its interests. In addition, member states have the opportunity to make more of an impact during their presidency, when they take the lead in negotiations.[13] The UK last held the EU presidency in the second half of 2005, when it played a constructive role in the Conference of the Parties (COP) in Montreal, maintaining the momentum for the Kyoto Protocol entry into force.[14] In earlier phases of the climate regime, the UK attempted to use the UNFCCC negotiations as a way to limit the extension of EU competence on climate policy.[15] This largely came from the UK's scepticism over the expansion of EU competence in areas outside the common market.[16] However, the UK has become more positive about working through the EU since the early 2000s, and has since played a more constructive role within EU climate diplomacy in the UNFCCC. It is therefore useful to briefly examine how the EU (and by extension the UK) has attempted to engage developing countries in the post-Kyoto climate negotiations.

The EU considers itself a climate leader, and has adopted a variety of policies to decrease its emissions in accordance with the UNFCCC and Kyoto Protocol. It has increasingly acknowledged, however, that emerging countries as large developing country emitters also need to take action to control their burgeoning emissions. How is the EU attempting to persuade emerging powers to take on mitigation measures? Are its efforts constructive and compatible with emerging countries' needs and priorities? Its record appears mixed: on the negative side, the EU tends to emphasise top-down, legally binding commitments, whereas emerging countries prefer voluntary commitments in order to avoid restricting their economic growth. In 2012 the EU attempted to "arm-twist" other emitters, including emerging powers, by extending its Emissions Trading Scheme (ETS) to aviation

---

9. Blue and Green Tomorrow, "EU 2030 Energy and Climate Targets: The Reaction" (22 January 2014), available: <http://blueandgreentomorrow.com/2014/01/22/eu-2030-energy-and-climate-targets-the-reaction/> (accessed 26 September 2014).

10. *Ibid.*

11. L. Van Schaik, "The Sustainability of the EU's Model for Climate Diplomacy", in S. Oberthur and M. Pallemaerts (eds.), *The New Climate Policies of the European Union: Internal Legislation and Climate Diplomacy* (Brussels: Brussels University Press, 2010), p. 262.

12. *Ibid.*, p. 265.

13. J. Vogler, "The European Union as an Environmental Policy Actor: Climate Change", in Wurzel and Connelly, *op. cit.*, p. 23.

14. Rayner and Jordan, *op. cit.*, p. 104.

15. L. Cass, "The Indispensable Awkward Partner: The United Kingdom in European Climate Policy", in P. Harris (ed.), *Europe and Global Climate Change* (Cheltenham: Edward Elgar, 2007), pp. 63–86.

16. *Ibid.*; Rayner and Jordan, *op. cit.*

and including all flights to and from Europe in the scheme. This added extra costs to foreign airlines, and created quite a lot of friction between the EU, the US and China, until the issue was moved to the International Civil Aviation Organisation (ICAO) and inclusion of these foreign airlines in the ETS was dropped.[17] Finally, the EU seemed quite isolated and lacked influence in the Copenhagen Conference of 2009. Its promise to move from 20% to 30% reductions if other emitters took action seemed to fall on deaf ears, and the final deal was hammered out between the US and BASIC (Brazil, South Africa, India and China) countries, leaving the EU's "leadership" image tarnished.[18]

On the positive side, however, the EU has been quite willing to explore the financial needs of developing countries and has contributed to the financial mechanisms of the UNFCCC, such as the Clean Development Mechanism (CDM), whose primary market is the EU ETS.[19] Most CDM projects and funding are located in emerging economies. In addition, the EU has been responsive to the demand by developing and emerging economies for a second Kyoto period, and has agreed to put its Copenhagen pledge for 20% reduction into this legally binding agreement. Therefore, although the EU is not entirely amenable to all the demands of emerging countries, it has been more flexible than other developed countries, such as the US. It has agreed to take more of the burden of mitigation under the common but differentiated responsibilities principle enshrined in the UNFCCC. And despite its insistence on legally binding commitments, in Durban it agreed to the term "legal force" being used for the future climate agreement in Paris in 2015, despite the ambiguity that the term implies. For these reasons the EU multilateral diplomacy, to which the UK contributes, provides an overall positive picture in relation to constructive engagement of emerging countries.

Outside its efforts within the EU and the UNFCCC, the UK has also made climate change a priority in other multilateral fora, like the UN and the G8. For example, in 2007 it introduced a discussion on climate change in the UN Security Council, even though other major powers like the US and China were opposed to discussing this issue at this high-level forum.[20] However, since the financial crisis and the unrest in the Middle East, climate change has diminished as a high-level politics issue on the international agenda. In addition, the Conservative-Liberal Democrat coalition government has not shown as much willingness to pursue the issue outside the UNFCCC.

From the discussion so far, the UK's behaviour in multilateral climate politics appears overall to be positive and progressive, particularly in the post-Kyoto period, but also at earlier points in time. In more recent years (post-2008) the UK has remained committed to climate action at the international level, but has not been pursuing it as vocally and strongly as before the financial crisis. In relation

---

17. J. Neely and K. Henderson, "EU Drops Plan to Extend CO2 Rules to International Flights", Reuters, 3 April 2014, available: <http://uk.reuters.com/article/2014/04/03/eu-carbon-aviation-idUKL5N0MV2KX20140403> (accessed 26 September 2014).

18. L. Groen, A. Niemann and S. Oberthur, "The EU as a Global Leader? The Copenhagen and Cancun UN Climate Change Negotiations", *Journal of Contemporary European Research*, Vol. 8, No. 2 (2012), pp. 173–191.

19. Sandbag, "The CDM is Still the Hostage of Ambition" (25 September 2012), available: <http://www.sandbag.org.uk/blog/2012/sep/25/cdm-still-hostage-ambition/> (accessed 29 September 2014).

20. Rayner and Jordan, *op. cit.*, p. 104.

to its engagement of emerging countries, however, there is little that can be gleaned from observing only its multilateral diplomacy, as this is mostly exercised via the EU. Looking at the UK's bilateral relations with emerging powers will be more useful in determining its level of engagement.

UK and EU Bilateral Climate Diplomacy with Emerging Powers

The UK's bilateral diplomacy with emerging countries is exercised at two levels: its own bilateral relations and the EU's bilateral relations with these countries. Both the EU and the UK seek to influence the climate policies of emerging countries through bilateral climate cooperation. The UK has also played a very active role in the EU's engagement of emerging countries and the signing of climate agreements between the EU and China in particular. Because the UK's and the EU's efforts are interconnected, this section will look at both sets of relationships.

EU Bilateral Climate Diplomacy

EU bilateral diplomacy with emerging countries mainly relies on financial and technical instruments, in accordance with its broader role as an economic and normative power. Between 2007 and 2014 the European Investment Bank funded climate change-related projects in China, India and Brazil for a total of 4.151 billion Euros (1.368 billion, 1.095 billion and 1.688 billion respectively).[21] The EU bilateral relationship with China includes several agreements, such as the EU–China Climate Change Partnership agreement (concluded during the UK presidency in 2005), the China–EU Action Plan on Energy Efficiency and Renewable Energies, the EU–China CDM Facilitation Project, the EU–China Near Zero Emissions Coal initiative (led by the UK) and a biennial EU–China Energy Conference.[22] All these initiatives aim to strengthen cooperation on climate change and in this way enhance China's interest and capacities for climate change mitigation. The extent to which these efforts are bearing fruit in terms of influence in Chinese climate policy is hard to trace. Torney found some evidence of policy diffusion from the EU to China, particularly in the form of lesson drawing:[23] the various initiatives described above are helpful in promoting policy learning and diffusion to China. For example, the Chinese government consulted extensively with the EU Commission in its design of emission trading pilot schemes.[24] Lee also finds that China uses EU initiatives and policies as inspiration and draws lessons from the EU's experience with climate policy:

21. The European Investment Bank, Projects Financed, available: <http://www.eib.org/projects/loans/regions/ala/index.htm?start=2007&end=2014> (accessed 29 September 2014).

22. House of Lords, European Union Committee, "Stars and Dragons: The EU and China" (9 March 2010), available: <http://www.publications.parliament.uk/pa/ld200910/ldselect/ldeucom/76/7610.htm> (accessed 29 September 2014).

23. D. Torney, "Assessing EU Leadership on Climate Change: The Limits of Diffusion in EU Relations with China and India", *KFG Working Paper No. 46* (2012), available: <http://userpage.fu-berlin.de/kfgeu/kfgwp/wpseries/WorkingPaperKFG_46.pdf> (accessed 29 September 2014).

24. *Ibid.*, p. 17.

Evidence of policy learning transfers abounds, from eco-labelling to support measures for renewable energy. The time lag between the EU enacting standards and China adopting them has gotten shorter in many policy areas, such as for vehicle emissions standards.[25]

Further to cooperation on technical issues, the EU and its member states also emphasised climate change in their meetings with high-level Chinese officials, keeping the issue on the agenda and thus helping to maintain the attention of the Chinese leadership on the issue.[26] However, Torney argues that "we cannot attribute too much influence to the EU"[27] because there is evidence that the increased attention to climate change and the commitment to adopt climate measures was also a result of developments in thinking of domestic actors, such as the new Chinese leadership in 2002[28] and the influence of domestic think tanks and institutes that supported climate action.[29] In this sense he finds that increased cooperation between China and the EU is a result of a change in domestic perceptions of interests in China rather than EU influence.[30] Lee comes to a similar conclusion:

> The EU (together with Japan and the US) has served as a "template" for China, and hand-held many agencies and companies in China through the process. That said, it is harder to prove that the partnership changed the level of ambition of China, even though it is difficult to conceive of more Chinese commitment to carbon emissions without international pressure from the EU and the like.[31]

On top of this, the EU's efforts in China are somewhat undermined by individual member states, who often compete with each other for commercial contracts in China, according to a House of Lords report.[32] The report suggests that more strategic cooperation and a long-term vision are needed in order for EU member states to work together.

The above discussion indicates that the EU is helping China in its development of climate policy, but has had limited influence in the change in the Chinese perception of interest in relation to its domestic climate policy. China's acceptance of climate mitigation as a legitimate policy goal has little to do with EU influence. Furthermore, an increased Chinese interest in climate mitigation, as well as increased climate cooperation between the EU and China, has not led to a convergence of positions of the two in climate negotiations. China continues to object to the dilution of the Common But Differentiated Responsibilities (CBDR) principle in post-Kyoto negotiations and continues to support the distinction between Annex

---

25. B. Lee, "The EU and China: Time for a Strategic Renewal?", in G. Grevi and T. Renard (eds.), *Hot Issues, Cold Shoulders, Lukewarm Partners: EU Strategic Partnerships and Climate Change* (European Strategic Partnership Observatory, November 2012), p. 30, available: <http://fride.org/download/RP2_EU_Strategic_Partnerships_and_Climate_Change.pdf> (accessed 30 January 2015).

26. Torney, *op. cit.*, p. 15.

27. *Ibid.*, p. 16.

28. *Ibid.*, p. 14.

29. *Ibid.*, p. 16.

30. *Ibid.*, p. 17.

31. Lee, *op. cit.*, p. 31.

32. House of Lords, *op. cit.*

I and non-Annex I parties, which the EU wants to eliminate.[33] China also continues to reject binding emissions targets for emerging countries. Therefore, the EU's influence in China is limited and constrained by the degree to which Chinese interests coincide with those of Europe.

In relation to India, the EU has also made efforts to create bilateral cooperation on climate change. Again during the UK presidency in 2005, an India–EU Initiative of Clean Development and Climate Change was signed. This agreement also created an EU–India Environment Forum and an EU–India Energy Panel. However, the policy goals in the EU–India agreement were very vague. In addition, not much action seems to have taken place to realise any of the terms of the agreement, as in 2008 the same goals were restated in a new agreement for a Joint Programme for Cooperation on Energy, Clean Development and Climate Change. However, not much has resulted from the Joint Programme either.[34] Cooperation on climate change between the EU and India is limited and more joint projects have taken place in other environmental issues rather than climate change.[35] India has cooperated with individual member states like Germany, Spain and the UK on renewable energy projects,[36] but it has resisted closer cooperation with the EU and it rejected the EU's offer to fund a Carbon Capture and Storage (CCS) demonstration plan.[37] Torney argues that this is because India has very different priorities to the EU in relation to climate change, and as a result is resisting policy diffusion from the EU.[38] In particular, India still prioritises economic growth and poverty alleviation *above* climate change mitigation and to the extent that it is interested in renewable energy this is mostly in order to achieve energy security and economic growth and less about achieving climate goals.[39] India therefore considers that its priorities are very different from those of the EU and this has also meant that India and the EU have quite divergent positions in climate negotiations: the EU supports legally binding commitments for all major emitters regardless of level of development, although it is in favour of differentiating the level of ambition; India, on the other hand, tends to emphasise its need for development and resists the agenda of legally binding commitments.[40] India also emphasises equality in the sense of equal access to the atmosphere and rejects the label of "major emitter" as it argues it is only responsible for 2.3% of total accumulated emissions.[41] Because of this large disparity in worldviews between the EU and India, Wagner concludes that it is not really possible, at least in the medium term, for the EU to influence the Indian negotiating position.[42] However, he argues that there is scope for cooperation to take place in relation to emission-reducing policies within India, particularly on renewable energy where there are common interests.[43]

---

33. Lee, *op. cit.*, p. 28.
34. Torney, *op. cit.*, p. 21.
35. C. Wagner, "The EU and India: Working from the Bottom Up", in Grevi and Renard, *op. cit.*, p. 41.
36. *Ibid.*, p. 40.
37. Torney, *op. cit.*, p. 21.
38. *Ibid.*; see also Wagner, *op. cit.*
39. Torney, *op. cit.*, p. 23.
40. Wagner, *op. cit.*, p. 39.
41. Torney, *op. cit.*, p. 20.
42. Wagner, *op. cit.*, p. 42.
43. *Ibid.*

Finally, the EU has also attempted to engage Brazil in bilateral climate cooperation. Initially this took place as part of the EU–Brazil Strategic Partnership that was launched in 2007, but in 2011 the EU–Brazil summit launched a separate climate change dialogue. The main areas of cooperation between the EU and Brazil centre on renewable energy and battling deforestation. So far these initiatives remain mostly aspirational and have failed to produce concrete policies and projects.[44] Perhaps this is a result of the recent nature of cooperation. There is significant potential for Brazil and the EU to cooperate on renewable energy, since both have shown a commitment to climate change mitigation.[45] Brazil is already cooperating with EU member states on renewable energy projects and the German government has funded a large part of a pilot programme on the protection of the Brazilian rainforest.[46] Both also have an interest in biofuels, but cooperation in this field has been frustrated slightly by the different commercial interests of the two sides: Brazilian sugarcane ethanol is considered environmentally damaging in the EU, who promotes rapeseed oil-based biodiesel.[47] Despite these differences it is considered that the scope for cooperation is significant and since both the EU and Brazil have an interest in climate mitigation, bilateral cooperation could increase in the future. At this point, however, it remains limited, and in addition Brazil has largely chosen to ally itself with the BASIC countries in the climate negotiations. Although its interests and positions are not as closely aligned to those of China and India, it also supports the CBDR and voluntary commitments. It is therefore too soon to speak of EU influence on Brazil, considering the lack of long-standing and genuine bilateral cooperation.

Overall, therefore, the EU is engaging emerging powers in bilateral as well as multilateral climate diplomacy. In this way it is making an effort to change the preferences of these states and create a higher level of interest in their governments towards battling climate change. The evidence suggests, however, that the ability of the EU to exert influence is limited and depends on the level of coincidence of interests between the EU and each of the emerging powers. Torney, for example, argues that the EU has had more influence in China than in India because of the different constellation of domestic interests in each country.[48] Because of this, India was more resistant than China to deepening cooperation. Another issue that limits the EU's influence is that its member states often compete with each other for commercial contracts in the various emerging economies, rather than working together.[49] Therefore, overall the picture on the EU's bilateral diplomacy with emerging countries is again mixed. It appears that it has been more successful with China, but the extent to which this is a direct result of influence and EU

44. S. Afionis and L.C. Stringer, "The Environment as a Strategic Priority in the European Union–Brazil Partnership: Is the EU Behaving as a Normative Power or Soft Imperialist?", *International Environmental Agreements: Politics, Law and Economics*, Vol. 14, No. 1 (2013), pp. 47–64.

45. *Ibid.*, p. 11.

46. S. Gratius and D. Gonzalez, "The EU and Brazil: Shared Goals, Different Strategies", in Grevi and Renard, *op. cit.*, p. 16.

47. *Ibid.*, p. 15.

48. Torney, *op. cit.*, p. 23.

49. N. Mabey and J. Mitchell, "Investing for an Uncertain Future: Priorities for UK Energy and Climate Security", Chatham House Briefing Paper, July 2010, p. 14, available: <http://www.chathamhouse.org/sites/default/files/public/Research/Europe/bp0710_mitchellmabey.pdf> (accessed 1 October 2014); J.-C. Gottwald, "Europe and China: Convergence, Politicization and Assertiveness", *East Asia*, Vol. 27, No. 1 (2010), pp. 79–97.

leadership rather than a coincidence of interests could be up for debate. China appears to be the most open to EU influence, and this is of course limited to joint projects. When it comes to translating this influence to China's negotiating position, no such claims appear valid. China remains firmly opposed to legally binding targets, which is what the EU is firmly committed to achieving.

UK Bilateral Climate Diplomacy

The UK bilateral climate diplomacy with emerging powers is at a rather under-developed stage. The highest level of cooperation on climate issues is with China. Most of this cooperation is on technical matters, such as helping with recording emissions, building carbon markets and business relations. Several formal agreements exist: the UK–China Action Plan on Climate Change and Energy was established in December 2007 and aims to aid China in its transition to a low carbon economy and to enhance China's role in delivering a global agreement;[50] a UK–China Climate Change Working Group was also established between the Chinese National Development and Reform Commission (NDRC) and the UK's Department for Environment Forestry and Rural Affairs (DEFRA) in December 2006. This working group aims to share knowledge on climate change, and focuses on issues like energy efficiency, adaptation and capacity-building activities around the CDM.[51] After the mandate of this group expired in 2011, a new memorandum of understanding was signed between the NDRC and the Department for Energy and Climate Change (DECC). This new agreement funded several low carbon pilots in China, with a budget of £200,000 a year until 2014.[52] The Foreign and Commonwealth Office (FCO) also funded 52 low carbon projects in China in 2012 as part of its China Prosperity Fund. Another initiative worth mentioning is the UK–China Energy Dialogue, launched in 2010. This included a meeting between the Ministers for Energy in both countries, as well as the opportunity for businesses from both sides to network.[53] This list of examples is not exhaustive of the cooperation initiatives with China.

In addition to formal intergovernmental agreements and initiatives between the two countries, bilateral diplomacy is also exercised by officials of the FCO. The embassy in Beijing has 20 staff members working on climate change as part of the global network of climate attachés.[54] The FCO complements the work of the DECC in relation to climate diplomacy by working to create the conditions for interest convergence between the UK and China. According to witnesses to the

50. K. Chmutina, "China's Participation in Global Climate Change Cooperation: From the 1980s to the Post-Kyoto Era", University of Nottingham China Policy Institute Briefing Series, Issue 63 (October 2010), pp. 11–12, available: <http://www.nottingham.ac.uk/cpi/documents/briefings/briefing-63-china-climate-change.pdf> (accessed 1 October 2014).

51. *Ibid.*, p. 12.

52. Energy and Climate Change Committee, House of Commons, "Low-Carbon Growth Links with China" (17 July 2012), p. 19, available: <http://www.publications.parliament.uk/pa/cm201213/cmselect/cmenergy/529/529.pdf> (accessed 1 October 2014).

53. W. Ke, "China, UK Hail Energy Dialogue", China.org, 10 November 2010, available: <http://www.china.org.cn/environment/2010-11/10/content_21312789.htm> (accessed 1 October 2014).

54. M. Darby, "UK Slashes Climate Diplomacy Budget", Responding to Climate Change, 9 August 2014, available: <http://www.rtcc.org/2014/07/31/uk-slashes-climate-diplomacy-budget/> (accessed 1 February 2015).

House of Commons Foreign Affairs Committee's inquiry into the role of the FCO in government, FCO officials showed an inventive style of diplomacy:

> The teams have reached beyond Governments to work with all sorts of non-state actors within both the business sector and the NGO sector. They have pioneered quite a different way of thinking about diplomacy.[55]

The climate relationship with China is also quite heavily based on economic interests, such as exporting British knowhow and technology to China. This is evident from the statements of a number of senior government officials. For example, the current Secretary of State for Energy and Climate, Ed Davey, emphasised the economic benefits of the "green industry" in his speech at Chatham House in July 2012:

> The UK is 6th in the world in the low-carbon sector, with an industry worth £122 billion. I want us to secure a greater share of this vibrant and growing sector ... Green business generated a trade surplus for the UK of £5 billion last year; if we play it right, it could halve our trade deficit before the next election.[56]

Similar testimonies are found in the Energy and Climate Change Committee's report to Parliament about UK–China climate cooperation. The Minister for Trade and Investment said that "alignment between the climate change agenda, UKTI and the business opportunities [...] is looked at and envied by a lot of other countries".[57] There also seems to be a new emphasis on commercial interests in the FCO since the coalition government took over in 2010, which the Foreign Affairs Committee report acknowledges.[58] This focus on trading opportunities is further exemplified by the hosting of the London Clean Energy Finance Summit, a UK government initiative to bring together investors (including from the City of London), developers and ministers from various countries to discuss investment opportunities in low energy.[59] Therefore the engagement with China does not only aim to enhance Chinese capacities and influence Chinese climate policy, but also aims to enhance business opportunities for the UK.

In relation to exercising influence, there is clear evidence of policy diffusion. A report by the House of Commons Committee on Energy and Climate Change on UK–China cooperation found that there was a lot of interest within China in the UK Climate Change Act and the concept of carbon budgets.[60] The UK was also the only country offering "dedicated partnership to China in its low carbon pilot

---

55. D. Steven, giving evidence to 'The Role of the FCO in UK Government', 7th Report of Session 2010-12, volume 1, House of Commons Foreign Affairs Committee (27 April 2011), p. 119, available: <http://www.publications.parliament.uk/pa/cm201012/cmselect/cmfaff/665/665.pdf> (accessed 1 February 2015).

56. E. Davey, "The UK's Vision for Tackling Climate Change", Chatham House speech transcript, 1 July 2012, available: <http://www.chathamhouse.org/publications/papers/view/184671> (accessed 1 October 2014).

57. Energy and Climate Change Committee, op. cit., p. 19.

58. "The Role of the FCO in UK Government", op. cit., p. 34.

59. Department of Energy and Climate Change, "Paris 2015: Securing our Prosperity through a Global Climate Change Agreement" (2014), available: <https://www.gov.uk/government/uploads/system/uploads/attachment_data/file/360596/hmg_paris_2015.pdf> (accessed 1 February 2015).

60. Energy and Climate Change Committee, op. cit., p. 10.

efforts"[61] and this seems to have enhanced the potential for UK influence. The diplomatic work of the FCO has also been praised in terms of promoting UK perceptions of climate policy solutions to China:

> The FCO has become engaged in building coalitions of interest to support ambitious outcomes among business, science, NGOs, faith groups and the media within key nations. This activity not only provides support for UK climate negotiators, but also gives us influence over others' economic and political choices. This was acknowledged, for example, by the Chinese government who have attributed the concept of low carbon economy they are now pursuing with vigour to the UK.[62]

On the other hand, the report of the Committee on Energy and Climate Change also found that there is a lack of strategic direction in UK–China cooperation, and too many projects are being pursued, but with limited financing and limited ability to make a difference.[63] In terms of coordination, the report proposes the creation of a cross-departmental committee to provide high-level strategic direction to the UK's low carbon cooperation with China.[64]

Equally important are the limitations on finance. Although the UK played a key role in establishing low carbon zones in China, it has not been able to provide enough funding for their successful implementation.[65] The money available is not enough to make an impact on such a large scale,[66] and due to the recession and austerity the pot is shrinking. For example, the FCO's Prosperity Fund spent £5 million to support climate change activities in China in 2011–12, itself not a very large amount, which then shrank to £4.5 million in 2012–13.[67] Further slashing of funding in the FCO climate budget has seen overall spending on climate activities reduced by 39% in the last three years (2011–14).[68] The Foreign Affairs Committee voiced concerns over the ability of the FCO to fulfil the ambitious mandate it has been given by the coalition government considering the increased lack of resources.[69] There are also concerns that climate change has been diminishing in priority since 2010 and that Philip Hammond, the new Foreign Secretary to replace William Hague, has even less of an interest in climate change.[70] This is likely to diminish the effectiveness of FCO diplomacy vis-à-vis China and other emerging countries.

The above discussion indicates that the UK has developed a beneficial climate relationship with China, is engaged in cooperation and able to diffuse policy and thus exercise some influence in relation to the development of domestic Chinese climate policy. Again, however, it is important not to overemphasise the UK's influence, since policy development in China is as much, if not more, a process of

---

61. *Ibid.*, p. 18.
62. "The Role of the FCO in UK Government", *op. cit.*, pp. 176–177.
63. Energy and Climate Change Committee, *op. cit.*, p. 5.
64. *Ibid.*, p. 21.
65. *Ibid.*, p. 28.
66. *Ibid.*, p. 22.
67. *Ibid.*, p. 20.
68. Darby, *op. cit.*
69. "The Role of the FCO in UK Government", *op. cit.*, p. 6.
70. Darby, *op. cit.*

domestic politics.[71] Perhaps the term "lesson drawing" is more appropriate than "policy diffusion". Equally, similarly to the EU efforts, bilateral cooperation and diplomacy has not moved China closer to the UK position on the adoption of a legally binding agreement in the context of climate negotiations.

UK climate diplomacy is less developed with India and even less so with Brazil. In relation to India, there are very few formalised levels of engagement, such as there are with China. An India–UK High-Level Dialogue on Sustainable Development exists, but there are no particular agreements on climate change. The office of the British High Commission in New Delhi includes a Climate Change and Energy Unit to coordinate the efforts of different government departments in India (DECC, DEFRA, Department for International Development [DFID] and FCO). However, parliamentary scrutiny of the engagement with India found that there was very little transparency in relation to what this office does, or how different issues are integrated between different departments.[72] The low level of formalisation of relations may be a result of the UK putting less emphasis on India than China, which reflects their relative contribution to global emissions (or the more limited business opportunities in India); or, as is the case with the EU, India might be resisting more formalised relations in order to avoid pressure to adjust its policies.

In relation to Brazil, again cooperation is less widespread than it is with China. A UK–Brazil High-Level Dialogue on Sustainable Development was established in 2006,[73] and some projects on biofuels and waste management have taken place through this framework. Surprisingly little information is available about UK–Brazil climate cooperation, either in the press or in government sources. Perhaps this reflects the fact that UK–Brazil relations were not a high priority for UK foreign policy in recent decades.[74] In more recent years more attention has been paid to enhancing this relationship, but it will take time to develop. Some encouraging signs include the fact that the UK and Brazil delegations found a lot of common ground and cooperated closely at the Cancun Climate Conference in 2010.[75] However, this signifies more a coincidence of interests rather than UK influence, since Brazil is the most progressive among the emerging countries when it comes to climate negotiations. The level to which the UK can influence Brazilian climate politics is limited because of the lack of a close diplomatic relationship between the two countries. In the words of Jeremy Browne MP, the FCO minister with responsibility for South America, "Brazil is well disposed towards us [the UK], but it does not give us automatic bonus points that are not earned in terms of our relationship with it".[76] Therefore, again the UK is making an effort to engage Brazil as an emerging power and important player in the climate regime, but this engagement is recent and not based on long-standing foundations.

---

71. See Torney and Lee on the previous discussion on EU–China bilateral cooperation and influence.

72. International Development Committee, House of Commons, "The Future of DFID's Programme in India" (7 June 2011), available: <http://www.publications.parliament.uk/pa/cm201012/cmselect/cmintdev/616/61602.htm> (accessed 1 October 2014).

73. Green Car Congress, "UK and Brazil Launch Working Group on Climate Change and Establish Dialogue on Sustainable Development" (7 March 2006), available: <http://www.greencarcongress.com/2006/03/uk_and_brazil_l.html> (accessed 1 October 2014).

74. Foreign Affairs Committee, House of Commons, "UK–Brazil Relations" (11 October 2011), p. 11, available: <http://www.publications.parliament.uk/pa/cm201012/cmselect/cmfaff/949/949.pdf> (accessed 1 October 2014).

75. *Ibid.*, p. 45.

76. *Ibid.*, p. 13.

Judging by the problems plaguing the efforts to engage China, particularly the lack of resources, the UK is likely to face issues with Brazil as well, especially in comparison with other European countries like Germany and Italy, who already have more established relations with Brazil.[77]

In conclusion, the UK's bilateral diplomacy with emerging powers is still at a relatively early stage of development, particularly in relation to India and Brazil. The efforts to engage these rising powers on a bilateral basis are plagued with problems of cross-departmental coordination, and, more importantly, a lack of resources, particularly in terms of financing projects in order to make an impact. These bilateral diplomatic efforts are also not emphasised in UK government discourse in terms of their contribution to a potential climate agreement. For example, the previous Secretary of State for Energy and Climate Change, Chris Huhne, emphasised the importance of working through the EU and the UNFCCC to achieve international cooperation on climate change in his speech at Chatham House in 2011, where he elaborated his "climate change doctrine".[78] No mention of bilateral diplomacy with the emerging powers figured in his speech, indicating that the emphasis lies elsewhere. His successor, Ed Davey, also gave a similar speech at Chatham House, where he also exalted the virtues of working with the EU and through multilateral mechanisms such as the UNFCCC, without really mentioning any bilateral diplomacy efforts with emerging powers.[79] Perhaps this is because the bilateral relations are meant to complement the multilateral process and aid the achievement of a global deal. And, as seen in the relationship with China, to some extent bilateral climate diplomacy is also meant to deliver economic gains in the form of business contracts.

All in all, the UK does engage emerging powers on climate change, both on a bilateral and multilateral basis. This engagement is relatively recent, reflecting an increased realisation of the importance of emerging countries in the climate regime and on other global issues. It might therefore take a while for these efforts to bear fruit, although some positive results are already evident in cooperation with China. In addition, since each emerging country forms its climate policy through a complex process, involving domestic politics, the multilateral process and a variety of external relations, UK and EU influence cannot be completely decisive, although it can play a constructive role.

It would appear that the best that can be hoped for from cultivating bilateral relationships with emerging countries would be an involvement in and influence on their domestic climate policy trajectories. Without underestimating the importance of this, the prospects of influencing the foreign climate policies of emerging countries appear less promising. The long-standing positions of BASIC countries on CBDR and voluntary as opposed to legally binding commitments do not at present seem open to change through diplomatic pressure or bilateral cooperation.

It is also important to recognise that emerging powers are not only passive receptors of climate diplomacy from established powers, but they are significant climate actors in their own right. Their increased economic clout and their rising interest in the issue of climate change means they are also promoting their own vision of

---

77. *Ibid.*, p. 11.

78. C. Huhne, "The Art and the Science of International Climate Change", Chatham House speech transcript, 21 July 2011, available: <http://www.chathamhouse.org/sites/files/chathamhouse/public/Meetings/Meeting%20Transcripts/210711huhne.pdf> (accessed 1 October 2014).

79. Davey, "The UK's Vision", *op. cit.*

climate governance and they exercise climate diplomacy of their own.[80] South-South cooperation on climate change is becoming more widespread and this signifies that emerging countries are not only receptors of influence but seek to influence developments in climate policy themselves. It is therefore important that EU and UK climate diplomacy with emerging countries is not approached as a top-down issue on the part of established powers, but as a matter of cooperation between equals.[81]

Conclusion

This article has discussed the leadership ambitions of the UK in the field of climate politics, and particularly scrutinised the level of engagement of the UK government with emerging countries. The UK's climate diplomacy does seem to suggest a recognition of the importance of emerging countries, and attempts are being made to secure climate cooperation with these countries. Much of this diplomacy is soft, focusing on development and economic/technological cooperation rather than direct diplomatic pressure to encourage more ambitious climate policies in those countries. This accurately reflects the UK's resources and limited leverage as an individual country, since it is not a significant emitter in its own right.

The UK also coordinates its efforts with EU states in order to increase its leverage in international negotiations. This is also a reasonable strategy, but could be further strengthened. Competition for commercial contracts between the EU member states harms the overall leverage that the EU can have in its climate relations with emerging countries. Since the UK wants to play a leading role within Europe, it could work with other member states that have strong climate credentials to create a more streamlined EU approach. It is important to note, however, that the potential for EU influence is also limited by the fact that emerging countries are largely symmetrical in power to the EU and have a strong embedded perception of their interests in the context of climate negotiations.

Despite the fact that the UK and the EU have limited ability to affect the negotiating position of emerging countries, continued cooperation and bilateral diplomacy efforts can bring benefits to both established and emerging powers. It is clear that commercial benefits are being sought on all sides, and policy emulation and lesson drawing is happening, particularly in the case of China. Emerging countries are also modifying their position on climate change based on their own assessment of their vulnerability, as well as the possible economic and energy security benefits of climate mitigation measures. Despite continued divergence in international negotiations, domestic agendas are showing signs of convergence, and further bilateral cooperation can only build on and ameliorate these trends.

---

80. S. Minas, "FPC Briefing: Climate Change Cooperation within the Global South: Finance, Policy and Institutions", Foreign Policy Centre (no date), available: <http://fpc.org.uk/fsblob/1628.pdf> (accessed 1 February 2015).

81. Lee, *op. cit.*, p. 31.

Interrogating States' Soft Power Strategies: A Case Study of Sports Mega-Events in Brazil and the UK

JONATHAN GRIX, PAUL MICHAEL BRANNAGAN and
BARRIE HOULIHAN

Central to this article is the use of sports mega-events as part of a state's "soft power" strategy. The article offers two things: first, a critique of the "soft power" concept and a clearer understanding of what it refers to by drawing on the political use of sports mega-events by states; second, the article seeks to understand how and why sports mega-events are attractive to states with different political systems and at different stages of economic development. To this end a case study of an advanced capitalist state (London Olympics, 2012) and a so-called "emerging" state (FIFA World Cup, 2014; Rio Olympics, 2016) will be undertaken in order to shed light on the role of sports events as part of soft power strategies across different categories of states.

Introduction

"Soft power" is in vogue. Not since the early 2000s has an academic concept been adopted so readily by politicians, policy-makers, media commentators and scholars alike. At that time, Robert Putnam's book, *Bowling Alone*,[1] and the attendant concept, "social capital", were both fashionable and influential, informing policy on both sides of the Atlantic. Then, as now, the original concept was picked up, bandied about, misused and abused to an extent that it was rendered meaningless. Three similarities with the social capital debate are of importance for the present discussion: first, Joseph Nye[2] clearly put his finger on something when coining the concept of "soft power"—there has evidently been a shift in attempts to manipulate the "politics of attraction" in international affairs among states of all political hues; second, the original concept was also ambiguous and unclearly defined; and third, there is still little agreement on what it is, whether and under what conditions either social capital or soft power can be created and maintained and if they actually have the impact on society and affairs that actors believe they have. Finally, there is little consensus as to whether "soft power" is a universal resource across ideologies, geographies, economies and cultures or simply a notion developed in, and pertaining to, the "West".

---

1. Robert Putnam, *Bowling Alone: The Collapse and Revival of American Community* (New York: Simon & Schuster Paperbacks, 2000).
2. J.S. Nye, *Bound to Lead: The Changing Nature of American Power* (New York: Basic Books, 1990).

The purpose of this article is, therefore, two-fold. First, it sets about a ground-clearing exercise by making some important distinctions between several strands of (the multi-disciplinary) literature which are often conflated in discussions of soft power. Second, it draws on the use of sports mega-events by states as part of their soft power strategies, using the UK (London, 2012) and Brazil (FIFA World Cup, 2014; Rio, 2016) as case studies of an "established" and "emerging" state respectively. In doing so, the article builds on the nascent International Relations (IR) literature analysing sport as a lens through which to shed light on wider inter-state political machinations[3] and contributes to turning the tide on the "neglect of sport within the study of IR".[4] Far from simply a "hobbyhorse",[5] the manipulation of sport and sports events by states for non-sporting aims offers unique insights into broader soft power strategies adopted by states to further their interests and improve their international standing.

The State of the Debate

The concept of "soft power" was coined in 1990 by the American political scientist, Joseph Nye. For Nye, the "power" aspect of the concept refers to one's ability to "effect the outcomes you want, and, if necessary, to change the behaviour of others to make this happen".[6] For national leaders, Nye suggests that political outcomes can be attained through a combination of both "hard" and "soft" strategies.[7] On the one hand, leaders may utilise forms of "hard power" through, for example, offering economic rewards or drawing on military force; on the other hand, leaders may indirectly adapt the political agenda in such a way that shapes the preferences of others through, for instance, emulating one's "intangible assets": attractive culture, pioneering ideologies and/or credible, legitimate and commendable institutions, values and policies.[8] It is this latter approach which Nye calls "soft power": "the ability to achieve goals through attraction rather than coercion".[9] Such attraction converts into power outcomes when those on the receiving end of the soft power strategy look to the state producing it for affirmation, guidance and leadership, or seek to imitate their domestic and/or international achievements.[10]

3. D. Black, "Dreaming Big: The Pursuit of 'Second Order' Games as a Strategic Response to Globalisation", *Sport in Society,* Vol. 11, No. 4 (2008), pp. 467–480; S. Cornelissen, "South Africa's 'Coming Out Party': Reflections on the Significance and Implications of the 2010 FIFA World Cup", in J. Grix (ed.), *Leveraging Legacies from Sports Mega-Events* (Basingstoke: Palgrave, 2014), pp. 142–153; R. Levermore and A. Budd (eds.), *Sport and International Relations* (London: Routledge, 2004).

4. L. Allison (ed.), *The Global Politics of Sport* (London: Routledge, 2005), p. 7.

5. J. Grix, "From Hobbyhorse to Mainstream: Using Sport to Understand British Politics ", *British Politics,* Vol. 5, No. 1 (2010), pp. 114–129.

6. J.S. Nye, "The Information Revolution and American Soft Power", *Asia-Pacific Review,* Vol. 9, No. 1 (2002), p. 2.

7. Nye, *Bound to Lead, op. cit.;* R.O. Keohane and J.S. Nye, "Power and Interdependence in the Information Age", *Foreign Affairs,* Vol. 77, No. 5 (1998), pp. 81–94.

8. Nye, "The Information Revolution", *op. cit.,* pp. 60–76; Nye, *Soft Power: The Means to Success in World Politics* (New York: Public Affairs, 2004); Nye, "Public Diplomacy and Soft Power", *The Annals of the American Academy of Political and Social Science,* Vol. 616, No. 1 (2008), p. 95.

9. Keohane and Nye , *op. cit.,* p. 98.

10. *Ibid.;* A. Vuving, "How Soft Power Works", Paper presented at the American Political Science Association Annual Meeting, Toronto, 3 September 2009, available: <http://www.apcss.org/Publications/Vuving%20How%20soft%20power%20works%20APSA%202009.pdf> (accessed 7 January 2015).

This is not to suggest, however, that soft power should necessarily replace the utilisation of hard power. In fact, national leaders should, whenever possible, endeavour to combine the soft dimension of attraction with the hard dimensions of coercion and inducement (what Nye terms "smart power").[11] Rather, Nye advocates that nation-states should take greater advantage of the former.[12] Nye's rationale for this is three-fold. First, since the end of the Cold War, nation-states have become far more concerned with forms of welfare over military glory, whereby, in the modern era, national leaders need greater public support before engaging in forceful pursuits.[13] Second, for the majority of powers, the use of force severely jeopardises their economic objectives and ability to maintain international competitiveness.[14] Finally, the increasing influence of the information revolution and globalisation has led to states' behaviour coming under closer scrutiny than ever before.[15] The result is that the use of force has become less tolerated in post-industrial (and, in particular, advanced capitalist) societies, leading to the increasing significance of soft forms of power.[16]

The consequence of this heightened significance has resulted in soft power becoming well and truly bound up within a multiplicity of contemporary discourses. First off is the academic group, those commentators who endeavour to unpick, understand and extend soft power conceptually, but in line with Nye's original thinking.[17] Second are those commentators who have used the concept to explain various socio-political phenomena in specific locales, for example Lam,[18] who situates Japan's successful export of manga and anime as part of a wider search for cultural attraction and soft power; Kalin,[19] who draws heavily on Nye's concept to explain some of the more recent socio-economic and political shifts in Turkey's foreign policy; Gallarotti and Al-Filali,[20] who examine the use by Saudi Arabia of investment in media, especially television and newspapers, to further their diplomatic interests; and finally, Pinkerton and Dodds,[21] who cite the BBC World Service as part of the UK's soft power "package". A third group

11. Nye, "Public Diplomacy and Soft Power", *op. cit.*, p. 94; Nye, "Think Again: Soft Power", *Foreign Policy* (2006), available: <http://www.foreignpolicy.com/articles/2006/02/22/think_again_soft_power> (accessed 12 January 2014).

12. Nye, *Bound to Lead, op. cit.*; Nye, "Soft Power and American Foreign Policy", *Political Science Quarterly*, Vol. 119, No. 2 (2004), pp. 255–270.

13. Nye, "The Information Revolution", *op. cit.*

14. *Ibid.*; P.G. Cerny, "Paradoxes of the Competition State: The Dynamics of Political Globalization", *Government and Opposition*, Vol. 32, No. 2 (1997), pp. 251–274.

15. Keohane and Nye, *op. cit.* ; J.S. Nye, "Propaganda Isn't the Way: Soft Power", Belfer Center for Science and International Affairs (2003), available: <http://belfercenter.ksg.harvard.edu/publication/1240/propaganda_isnt_the_way.html> (accesed 12 January 2015).

16. Nye, "The Information Revolution", *op. cit.*

17. See, for example, E. Lock, "Soft Power and Strategy: Developing a 'Strategic' Conception of Power", in I. Parmar and M. Cox (eds.), *Soft Power and US Foreign Policy: Theoretical, Historical, and Contemporary Perspectives* (London: Routledge, 2009), pp. 32–50; Vuving, *op. cit.*

18. P.E. Lam, "Japan's Quest for 'Soft Power': Attraction and Limitation ", *East Asia*, Vol. 24, No. 4 (2007), pp. 349–363.

19. I. Kalin, "Soft Power and Public Diplomacy in Turkey ", *Perceptions: Journal of International Affairs*, Vol. 16 (2011), pp. 5–24.

20. G. Gallarotti and I.Y. Al-Filali, "Saudi Arabia's Soft Power", *International Studies*, Vol. 49, Nos. 3&4 (2012), pp. 233–261.

21. A. Pinkerton and K. Dodds, "Radio Geopolitics: Broadcasting, Listening and the Struggle for Acoustic Spaces ", *Progress in Human Geography* (2008), available: <http://phg.sagepub.com/content/early/2008/09/02/0309132508090978.short> (accessed 17 January 2015).

are those commentators in a myriad of media channels in which soft power is cited on a daily basis. This ranges from mainstream newspapers in which lip service to "soft power" is paid, but little explanation or definition is offered,[22] to the more academically focused magazines, blogs and online articles that, at least more frequently, do attempt to provide a partial conceptual explanation.[23] Finally, a variety of political leaders and national governments have employed the concept, examples including former Chinese president Hu Jintao's argument for China to enhance its soft power output at the 17th National Congress of the Communist Party of China in 2007;[24] Hillary Clinton's reference to both soft power and smart power during her speech at the 2013 Council of Foreign Affairs;[25] and the British Parliament's 2013 establishment of its "Committee on Soft Power and the UK's Influence", which led to the publication of two extensive volumes in March 2014.[26]

Perhaps most significantly here, however, is the increasing discussion of soft power in the context of the so-called emerging nation-states. Nye himself has drawn heavily on the soft power of the US, detailing the overarching reach of it cultural products, educational and technological excellence, tolerant immigration policies and political stability.[27] However, due to the inability to fight global poverty, the protection of the environment, the use of force outside its borders and the failure of the so-called "Wall Street model", Nye suggests that the general perception is that America's soft power is in decline.[28] This is complemented, of course, by the rising economic and technological might of countries such as Brazil, Russia, India and China, which, as academic discourse suggests, all have soft power ambitions of their own.

Chinese authorities, for example, are currently engaged in a soft power offensive in order to project a more benevolent and less threatening image of the country.[29]

---

22. See, for example, C. Tryhorn, "BBC is in a 'Soft Power' Battle with International Broadcasters", *The Guardian*, 13 November 2013, available: <http://www.theguardian.com/media/media-blog/2013/nov/13/bbc-broadcasters-tony-hall-worldwide-audience-cctv-al-jazeera> (accessed 10 October 2014); N. Norton-Taylor, "'Soft Power'—A Key Asset in New International Order", *The Guardian*, 28 March 2014, available: <http://www.theguardian.com/world/defence-and-security-blog/2014/mar/28/power-military-culture> (accessed 11 October 2014).

23. See T. Moss, "Soft Power? China Has Plenty", *The Diplomat*, 4 June 2013, available: <http://thediplomat.com/2013/06/soft-power-china-has-plenty/> (accessed 13 October 2014).

24. J.S. Nye, "American and Chinese Power after the Financial Crisis ", *The Washington Quarterly*, Vol. 33, No. 4 (2010), pp. 143–153.

25. L. Madison, "In Farewell Speech, Clinton Calls for 'Smart Power' on Global Stage", CBS News, 1 February 2013, available: <http://www.cbsnews.com/news/in-farewell-speech-clinton-calls-for-smart-power-on-global-stage/> (accessed 17 October 2014).

26. House of Lords, *Soft Power and the UK's Influence Committee* (Vols. 1 and 2) (online, 2014), available: <http://www.parliament.uk/documents/lords-committees/soft-power-uk-influence/soft-power-ev-vol1-a-g.pdf> and <http://www.parliament.uk/documents/lords-committees/soft-power-uk-influence/SoftPowerEvVol2.pdf> (accessed 23 January 2015).

27. Nye, "Soft Power and American Foreign Policy", *op. cit.*; Nye, *Soft Power: The Means to Success, op. cit.*; Nye, "The Futures of American Power: Dominance and Decline in Perspective", *Foreign Aff airs*, Vol. 89, No. 2 (2010), pp. 1–10.

28. Nye, "Soft Power and American Foreign Policy", *op. cit.*; Nye, "The Futures of American Power", *op. cit.* See also M. Kroenig, M. McAdam and S. Weber, "Taking Soft Power Seriously", *Comparative Strategy*, Vol. 29, No. 5 (2010), pp. 412–431.

29. J. Kurlantzick, *Charm Offensive: How China's Soft Power is Transforming the World* (Grand Rapids, MI: Yale University Press, 2007); Y. Wang, "Public Diplomacy and the Rise of Chinese Soft Power ", *The Annals of the American Academy of Political and Social Science*, Vol. 616, No. 1 (2008), pp. 257–273; D.A.

Central here has been the promotion of the Chinese language abroad through the numerous Confucius Institutes based overseas; the prestige and respect gained by various states—mainly in Africa and South America—as a result of the success of the "Beijing Consensus" in relative comparison to the Washington Consensus; the country's involvement in United Nations peacekeeping missions, humanitarian assistance and disaster relief; and the impressive international reach of its largest media outlets, Central China Television (CCTV) and Xinhua News Agency.[30]

India's drive for soft power rests on attempting to escape its disconnected and extensively deprived past, as well as its belligerence towards Pakistan.[31] Today, India conjures up notions related to film, business and technology: Bollywood regularly produces more films than its Western counterpart, Hollywood; India's extensive expatriate communities in Europe and America play critical roles in business, healthcare and politics in their newfound homes; and, perhaps most significantly, in the field of information technology, India's Infosys Technologies, Wipro, the Tata Group, the Reliance Group, the Indian Institute of Management and the Indian Institute of Technology have become global names.[32]

Likewise, Brazil has become particularly adept at leveraging soft power, arguably due to its relative lack of military capacity.[33] Central here has been Brazil's desire to play a leading role in successfully negotiating two agreements clarifying the right of World Trade Organization member states to apply various flexibilities available under the Trade Related Intellectual Property Rights and to protect public health. Furthermore, in 2001, the Brazilian National AIDS Programme won UNESCO's Human Rights and Culture of Peace Award, earning Brazil much respect and recognition as a global leader in this regard. Brazil is also one of the world's largest aid donors, with an annual spend of roughly US$4 billion.[34]

Sports Mega-Events as Part of a Nation's Soft Power Strategy

While it is clear that soft power now forms part of many nation-states' foreign policy strategies, attention has only recently turned to the role of sports mega-events (SMEs) in this process. For the purpose of this article a simple definition of what constitutes a mega-event is used, based on the work of Roche, who

Bell, "War, Peace, and China's Soft Power: A Confucian Approach", *Diogenes*, Vol. 56, No. 1 (2009), pp. 26–40.

30. B. Gill and Y. Huang, "Sources and Limits of Chinese 'Soft Power'", *Survival*, Vol. 48, No. 2 (2006), pp. 17–36; J. Gil, "The Promotion of Chinese Language Learning and China's Soft Power", *Asian Social Science*, Vol. 4, No. 10 (2008), p. 116; J. DeLisle, "Soft Power in a Hard Place: China, Taiwan, Cross-Strait Relations and US Policy ", *Orbis*, Vol. 54, No. 4 (2010), pp. 493–524; S. Ding, "Analyzing Rising Power from the Perspective of Soft Power: A New Look at China's Rise to the Status Quo Power ", *Journal of Contemporary China*, Vol. 19, No. 64 (2010), pp. 255–272.

31. J. Pocha, "The Rising 'Soft Power' of India and China", *New Perspectives Quarterly*, Vol. 20, No. 1 (2003), pp. 4–13.

32. *Ibid.*; J.E. Hymans, "India's Soft Power and Vulnerability", *India Review*, Vol. 8, No. 3 (2009), pp. 234–265; Nicolas Blarel, "India: The Next Superpower? India's Soft Power: From Potential to Reality ?", *IDEAS Reports* (2012), available: <http://eprints.lse.ac.uk/43445/> (accessed 25 January 2015).

33. P. Dauvergne and D.B.L. Farias, "The Rise of Brazil as a Global Development Power", *Third World Quarterly*, Vol. 33, No. 5 (2012), pp. 903–917.

34. Cf. K. Lee and E.J. Gomes, "Brazil's Ascendance: The Soft Power Role of Global Health Diplomacy", *European Business Review* (2010), available: <http://www.aberystwyth.ac.uk/en/media/departmental/interpol/chair/KL—Brazil's-ascendance-article.pdf> (accessed 19 October 2014).

considered these events to be "[l]arge-scale, cultural (including commercial and sporting) events, which have a dramatic character, *mass popular appeal* and *international significance*".[35] Such a definition does not, however, take into account the number of visitors an event attracts, the tickets sold, the broadcasting rights around the event or the capital investment budget.[36] Nevertheless, in general, an SME of the first order pertains to the FIFA World Cup and the Olympics; smaller events—often with a major regional impact—are the so-called second-order SMEs (for example, the Commonwealth or Pan American Games). Whichever definition is used, sports megas are increasingly being used by states of all political hues to project an image to the outside world, and acquiring and hosting them have become key factors in local and national development strategies.[37]

Most specifically in this context are the potential "legacies" that are said to come with both applying for and hosting SMEs.[38] A cursory glance at the sport studies literature on SMEs suggests that such legacies range from an increase in the number of a state's citizens participating in sport,[39] to city regeneration,[40] employment,[41] tourism gains[42] and a "feel-good" factor among the host's population.[43] In the much-cited case of Los Angeles, for example, the staging of the 1984 Summer Olympic Games brought the city a surplus of approximately US $338m;[44] in the case of the 1992 Barcelona Summer Olympic Games, the rate of unemployment around the city fell from 18.4% to 9.6%;[45] and one of the central objectives behind the hosting of the London 2012 Summer Olympic Games was to increase the rate of sports participation, leading to a fitter and healthier society.[46]

35. M. Roche, *Mega-Events and Modernity: Olympics and EXPOS in the Growth of Global Culture* (London: Routledge, 2002), p. 1; emphasis added.

36. See M. Muller, "What Makes an Event a Mega-Event? Definitions and Sizes", *Leisure Studies* (2015), doi: 10.1080/02614367.2014.993333, available: <http://www.tandfonline.com/doi/full/10.1080/02614367.2014.993333#abstract> (accessed 2 February 2015).

37. J. Nauright and K.S. Schimmel, *The Political Economy of Sport* (Basingstoke: Palgrave Macmillan, 2005).

38. J.J. MacAloon, "'Legacy' as Managerial/Magical Discourse in Contemporary Olympic Affairs", *The International Journal of the History of Sport*, Vol. 25, No. 14 (2008), pp. 2060–2071.

39. V. Girginov and L. Hills, "A Sustainable Sports Legacy: Creating a Link between the London Olympics and Sports Participation", *The International Journal of the History of Sport*, Vol. 25, No. 14 (2008), pp. 2091–2116.

40. B. Chalkley and S. Essex, "Urban Development through Hosting International Events: A History of the Olympic Games", *Planning Perspectives*, Vol. 14, No. 4 (1999), pp. 369–394.

41. Roche, *op. cit.*

42. L. Chalip and J. McGuirty, "Bundling Sport Events with the Host Destination", *Journal of Sport & Tourism*, Vol. 9, No. 3 (2004), pp. 267–282; N.S. Kim and L. Chalip, "Why Travel to the FIFA World Cup? Effects of Motives, Background, Interest, and Constraints", *Tourism Management*, Vol. 25, No. 6 (2004), pp. 695–707.

43. H. Preuss, "The Conceptualisation and Measurement of Mega Sport Event Legacies ", *Journal of Sport & Tourism*, Vol. 12, Nos. 3–4 (2007), pp. 207–228; J. Grix and F. Carmichael, "Why Do Governments Invest in Elite Sport? A Polemic", *International Journal of Sport Policy and Politics*, Vol. 4, No. 1 (2012), pp. 73–90.

44. C. Gratton, N. Dobson and S. Shibli, "The Economic Importance of Major Sports Events: A Case-Study of Six Events", *Managing Leisure*, Vol. 5, No. 1 (2000), pp. 17–28.

45. F. Miguélez and P. Carrasquer, "The Repercussion of the Olympic Games on Labour", in M. Moragas and M. Botela (eds.), *The Keys to Success* (Barcelona: Centre d'Estudis Olimpics i de l'Esport, Universitat Autonoma de Barcelona, 1995), pp. 1–22.

46. Girginov and Hills, *op. cit.*

However, it should be made explicit here that, in the majority of cases, SMEs fail to produce the legacies trumpeted in the pre-event rhetoric and that any positive impacts are often difficult to attribute, with confidence, to the event. Moreover, SMEs can actually leave behind a number of negative economic and social consequences for their hosts.[47] For example, although sport events have been considered to be effective additions to the economic development of cities and states, in numerous cases they result in a post-event legacy of "white elephants", that is, underused sporting facilities. In addition, most mega-events cost billions of dollars to stage and often result in a large financial burden for the host cities and states.[48] The 1972 Olympic Games, for example, left Munich with debts of up to US$ 279 million; and four years later in Montreal the Games provided debts of up to US$ 1086,[49] famously taking 30 years for taxpayers to redeem. Furthermore, beliefs surrounding positive legacy regeneration,[50] employment,[51] the so-called feel-good factor[52] and increases in sports participation[53] have also been questioned by countless academics. Supposed tourism gains, too, are said to be drastically overstated: the 2002 FIFA World Cup in Japan and South Korea, for example, proved to be wildly optimistic, with Japan attracting only 30,000 more visitors and South Korea reporting the same number as the previous year.[54]

The reason why states continue to strive to host SMEs is understood by many as an attempt to improve their nation's image by profiling and showcasing themselves globally and "attracting" others.[55] As such, numerous scholars consider SMEs to be a vital part of a government's contemporary soft power strategy.[56] Indeed, with their unprecedented global audiences,[57] and valuable promotional opportunities

47. T. Mules and B. Faulkner, "An Economic Perspective on Special Events", *Tourism Economics*, Vol. 2 (1996), pp. 314–329; G. Andranovich, M.J. Burbank and C. Heying, "Olympic Cities: Lessons Learned from Mega-Event Politics", *Journal of Urban Affairs*, Vol. 23, No. 2 (2001), pp. 113–131.

48. S. Essex and B. Chalkley, "Mega-Sporting Events in Urban and Regional Policy: A History of the Winter Olympics", *Planning Perspectives*, Vol. 19, No. 2 (2004), pp. 201–204.

49. Gratton, Dobson and Shibli, *op. cit.*

50. Preuss, *op. cit.*

51. K. Toohey and A.J. Veal, *The Olympic Games: A Social Science Perspective*, 2nd edition (Wallingford: CABI Publishing, 2007).

52. Grix and Carmichael, *op. cit.*

53. Girginov and Hills, *op. cit.*

54. J.D. Horne and W. Manzenreiter, "Accounting for Mega-Events: Forecast and Actual Impacts of the 2002 Football World Cup Finals on the Host Countries Japan/Korea", *International Review for the Sociology of Sport*, Vol. 39, No. 2 (2004), pp. 187–203.

55. Cf. P. Horton, "Sport as Public Diplomacy and Public Disquiet: Australia's Ambivalent Embrace of the Beijing Olympics", *The International Journal of the History of Sport*, Vol. 25, No. 7 (2008), pp. 851–875; A. Deos, "Sport and Relational Public Diplomacy: The Case of New Zealand and Rugby World Cup 2011 ", *Sport in Society*, Vol. 17, No. 9 (2013), pp. 1–17; B. Knott, A. Fyall and I. Jones, "The Nation-Branding Legacy of the 2010 FIFA World Cup for South Africa ", *Journal of Hospitality Marketing & Management*, Vol. 22, No. 6 (2013), pp. 569–595.

56. C.J. Finlay and X. Xin, "Public Diplomacy Games: A Comparative Study of American and Japanese Responses to the Interplay of Nationalism, Ideology and Chinese Soft Power Strategies around the 2008 Beijing Olympics", *Sport in Society*, Vol. 13, No. 5 (2010), pp. 876–900; W. Manzenreiter, "The Beijing Games in the Western Imagination of China: The Weak Power of Soft Power", *Journal of Sport and Social Issues*, Vol. 34 (2010), pp. 29–48; K. Freeman, "Sport as Swaggering: Utilizing Sport as Soft Power ", *Sport in Society*, Vol. 15, No. 9 (2012), pp. 1260–1274; J. Grix and B. Houlihan, "Sports Mega-Events as Part of a Nation's Soft Power Strategy: The Cases of Germany (2006) and the UK (2012)", *The British Journal of Politics & International Relations*, Vol. 16, No. 4 (2014), pp. 572–596.

57. Roche, *op. cit.*; D.L. Andrews, "Sport and the Transnationalizing Media Corporation", *The Journal of Media Economics*, Vol. 16, No. 4 (2003), pp. 235–251.

for cities and states,[58] national leaders regularly justify their investment in SMEs in terms of promoting their country's image and gaining international prestige, transcending provincialism and historic insecurities, and embracing globality, competitiveness and excellence.[59]

Most precisely here, hosting SMEs successfully is increasingly acknowledged to be a highly visible and potentially positive signal to other countries,[60] acting as a valuable asset in accelerating their entry to, and acceptance within, the world's mature economies.[61] In this sense, international sporting success, whether by athletic competition or the effective staging of an SME, provides the perfect opportunity for national leaders who seek to "attract" others with their values and culture and persuade them to want what they want by projecting specific images, principles, achievements and visions to foreign publics,[62] echoing, in many cases, descriptions of excellence, fairness and, most importantly in a soft power context, universal friendship and mutual cooperation and exchange.[63]

Australia is an example of a state successfully using an SME to project a positive image of itself. With home-team advantage, the Australians were able both to perform above expectations in sport and host a highly successful Summer Olympic Games in 2000.[64] Equally, the co-hosting of the 2002 FIFA World Cup laid the groundwork for future internationalism and cooperation between Japan and South Korea — nations that had a long historical opposition towards one another.[65] Additionally, the case of Germany, whose image was severely tarnished by the legacy of the Third Reich and the barbarity of the Nazis, indicates how the 2006 FIFA World Cup was able to go some considerable way in altering foreign publics' negative view of the country.[66] Finally, the 2010 FIFA World Cup was able to portray the tournament as an "African showpiece" — an instrument of continental unity, friendship, solidarity and peace between the state and the rest of the African continent.[67]

Methods

Our data collection strategy involved a series of three stages with which to unpack the role of SMEs in the Brazilian and UK soft power strategies.

58. D. Black and J. Van der Westhuizen, "The Allure of Global Games for 'Semi-peripheral' Polities and Spaces: A Research Agenda", *Third World Quarterly*, Vol. 25 (2004), pp. 1195–1214; J. Nauright, "Global Games: Culture, Political Economy and Sport in the Globalised World of the 21st Century ", *Third World Quarterly*, Vol. 25, No. 7 (2004), pp. 1325–1336.

59. J. Grix and D. Lee, "Soft Power, Sports Mega-Events and Emerging States: The Lure of the Politics of Attraction", *Global Society*, Vol. 27, No. 4 (2013), pp. 521–536.

60. Finlay and Xin, *op. cit.*; S. Cornelissen, "More than a Sporting chance? Appraising the Sport for Development Legacy of the 2010 FIFA World Cup", *Third World Quarterly*, Vol. 32, No. 3 (2011), pp. 503–529.

61. Grix and Lee, *op. cit.*

62. *Ibid.*

63. Manzenreiter, *op. cit.*

64. D. Black, "The Symbolic Politics of Sport Mega-Events: 2010 in Comparative Perspective", *Politikon*, Vol. 34, No. 3 (2007), pp. 261–276.

65. G. Jarvie, "Internationalism and Sport in the Making of Nations", *Identities: Global Studies in Culture and Power*, Vol. 10, No. 4 (2003), pp. 537–551; see also Horne and Manzenreiter, *op. cit.*

66. Grix and Houlihan, *op. cit.*

67. Cornelissen, "South Africa's 'Coming Out Party'" , *op. cit.*; U. Pillay and O. Bass, "Mega-Events as a Response to Poverty Reduction: The 2010 FIFA World Cup and its Urban Development Implications", *Urban Forum*, Vol. 19 (2008), pp. 329–346.

Table 1. Document Collection Inclusion-Exclusion Criteria.

	Included	Excluded
Newspapers	Broadsheets (*The Guardian, The Telegraph, The Times*, etc.)	Tabloids (*The Sun, The Daily Mirror, The Daily Star*, etc.)
Virtual	Other international news agencies (BBC, Reuters, Al Jazeera, etc.)	All "social media" (forums, blogs, networks, etc.)
Government Documents	Documents published directly from—or backed up by—official state departments	Documents unable to be backed up by official state publications
Non-state Documents	Documents published directly from—or backed up by—well-known NGOs (Amnesty, Green Peace, Transparency International, etc.)	Documents from unknown NGOs and/or those unable to be backed up by well-known NGO publications
Private-Sector Documents	Documents published directly from—or backed up by—well-known private-sector companies (Nike, Adidas, GfK Group, etc.).	Documents from unknown private-sector companies and/or those unable to be backed up by publications from well-known private-sector companies

First, we conducted a thorough analysis of documents surrounding London's hosting of the 2012 Olympic Games and Brazil's staging of the 2014 FIFA World Cup and acquisition of the 2016 Summer Olympic Games. In looking to ensure that we only incorporated into our sample documents that had an authentic origin and provided credible and factual accuracy, we followed the inclusion-exclusion criteria as shown in Table 1.

Second, we conducted a number of informal interviews with key officials from the Brazilian Ministry of Sport in April 2013 and November 2014 in Brasilia and Sao Paulo, where one of the authors held academic workshops and meetings. Finally, during both visits to Brazil, field notes were taken whereby we visited key cultural sites and sporting venues and attended various conferences and seminars.

The London Olympics, 2012

The British Foreign and Commonwealth Office (FCO) has generally adopted a disdainful attitude towards the concept of soft power in part because the habits of hard power are difficult to break. Since 1914 there have been few if any years when British forces have not been at war in some part of the world.[68] Nevertheless, soft power resources have not been totally absent from the foreign policy repertoire, with the work of the British Council and the BBC World Service being long-standing examples.[69] Even sport, initially in the form of the British Empire Games and currently the Commonwealth Games, has been used as a soft power resource for over 80 years. While the initial form of the Games was a celebration of the British Empire, the more recent iterations have become the most visible indication of the

---

68. "Britain's 100 Years of Conflict", *The Guardian*, 11 February 2014, available: <http://www.theguardian.com/uk-news/ng-interactive/2014/feb/11/britain-100-years-of-conflict> (accessed 21 October 2014).

69. Foreign and Commonwealth Office, *Changing Perceptions—Review of Public Diplomacy* (London: Foreign and Commonwealth Office, March 2002; also referred to as the Wilton Review).

survival of the Commonwealth as a political institution. However, the increased symbolic importance of the Commonwealth Games for Britain and for other Commonwealth member states has been inadvertent rather than planned and a consequence of the increasingly sclerotic nature of the Commonwealth as an institution which has allowed symbolism to compensate for the lack of substance.

It was against this backdrop of a preference for hard power and a lack of obvious interest in the utilisation of soft power that Britain was awarded in 2005 the right to host the world's most important sport event—the Summer Olympic and Paralympic Games—and, in consequence, the opportunity to exploit a significant soft power opportunity. The embrace of this opportunity by the British Foreign Office and Commonwealth was dutiful rather than enthusiastic. The Carter Report into public diplomacy commented on the "untapped potential" of sport to "reach a wide range of target audiences with diverse economic and social backgrounds" and suggested that the potential value of sport should "continue to be explored".[70] A report to the House of Commons Foreign Affairs Committee by the British Council in the same year noted the opportunity presented by the hosting of the Olympic and Paralympic Games to build international understanding among young people in Britain and in other countries.[71] Despite the lack of a tradition of using soft power resources, the FCO did allocate a small budget to exploit the opportunity that the 2012 Games presented and the high profile that Team GB would have during the Games. The starting point for the sport soft power strategy was an assessment of the then current international image of the UK commissioned by the FCO in 2005. The evidence, as reported to the House of Commons Foreign Affairs Committee,[72] painted a mixed picture. The international profile of the UK was sharply defined, but the positive elements—that the country was "fair, innovative, diverse, confident and stylish"—were set against a more negative perception of a country that was "arrogant, stuffy, old-fashioned and cold". The image that the FCO wanted to project was of a "modern Britain ... open (welcoming, diverse, tolerant), connected (through our involvement in the UN and G20, politically, geographically, in terms of trade and travel), creative and dynamic".[73] The 2012 Games were acknowledged by the FCO as an opportunity not only to address the negative elements in the international perception of the UK and engineer a repositioning of the UK brand, but also to target particular issues and countries. In response to this opportunity the FCO devised a strategy for the two years prior to the Games, designed to achieve a range of objectives, namely: enhancing the general brand image of the country; encouraging inward investment and boosting exports; and addressing national security issues. More specifically the FCO was concerned to redefine brand UK and to use the Olympics "to promote British culture at home and abroad [and to] cement Britain's reputation as a ... vibrant, open and modern society, a global hub in a networked world". The second objective was to "bolster the UK economy, increase commercial opportunities for British business in target countries and secure high value inward investment" and it could also be considered to be similarly concerned with shaping the perception of the UK among potential inward investors.

---

70. Lord Carter of Coles, *Public Diplomacy Review* (London: Foreign and Commonwealth Office, 2005), pp. 30–31.

71. House of Commons, Foreign Affairs Committee, *3rd Report, Public Diplomacy* (London: The Stationery Office, 2005–2006), Ev5.

72. *Ibid.*, FCO Written Evidence, para. 20, 2011.

73. *Ibid.*

The third objective was more specifically targeted and was to "enhance our security by harnessing the global appeal of the Olympics, particularly among the young, to reinforce values of tolerance, moderation and openness".[74]

The expectation that a nation's brand can be significantly affected by a single event is perhaps overly optimistic, unless of course the event has problems. The Olympic Games in 2004 and the Commonwealth Games in 2010 tended to impact negatively on the brand image of Athens and Delhi respectively in terms of efficiency and effectiveness and the 2014 Sochi Winter Olympics tended to project an image of profligacy and corruption. The problem facing the UK was that, unlike Greece, India and Russia, the country had enjoyed a generally positive international image for some time, as measured by the Anholt-Gfk Roper Index.[75] In both 2009 and 2010 the UK ranked fourth. Consequently a successful Olympic and Paralympic Games was unlikely to significantly improve the nation's image, while an unsuccessful Games could certainly damage the brand. As it turned out, the international media perception of the 2012 Games was almost uniformly positive.[76] London benefitted, in particular, and was seen as a good place to do business. There is no evidence that the Games negatively affected that perception. In the element of the Anholt-Gfk Roper Index which specifically measures investment appeal, the UK ranked third in both 2012 and 2013 (behind Germany, Canada and the USA).[77]

The third sport soft power objective related to threats to domestic and international security arising from conflicts in the Middle East. The UK government has supported, either directly or indirectly, a number of Olympic legacy projects targeted at countries in the Middle East. The International Inspirations project, which is managed by the British Council in conjunction with UNESCO, the Youth Sport Trust (a UK-based sport charity) and UK Sport, aims to improve the quality of physical education available to children. The project was launched in 2005 following the award of the Olympic and Paralympic Games to London and has delivered programmes in over 20 countries including Egypt, Jordan, Pakistan and Turkey. A second, but contrasting sport soft power initiative is the financial support given by the British Consulate in Jerusalem to the Speed Sisters, an all-female rally team based in Palestine. More directly related to the Olympics is the recruitment of well-known Olympians and Paralympians such as Sir Steve Redgrave, Lady Tanni Grey-Thompson and Chris Holmes as "Olympic Ambassadors". In recent years these ambassadors have visited selected countries including Israel, Jordan and Palestine.

While the domestic and international perception of the London 2012 Games was generally very positive, it is difficult to assess the utility of the diplomatic value of sport as a soft power resource. While it is doubtful that UK sport diplomacy had a negative impact on the pursuit of the UK government's foreign policy objectives, it is difficult to determine the extent to which a positive impact was generated. Where

---

74. House of Commons, Foreign Affairs Committee, *2nd Report, FCO Public Diplomacy: The Olympic and Paralympic Games 2012* (London: The Stationery Office, 2010–2011), Ev19.

75. Developed by Simon Anholt, this index measures the image and reputation of nations across the world.

76. Grix and Houlihan, *op. cit.*

77. "US Voted Top Country for Attracting Talent and Investment but with a Reducing Lead", GfK Press Release, 14 November 2013, available: <http://www.gfk.com/news-and-events/press-room/press-releases/pages/nation-brand-index-2013-latest-findings.aspx> (accessed 22 October 2014).

countries have either eschewed the use of hard power, as is the case with Germany and Japan, or simply do not possess a significant hard power capability, sport soft power is, by default, a relatively significant resource and potentially effective resource. However, where a country is still giving prominence to the hard power resources in its diplomatic portfolio, as is the case with the UK, it is doubtful whether the deployment of sport soft power resources is capable of doing more than reinforcing hard power objectives.

Brazil's "Double Host" Status

On the surface Brazil would appear to fit the classic typology of an "emerging state" or "rising power", one that attempts to use a variety of strategies to announce its arrival on the world stage, often burnishing its image and attracting tourists to its shores. As discussed, hosting SMEs is certainly part of a broader concerted "soft power" strategy;[78] however, there are a number of issues that set Brazil apart from other so-called "BRICS" countries (Russia, India, China and South Africa). Generic themes of "image leveraging" bind hosting states across the political spectrum from the UK to Qatar—especially after Germany's successful image overhaul, in part through staging the FIFA World Cup in 2006—but Brazil is unique in a number of ways. In Brazil's case, for instance, hosting SMEs is not simply a way to announce that it is ready "to signal [its] 'graduation' to the status ... of advanced state"[79]—that is, move from the periphery to the core—but to indicate its shift from a regional actor to a global actor in international affairs. In what follows we focus on both the international and domestic legacies deriving from what we term Brazil's "double host" status.

Brazil is at the forefront of the emerging powers discourse, although at the time of writing attempts were being made to distinguish the next batch of economic powerhouses, the "MINT" group (Mexico, Indonesia, Nigeria and Turkey). A sign of Brazil's global economic power came towards the end of 2011 when it overtook the UK to become the world's sixth largest economy.[80] Brazil's rise is clearly not just economic. Its ambition is to play a role in international affairs commensurate with its size, as evident in:

1. its recent attempt to gain a permanent seat at the UN Security Council;
2. taking over the command of a peacekeeping mission in Haiti; and
3. its recent attempt, along with Turkey, to intermediate a nuclear deal with Iran.

While wider debates rage about the ways in which Brazil will exercise its newly found power in the international system, the unprecedented hosting of the two largest SMEs in the world has received far less scrutiny. Brazil's double host status is likely to be matched by political influence on the world stage, as former hosts China and South Africa have demonstrated. The latter are, post event, established participants in multilateral summits such as the G20.

---

78. Grix and Houlihan, *op. cit.*

79. Black and Van Der Westhuizen, *op. cit.*, p. 1206.

80. Phillip Inman, "Brazil's Economy Overtakes UK to Become World's Sixth Largest", *The Guardian*, 6 March 2012, available: <http://www.theguardian.com/business/2012/mar/06/brazil-economy-worlds-sixth-largest> (accessed 3 March 2015).

On hearing that Rio would host the 2016 Olympics, the then president of Brazil, Luiz Inácio Lula da Silva, stated: "The world has recognised that the time has come for Brazil". He went on to suggest in an emotional address that, "Today I've felt prouder of being Brazilian than on any other day. Today is the day that Brazil gained its international citizenship … Today we earned respect".[81] Rohter puts this in perspective and suggests that Brazilians want Brazil to be taken seriously, "especially by the countries it views as great powers".[82] International recognition is, as discussed above, central to a soft power strategy.

Brazil is, of course, no novice at showcasing itself through large-scale events. The successful (from the outside) staging of the 2007 Pan American Games was clearly a precursor to winning the right to host both the 2014 World Cup and the 2016 Olympic Games. This was followed by the successful hosting of the global Rio +20 Sustainable Development Conference in 2012 and the World Youth Journey, a Catholic event held in Rio in 2013, an event that Pope Francis deemed important enough to attend.[83]

However, winning the bidding process for the Olympics or World Cup usually sends out a number of positive signals of inclusion and acceptance in the international system; being chosen for two in short succession suggests that the International Olympic Committee (IOC) and FIFA have enough trust in Brazil to put on successful events and a belief that it can put its "historical in-fighting to one side, streamline its culture of opaque bureaucracy and clamp down on the rampant corruption linked to its political elite".[84] That is, it needs to refashion the unattractive elements of its political culture. The latter is reflected in Brazil's 72nd spot in the 2013 "corruption index" put together by the non-governmental organisation (NGO) Transparency International,[85] joint with South Africa and eight places above China.

Apart from international legacies, Brazil's motives for hosting are as much about "domestic" legacies as anything else. While global exposure is central to Brazil's soft power strategy, there is a feeling that this large country of almost 200 million inhabitants has, for too long, been a "sleeping giant". Brazil has, since Stefan Zweig's prognosis of Brazil as the "Land of the Future" in 1941, struggled under a sense of burden of expectation.[86] Carvalho, in his analysis of Brazilian national myths and heroes, argues that the original myth of Brazil (as a country) is not related to political institutions, for example democracy and the monarchy in the UK, but is rather related to its nature and its enormous size.[87] The Brazilian national consciousness has been linked, since the nation's creation, to the expanse of the country's nature and the expectation of a bright future. Carvalho gets to the root of the Brazilian paradox when he suggests that:

81. Luiz Inácio Lula da Silva, quoted in Larry Rohter, *Brazil on the Rise. The Story of a Country Transformed* (Basingstoke: Palgrave Macmillan, 2012), p. 223.

82. Larry Rohter, *ibid.*, p. 224.

83. World Youth Journey Organisation (2014), available: <http://wydcentral.org/> (accessed 13 February 2014).

84. *Ibid.*

85. Transparency International, "Corruption Perception Index 2013", available: <http://www.transparency.org/cpi2013/results> (accessed 13 February 2014).

86. Rohter , *op. cit.*

87. José Murilo de Carvalho, "Nação imaginária: memória, mitos e heróis", in Adauto Novaes (ed.), *A crise do estado-nação* (Rio de Janeiro: Civilização Brasileira, 2003), pp. 395–418.

The drama of the country lies in the contrast between dream and reality, aspiration and achievement. [...]. Aspirations are not accompanied by appropriate actions to accomplish them. People do not trust in their leaders and institutions, but do not do anything to make the former more responsible for public social needs and to change the development of the latter [...] Hence a feeling of frustration, disappointment with the government and institutions, and the permanence of a vague hope that a possible messiah can come up with the solution to all problems.[88]

During his two terms in office (2003–2006 and 2007–2010), the former president, Lula, used to refer to himself as this messiah, arguing that his government would do for the country much more than the previous governments in Brazil's history put together. It was (and has been) a very effective rhetorical tool, which contributed to his charismatic legitimacy. Lula adopted a political strategy based on a discourse made up of this imagery of Brazil as the "land of the future" and enacted measures that underpinned this imagery in practice.

It is worth noting that Lula's rhetoric, drawing on the "land of the future" notion discussed above, came particularly to the fore when he was speaking of SMEs. For example, at the ceremony in which the Brazilian federal government officially announced its support for Rio's Olympic bid, Lula used his trademark superlatives, stating:

> If this country could organize the Pan-American Games like it did, in such a short space of time, why can't we organize the best Olympic Games that has ever taken place in any country?[89]

After winning the right to host the 2014 FIFA World Cup and the 2016 Olympics in 2006, the next stage was to implement the commitments set out in the respective bids. To ensure the completion of both events according to the proposed guidelines, a set of measures has been adopted by the Local Organising Committees as well as by municipal, state and federal governments. Among them, the most relevant are: 1) the construction and/or reform of sports facilities; 2) investment in infrastructure, especially that related to transport, such as airports and underground train systems; 3) the adaptation of the Brazilian legal framework, in order to ensure a "fit" with the requirements demanded by FIFA and the IOC.

In 2007 President Lula had suggested that no public money would be spent on the World Cup. At this time there was considerable debate about budget overspend and corruption, with monies belonging to the people being siphoned off. Subsequent events made hollow Lula's promise: the federal government not only had to pump resources into the construction of stadia, but had to make up the shortfall of ever increasing regional budgets. Officially, the exponential rise in costs for the World Cup has been attributed to FIFA's demands; the late delivery of the World Cup infrastructure, unfinished at the time of writing, reveals the gap between government rhetoric and the reality on the ground.

---

88. *Ibid.*, p. 14.

89. BRASIL. Discurso do Presidente da República, Luiz Inácio Lula da Silva, durante a solenidade de anúncio de medidas de apoio á candidatura do Rio de Janeiro aos Jogos Olímpicos e Paraolímpicos de 2016. Rio de Janeiro, 23 June 2008, available: http://imprensaacervo.planalto.gov.br/download/discursos/pr737-2@.doc (accessed 18 May 2015).

The building of transport infrastructure, designed to provide better mobility to and within host cities, is also presenting many problems. One of the primary legacies promised was the construction or reform of airports, underground trains, high-speed train systems and so on. These projects have taken much longer than initially planned. Furthermore, a number of projects have been postponed (until after the World Cup) or even cancelled. Finally, the adaptation of the Brazilian legal framework was necessary because some of the commitments taken on by Brazil were not covered by national legislation. These "pre-event institutional legacies"[90] resulted in the enactment of two laws: the so-called Olympic Act (Law n° 12.035, 1 October 2009) and the General Law of the World Cup (Law n° 12.663, 5 June 2012). Both set out special rules for, respectively, the 2016 Olympics and 2013 FIFA Confederations Cup/2014 FIFA World Cup, allowing the removal of any known legal rule which, in the eyes of FIFA or the IOC, could represent an obstacle to the completion of their events in Brazil.

All of the above impact on the potential for any long-term legacies from Brazil's two SMEs. The effect has been growing popular dissatisfaction with the rising costs and expenditure related to both events. Demonstrators took to the streets to protest against the lack of resources for basic educational and health policies. An example of this dissatisfaction could be observed during the 2013 Confederations Cup, held in five of the 12 host cities of the 2014 World Cup. There were many popular protests against the costs of the latter, with demands for resources for schools and hospitals. Both the Brazilian and FIFA presidents, Dilma Rousseff and Joseph Blatter, were booed by the crowd at the opening ceremony and FIFA's representatives were harassed by protesters. It is this type of public reaction that has led some to label SMEs "double-edged swords", simultaneously holding the capacity to result in both soft power and soft "disempowerment".[91]

Conclusion

This article has set out to interrogate the use of sports mega-events as part of states' soft power strategies by focusing on both an advanced capitalist state (the UK) and an "emerging" state (Brazil). The rationale behind this endeavour was to shed light on, and clarify, the concept of "soft power", which has, up until now, not been used widely in relation to sport.

The acquisition and successful hosting of such SMEs is now looked upon as a significant "litmus test" for would-be leading states globally. Although the precise mechanisms through which a state is said to gain in soft power due to hosting a successful SME are not clear, showcasing the ability to deal with the logistics of such an event appears to be crucial to how hosts are viewed by others.

While the concept of soft power, as suggested in this article, is of use as a lens through which to understand why states wish to host sports mega-events, it is a

90. R.M. Toledo, J. Grix and M.T.S. Bega, *Megaeventos Esportivos e seus Legados: uma análise dos efeitos institucionais da dupla condição do Brasil de país-sede* (Revista de Sociologia e Política, in press).

91. J. Grix, "The Risks and Rewards of Hosting Sports Mega-Events", *ICC Journal* (International Centre for Sport Security), Vol. 1, No. 1 (2013), pp. 22–27; P.M. Brannagan and R. Giulianotti, "Qatar, Global Sport, and the 2022 FIFA World Cup", in Grix, *Leveraging Legacies, op. cit.*, pp. 154–165; Brannagan and Giulianotti, "Soft Power and Soft Disempowerment: Qatar, Global Sport and Football's 2022 World Cup Finals", *Leisure Studies*(2014), available: <http://www.tandfonline.com/doi/full/10.1080/02614367.2014.964291#> (accessed 9 January 2015).

broad-brush concept that does not allow for the nuances between states. Whereas the UK's image abroad was very positive before the event and to better this was not the key aim, Germany used the 2006 World Cup to alter a tarnished image; Brazil, on the other hand, does not suffer from a negative image abroad, but wishes to consolidate its regional power position on the global stage. Thus, the use of similar SMEs is not always for parallel reasons, despite being part of states' much wider soft power strategies. There are a number of ways in which a state's use of SMEs could be compared across cases, but a direct, comparative method of analysis misses a number of key points. First, as we have sought to make clear, successful and wealthy advanced capitalist states, such as Germany, have a very different resource base, including infrastructure, from which to launch a sports-related soft power strategy than a so-called "emerging state". Germany did not need to convince a doubtful electorate of the need to invest in roads, transport links and other logistics, as all these existed before the event took place.[92] Equally, given that Germany has little "hard power" to speak of, it was able to focus almost exclusively on leveraging a positive image globally. Brazil, on the other hand, is not in the same position financially and does not have over 50 years of democratic rule under its belt. Equally, it would be a mistake to assume that Brazil is simply using its double host status as a Trojan Horse for neoliberal reforms that will push the country towards a more "developed" status. Such a reading is a narrow and linear understanding of development in terms of a growing global power. What is clear, however, is that while the use of sports mega-events appears to have become part and parcel of most states' soft power packages, the benefits that are said to derive from hosting them remain overstated, over-inflated and under-researched. It is hoped that the ideas put forward in this article can form the basis of future work on the role of sports mega-events in states' soft power strategies. It is clear, however, that there is a need to understand the mechanisms by which soft power actually assists states in gaining international prestige, and how they can prevent such strategies backfiring and leading to "soft disempowerment".[93]

Past research indicates that societies with deep structural divides and fault lines —inequality in society, poverty, high crime, corruption etc.—are very unlikely to change as a result of an SME or any hoped-for legacy. Shortly before, during and after, sport certainly papers over such cracks, but without fundamental reform and the will to change, cracks soon reappear once the perennial sport circus rolls out of town and on to the next.

Acknowledgements

The authors would like to thank Renata Toledo for her help with the section on Brazil, in particular for providing the legal documents to make our argument.

Disclosure statement

No potential conflict of interest was reported by the authors.

---

92. Grix and Houlihan, *op. cit.*
93. Brannagan and Giulianotti, "Soft Power and Soft Disempowerment", *op. cit.*

Index

For Product Safety Concerns and Information please contact our EU
representative GPSR@taylorandfrancis.com
Taylor & Francis Verlag GmbH, Kaufingerstraße 24, 80331 München, Germany

www.ingramcontent.com/pod-product-compliance
Lightning Source LLC
Chambersburg PA
CBHW081434270326
41932CB00019B/3197

* 9 7 8 1 1 3 8 3 9 1 9 5 6 *